Frommer's®

PORTABLE
Bahamas

D1280768

by Darwin Porter & Danforth Prince

WILEY

Wiley Publishing, Inc.

Published by:

WILEY PUBLISHING, INC.

111 River St.
Hoboken, NJ 07030-5774

ISBN-13: 978-0-7645-9882-1
ISBN-10: 0-7645-9882-1

Editor: Jennifer Anmuth
Production Editor: Eric T. Schroeder
Cartographer: Elizabeth Puhl
Photo Editor: Richard Fox
Production by Wiley Indianapolis Composition Services

Front cover photo: Snorkeler observes a school of French and blue-striped grunts in New Providence.

For information on our other products and services or to obtain technical support, please contact our Customer Care Department within the U.S. at 800/762-2974, outside the U.S. at 317/572-3993 or fax 317/572-4002.

Wiley also publishes its books in a variety of electronic formats. Some content that appears in print may not be available in electronic formats.

Manufactured in the United States of America

5   4   3   2   1

Contents

List of Maps

ABOUT THE AUTHORS

As a team of veteran travel writers, **Darwin Porter** and **Danforth Prince** have produced numerous titles for Frommer's, including best-selling guides to Italy, France, the Caribbean, England, and Germany. Porter, a former bureau chief of *The Miami Herald,* is also a Hollywood biographer, and his most recent release is *Howard Hughes: Hell's Angel.* Prince was formerly employed by the Paris bureau of *The New York Times,* and is today the president of Blood Moon Productions and other media-related firms.

An Invitation to the Reader

In researching this book, we discovered many wonderful places—hotels, restaurants, shops, and more. We're sure you'll find others. Please tell us about them, so we can share the information with your fellow travelers in upcoming editions. If you were disappointed with a recommendation, we'd love to know that, too. Please write to:

Frommer's Portable Bahamas, 5th Edition
Wiley Publishing, Inc. • 111 River St. • Hoboken, NJ 07030-5774

An Additional Note

Please be advised that travel information is subject to change at any time—and this is especially true of prices. We therefore suggest that you write or call ahead for confirmation when making your travel plans. The authors, editors, and publisher cannot be held responsible for the experiences of readers while traveling. Your safety is important to us, however, so we encourage you to stay alert and be aware of your surroundings. Keep a close eye on cameras, purses, and wallets, all favorite targets of thieves and pickpockets.

Other Great Guides for Your Trip:

Frommer's Bahamas
Frommer's Caribbean
Frommer's Caribbean Cruises & Ports of Call
Frommer's Caribbean Ports of Call

FROMMER'S STAR RATINGS, ICONS & ABBREVIATIONS

Every hotel, restaurant, and attraction listing in this guide has been ranked for quality, value, service, amenities, and special features using a **star-rating system.** In country, state, and regional guides, we also rate towns and regions to help you narrow down your choices and budget your time accordingly. Hotels and restaurants are rated on a scale of zero (recommended) to three stars (exceptional). Attractions, shopping, nightlife, towns, and regions are rated according to the following scale: zero stars (recommended), one star (highly recommended), two stars (very highly recommended), and three stars (must-see).

In addition to the star-rating system, we also use **seven feature icons** that point you to the great deals, in-the-know advice, and unique experiences that separate travelers from tourists. Throughout the book, look for:

Finds	Special finds—those places only insiders know about
Fun Fact	Fun facts—details that make travelers more informed and their trips more fun
Kids	Best bets for kids and advice for the whole family
Moments	Special moments—those experiences that memories are made of
Overrated	Places or experiences not worth your time or money
Tips	Insider tips—great ways to save time and money
Value	Great values—where to get the best deals

The following **abbreviations** are used for credit cards:

AE	American Express	DISC	Discover	V	Visa
DC	Diners Club	MC	MasterCard		

FROMMERS.COM

Now that you have the guidebook to a great trip, visit our website at **www.frommers.com** for travel information on more than 3,000 destinations. With features updated regularly, we give you instant access to the most current trip-planning information available. At Frommers.com, you'll also find the best prices on airfares, accommodations, and car rentals—and you can even book travel online through our travel booking partners. At Frommers.com, you'll also find the following:

- Online updates to our most popular guidebooks
- Vacation sweepstakes and contest giveaways
- Newsletter highlighting the hottest travel trends
- Online travel message boards with featured travel discussions

The Best of The Bahamas

The Bahamas is one of the most geographically complicated nations of the Atlantic. A coral-based archipelago, it is composed of more than 700 islands, 2,000 cays (pronounced "keys," from the Spanish word for small islands), and hundreds of rocky outcroppings that have damaged the hulls of countless ships since colonial days.

But don't worry: We're here to help you plan the perfect getaway. In this chapter, you'll find clear and concise lists of The Bahamas' best beaches, honeymoon resorts, family vacations, and restaurants.

For more information on choosing the island that best suits your taste and budget, refer to "The Islands in Brief" in chapter 2. There, we'll explain the pros and cons of each island in detail.

1 The Best Beaches

- **Cable Beach** (New Providence Island): The glittering shoreline of Cable Beach has easy access to shops, casinos, restaurants, watersports, and bars. It's a sandy 6.5km-long (4-mile) long strip, with a great array of facilities and activities. See "Beaches, Watersports & Other Outdoor Pursuits" in chapter 3.
- **Cabbage Beach** (Paradise Island): Think Vegas in the Tropics. It seems as if most of the sunbathers dozing on the sands here are recovering from the previous evening's partying, and it's likely to be crowded near the megahotels, but you can find a bit more solitude on the beach's isolated northwestern extension (Paradise Beach), which is accessible only by boat or on foot. Lined with palms, sea grapes, and casuarinas, the sands are broad and stretch for at least 3km (2 miles). See "Beaches, Watersports & Other Outdoor Pursuits" in chapter 4.
- **Xanadu Beach** (Grand Bahama Island): Grand Bahama has 97km (60 miles) of sandy shoreline, but Xanadu Beach is most convenient to Freeport's resort hotels, several of which offer shuttle service to Xanadu. There's more than a kilometer of white sand and (usually) gentle surf. Don't expect to have Xanadu to yourself, but if you want more quiet and privacy, try

The Best Beaches of The Bahamas

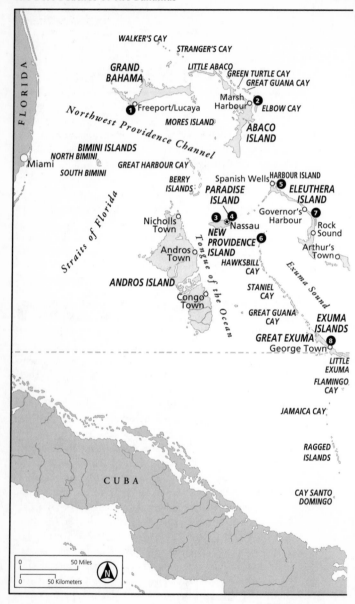

ATLANTIC

OCEAN

CAT ISLAND
9

Cockburn Town **SAN SALVADOR**

Stella Maris **RUM CAY**

Tropic of Cancer

LONG ISLAND
Deadman's Cay

CROOKED ISLAND

ACKLINS ISLAND

MAYAGUANA ISLAND

TURKS AND CAICOS ISLANDS
NORTH (U.K.)
CAICOS
PINE CAY *MIDDLE CAICOS*
EAST CAICOS
PROVIDENCIALES
Grace Bay *CAICOS ISLANDS*
GRAND TURK ISLAND
SOUTH CAICOS
SALT CAY *TURKS ISLANDS*

LITTLE INAGUA

GREAT INAGUA

any of the beaches that stretch from Xanadu for many miles in either direction. See "Beaches, Watersports & Other Outdoor Pursuits" in chapter 5.

2 The Best Honeymoon Resorts

- **Sandals Royal Bahamian Hotel** (Cable Beach, New Providence Island; ✆ **800/SANDALS** or 242/327-6400; www. sandals.com): This Jamaican chain of couples-only, all-inclusive hotels is a honeymooners' favorite. The Bahamas's branch of the chain is more upscale than many of its Jamaican counterparts, and it offers 27 secluded honeymoon suites with semiprivate plunge pools. Staff members lend their experience and talent to on-site wedding celebrations; Sandals will provide everything from a preacher to flowers, as well as champagne and a cake. It's more expensive than most Sandals resorts, but you can usually get better rates through a travel agent or a package deal. See p. 64.

- **Compass Point** (New Providence Island; ✆ **800/633-3284** or 242/327-4500; www.compasspointbahamas.com): This choice is a charming and personalized statement for those who shun megaresorts. The accommodations are found in floridly painted huts or cottages, some of which have kitchenettes and some of which are raised on stilts. Completely in harmony with the lovely natural setting, it's nevertheless state of the art. See p. 71.

- **One&Only Ocean Club** (Paradise Island; ✆ **800/321-3000** in the U.S. only, or 242/363-2501; www.oneandonlyresorts.com): It's elegant, low-key, and low-rise, and it feels exclusive. The guests include many older couples celebrating honeymoons. With waterfalls, fountains, reflecting pools, and a stone gazebo, the Ocean Club's formal terraced gardens were inspired by the club's founder (an heir to the A&P fortune) and are the most impressive in The Bahamas. At the center is a French cloister, with carvings from the 12th century. See p. 110.

- **Old Bahama Bay** (Grand Bahama Island; ✆ **800/572-5711** or 800/444-9469; www.oldbahamabay.com): Perfect for honeymooners seeking a quiet hideaway in a boutique-style hotel with cottages adjacent to a marina. The casinos, entertainment, shopping, and dining of Freeport/Lucaya are 40km (25 miles) away, but here you can sneak away to luxury, solitude, and romance. See p. 146.

3 The Best Family Vacations

- **Radisson Cable Beach Hotel** (Cable Beach, New Providence Island; ℂ **800/333-3333** or 242/327-6000; www.radisson-cablebeach.com): A family could spend their entire vacation on the grounds of this vast resort. There's a pool area that features the most lavish artificial waterfall this side of Tahiti; a health club at the nearby Crystal Palace that welcomes both guests and their children; Camp Junkanoo, with supervised play for children 3 through 12; and a long list of in-house activities that includes dancing lessons. See p. 68.

- **Atlantis Paradise Island Resort & Casino** (Paradise Island; ℂ **800/ATLANTIS** in the U.S., or 242/363-3957; www.atlantis.com): This is one of the largest hotel complexes in the world, with endless rows of shops and watersports galore. Both children and adults will enjoy the 5.6-hectare (14-acre) sea world with water slides, a lagoon for watersports, white sandy beaches, and underground grottoes plus an underwater viewing tunnel and 240m (787 ft.) of cascading waterfalls. Its children's menus and innovative, creative children's programs are the best in The Bahamas and perhaps even in the Caribbean. See p. 123.

- **Crowne Plaza Golf Resort & Casino at the Royal Oasis** (Grand Bahama Island; ℂ **800/545-1300** or 242/350-7000): Many guests come here just to gamble and work on their tans, but others bring their kids. To divert them, the hotel maintains a pair of playgrounds and a swimming pool inspired by a tropical oasis, and offers children's platters in some of the restaurants. The architecture features lots of "Aladdin and His Lamp" accessories, such as minarets above a decidedly non-Islamic setting. See p. 138.

- **Best Western Castaways** (Grand Bahama Island; ℂ **800/780-7234** in the U.S., or 242/352-6682; www.bestwestern.com): Here's a good choice for families on a budget. The pagoda-capped lobby is set a very short walk from the ice-cream stands, souvenir shops, and fountains of the International Bazaar. Children under 12 stay free in their parent's room, and the in-house lounge presents limbo and fire-eating shows several evenings a month. The hotel offers a babysitting service and a free shuttle to Xanadu Beach. See p. 139.

4 The Best Restaurants

- **Chez Willie** (Nassau, New Providence Island; ✆ 242/322-5364): This is one of the newest, but also the classiest, restaurants on New Providence Island, overshadowing its competitors on Cable Beach. It's a throwback to the grandeur of Old Nassau in its Duke and Duchess of Windsor cafe society heyday. Your host, Willie Armstrong, oversees a smoothly run operation serving some of the best French and Bahamian cuisine found on the island. See p. 73.

- **Buena Vista** (Nassau, New Providence Island; ✆ 242/322-2811; www.buenavista-restaurant.com): Overlooking Nassau Harbour, this restaurant retains the elegance that the city had when the Duke and Duchess of Windsor were in the governor's mansion. Its take on both a continental and Bahamian cuisine still attracts the serious foodie drawn both to the cuisine and the expert service by tuxedo-clad waiters. See p. 72.

- **Dune Bar** (in the One&Only Ocean Club, Paradise Island; ✆ 242/363-2501, ext. 64739): The most cutting-edge restaurant in either Paradise Island or Nassau is this creation of French-born restaurant guru Jean-Georges Vongerichten, he of several of New York City's leading lights. Every dish served here is something special—from shrimp dusted with orange powder to chicken and coconut milk soup with shiitake cakes. See p. 126.

- **Bahamian Club** (Paradise Island; ✆ 242/363-3000): A notch down from the superb Dune, this establishment is one of the leading restaurants in The Bahamas and our favorite at the sprawling megaresort of Atlantis. Strictly upscale, it presents a superb French and international cuisine nightly against a backdrop that evokes the British Colonial era. The restaurant serves the island's finest cuts of meats. See p. 115.

- **Villa d'Este** (in the Atlantis Paradise Island Resort and Casino, Paradise Island; ✆ 242/363-3000): This is the finest Italian restaurant on Paradise Island, with nothing in Nassau to top it, either. The setting is gracious, tasteful, and Old World, but it's the food that keeps visitors and locals alike clamoring for reservations. All the old favorites are here, including veal parmigiana and fettuccine Alfredo as fine as any you'd find in Rome. Fresh herbs add zest to many dishes, and the pasta dishes are particularly good. See p. 119.

2

Planning Your Trip to The Bahamas

You can be in The Bahamas after a quick 35-minute jet hop from Miami, but don't forget to bring your passport. Under new Homeland Security regulations, Americans traveling to The Bahamas must show passports starting December 31, 2005, upon their return to the United States. Those returning to Canada will have to show passports starting December 31, 2006. A driver's license or a birth certificate will not be acceptable. See section 3, "Entry Requirement & Customs," for more details.

1 The Islands in Brief

The Bahamian chain of islands, cays, and reefs stretches from Grand Bahama Island, 121km (75 miles) almost due east of Palm Beach, Florida, to Great Inagua, the southernmost island, which lies about 97km (60 miles) northeast of Cuba and fewer than 161km (100 miles) north of Haiti.

The most developed islands for tourism in The Bahamas are **New Providence Island,** site of Nassau (the capital) and Cable Beach; **Paradise Island;** and **Grand Bahama,** home of Freeport and Lucaya. If you're after glitz, gambling, bustling restaurants, nightclubs, and a beach-party scene, these big three islands are where you'll want to be. Package deals are easily found here.

Set sail (or hop on a short commuter flight) for one of the **Out Islands,** such as Andros, the Exumas, or the Abacos, and you'll find fewer crowds—and often lower prices, too. Though some of the Out Islands are accessible mainly (or only) by boat, it's still worth your while to make the trip if you like the idea of having an entire beach to yourself. Space doesn't permit us to cover all these islands in this small guide, so if you're interested, please pick up a copy of *Frommer's Bahamas* for complete coverage.

NEW PROVIDENCE ISLAND (NASSAU/CABLE BEACH)

New Providence isn't the largest of the Bahamian Islands, but it's the historic heart of the nation, with a strong maritime tradition and the largest population in the country. Home to more than 125,000 residents, it offers groves of pines and casuarinas; sandy, flat soil; the closest thing in The Bahamas to urban sprawl; and superb anchorages sheltered from rough seas by the presence of nearby Paradise Island. New Providence has the country's busiest airport and is dotted with hundreds of villas owned by foreign investors. Its two major resort areas are Cable Beach and Nassau.

The resort area of **Cable Beach** is a glittering beachfront strip of hotels, restaurants, and casinos; only Paradise Island has been more developed. Its center is the Marriott Resort & Crystal Palace Casino. Often, deciding between Cable Beach and Paradise Island isn't so much a choice of which island you prefer as a choice of which hotel you prefer. But it's easy to sample both, since it takes only about 30 minutes to drive between the two.

Nassau, the Bahamian capital, isn't on a great stretch of shoreline and doesn't have as many first-rate hotels as either Paradise Island or Cable Beach—with the exception of the Bahama Hilton, which has a small private beach. The main advantages of Nassau are colonial charm and price. Its hotels may not be ideally located, but they are relatively inexpensive; some offer low prices even during the winter high season. You can base yourself here and commute easily to the beaches at Paradise Island or Cable Beach. Some travelers even prefer Nassau because it's the seat of Bahamian culture and history—not to mention the shopping mecca of The Bahamas.

PARADISE ISLAND   If high-rise hotels and glittering casinos are what you want, along with some of the best beaches in The Bahamas, there is no better choice than Paradise Island, directly off the coast of Nassau. It has the best food, the best entertainment, terrific beaches, casinos, and the best hotels. Its major drawbacks are that it's expensive and often overcrowded. Boasting a colorful history, yet a host of unremarkable architecture, Paradise Island remains perhaps the most intensely marketed piece of real estate in the world. The sands and shoals of the elongated and narrow island protect the wharves and piers of Nassau, which rise across a narrow channel only 180m (590 ft.) away.

Owners of the 277-hectare (684-acre) island have included brokerage mogul Joseph Lynch (of Merrill Lynch) and Huntington Hartford, heir to the A&P supermarket fortune. More recent investors have included Merv Griffin. The island today is a carefully landscaped residential and commercial complex with good beaches, lots of glitter (some of it tasteful, some of it way too over-the-top), and many diversions.

GRAND BAHAMA ISLAND (FREEPORT/LUCAYA) The island's name derives from the Spanish term *gran bajamar* (great shallows), which refers to the shallow reefs and sandbars that, over the centuries, have destroyed everything from Spanish galleons to English clipper ships on Grand Bahama's shores. Thanks to the tourist development schemes of U.S. financiers such as Howard Hughes, Grand Bahama boasts a well-developed tourist infrastructure. Casinos, beaches, and restaurants are now plentiful here.

Grand Bahama's **Freeport/Lucaya** resort area is another popular destination for American tourists, though it has a lot more tacky development than Paradise Island or Cable Beach. The compensation for that is a lower price tag on just about everything. Freeport/ Lucaya offers plenty of opportunities for fine dining, entertainment, and gambling. Grand Bahama also offers the best hiking in The Bahamas and has some of the finest sandy beaches. Its golf courses attract players from all over the globe, and the island hosts major tournaments several times a year. You'll find some of the world's best diving here, as well as UNEXSO, the internationally famous diving school. Grand Bahama Island is especially popular with families.

2 Visitor Information

The "Planning Your Trip Online" section that begins on p. 25 is packed with invaluable advice about how to search for late-breaking information on the Web.

However, travel conditions are ever changing, and you'll want to marshal other resources as well. The two best sources to try before you leave home are your travel agent and **The Bahamas Tourist Office** nearest you. Visit the nation's official tourism office at www. bahamas.com, or call ✆ **800/BAHAMAS** or 242/302-2000. You can also walk in at the following branch offices:

Chicago: 8600 W. Bryn Mawr Ave., Suite 580, North Chicago, IL 60631 (✆ **773/693-1500**)

Los Angeles: 11400 W. Olympic Blvd., Suite 204, Los Angeles, CA 90064 (✆ **800/439-6993** or 310/312-9544)

Florida: 1200 S. Pine Island Rd., Suite 750, Plantation, FL 33324 (✆ **954/236-9292**)

New York: 150 E. 52nd St., New York, NY 10022 (✆ **212/ 758-2777**)

Toronto: 121 Bloor St. E., Suite 1101, Toronto, ON M4W 3M5 (© **416/968-2999**)
United Kingdom: 10 Chesterfield St., London W1J 5JL (© **020/7355-0800**)

You may also want to contact the U.S. State Department for background bulletins, which supply up-to-date information on crime, health concerns, import restrictions, and other travel matters. Call © **202/512-1800** or visit www.travel.state.gov.

A travel agent can be a great source of information. Make sure your agent is a member of the American Society of Travel Agents (ASTA). If you get poor service from an ASTA agent, you can write to the ASTA Consumer Affairs Department, 1101 King St., Alexandria, VA 22314 (© **800/440-ASTA** or 703/739-2782; www. astanet.com).

SEARCHING THE WEB

Bahamas websites include:

The Bahamas Ministry of Tourism (www.bahamas.com or www.tourismbahamas.org): Official tourism site.
Bahamas Tourist Guide (www.interknowledge.com/bahamas): Travelers' opinions.
Bahamas Vacation Guide (www.bahamasvg.com): Service listings.
Nassau/Paradise Island Promotion Board (www.nassauparadise island.com): Service listings.

3 Entry Requirements & Customs

ENTRY REQUIREMENTS
DOCUMENTS

To enter The Bahamas, **citizens of the United States, Britain,** and **Canada** coming in as visitors *must* bring a passport to demonstrate proof of citizenship. Under new Homeland Security regulations, starting December 31, 2005, Americans must show passports upon their return to the United States. A driver's license or a birth certificate will not be acceptable. Those returning to Canada will have to show passports starting December 31, 2006.

Onward or return tickets must be shown to immigration officials in The Bahamas. Citizens of other countries, including Australia, Ireland, and New Zealand, should carry a valid passport.

You can find more information on passports in the Fast Facts section, below. For a complete up-to-date country-by-country listing of passport requirements around the world, go to **www.travel. state.gov**.

The Commonwealth of The Bahamas does not require visas. On entry to The Bahamas, you'll be given an Immigration Card to complete and sign. The card has a carbon copy that you must keep until departure, at which time it must be turned in. You'll also have to pay a departure tax before you can exit the country (see "Taxes" under "Fast Facts: The Bahamas," later in this chapter).

CUSTOMS
What You Can Bring into The Bahamas

Bahamian Customs allow you to bring in 200 cigarettes, 50 cigars, or 1 pound of tobacco, plus 1 quart of spirits (hard liquor). You can also bring in items classified as "personal effects," and all the money you wish.

What You Can Take Home from The Bahamas

Visitors leaving Nassau or Freeport/Lucaya for most U.S. destinations clear U.S. Customs and Immigration before departing The Bahamas. Charter companies can make special arrangements with the Nassau or Freeport flight services and U.S. Customs and Immigration for preclearance. No further formalities are required upon arrival in the United States once the preclearance has taken place in Nassau or Freeport.

Collect receipts for all the purchases you make in The Bahamas. *Note:* If a merchant suggests giving you a false receipt, misstating the value of the goods, beware—the merchant might be an informer to U.S. Customs. You must also declare all gifts received during your stay abroad.

Tips Passport

Allow plenty of time before your trip to apply for a passport; the processing normally takes 3 weeks, and can take longer during busy periods (especially spring). Also keep in mind that if you need a passport in a hurry, you'll pay a higher processing fee. When traveling, safeguard your passport in an inconspicuous, inaccessible place like a money belt; keep a copy of the critical pages (including your passport number) in a separate place. If you lose your passport, visit the nearest consulate of your native country as soon as possible for a replacement.

If you purchased an item during an earlier trip abroad, carry proof that you have already paid customs duty on the item at the time of your previous reentry. To be extra careful, compile a list of expensive carry-on items and ask a U.S. Customs agent to stamp your list at the airport before your departure.

Returning U.S. citizens who have been away for 48 hours or more are allowed to bring back, once every 30 days, $800 worth of merchandise duty-free. You'll be charged a flat rate of 10% duty on the next $1,000 worth of purchases. Be sure to have your receipts handy. On gifts, the duty-free limit is $100. You cannot bring fresh foodstuffs into the United States; canned or packaged foods, however, are allowed, and you can bring back 1 liter of alcohol.

For specifics on what you can bring back, download the invaluable free pamphlet *Know Before You Go* online at **www.cbp.gov**. (Click on "Travel" then "Know Before You Go Online Brochure.") Or contact the **U.S. Customs & Border Protection (CBP),** 1300 Pennsylvania Ave. NW, Washington, DC 20229 (② **877/287-8667**) and request the pamphlet.

For a clear summary of **Canadian** rules, write for the booklet *I Declare,* issued by the **Canada Border Services** (② **800/461-9999** in Canada, or 204/983-3500; www.cbsa-asfc.gc.ca). Canada allows its citizens a C$750 exemption, and you're allowed to bring back duty-free one carton of cigarettes, one can of tobacco, 40 imperial ounces of liquor, and 50 cigars. In addition, you're allowed to mail gifts to Canada valued at less than C$60 a day, provided they're unsolicited and don't contain alcohol or tobacco (write on the package "Unsolicited gift, under $60 value"). All valuables should be declared on the Y-38 form before departure from Canada, including serial numbers of valuables you already own, such as expensive foreign cameras. *Note:* The C$750 exemption can only be used once a year and only after an absence of 7 days.

U.K. citizens returning from **a non-E.U. country** have a customs allowance of 200 cigarettes; 50 cigars; 250g of smoking tobacco; 2 liters of still table wine; 1 liter of spirits or strong liqueurs (over 22% volume); 2 liters of fortified wine, sparkling wine or other liqueurs; 60cc (ml) perfume; 250cc (ml) of toilet water; and £145 worth of all other goods, including gifts and souvenirs. People under 17 cannot have the tobacco or alcohol allowance. For more information, contact **HM Customs & Excise** at ② **0845/010-9000** or 020/8929-0152) or consult U.K.'s customs website at www.hmce. gov.uk.

The duty-free allowance in **Australia** is A$400 or, for those under 18, A$200. Citizens can bring in 250 cigarettes or 250 grams of loose tobacco, and 1,125 milliliters of alcohol. If you're returning with valuables you already own, such as foreign-made cameras, you should file Form B263. A helpful brochure available from Australian consulates or Customs offices is *Know Before You Go.* For more information, call the **Australian Customs Service** at (C) **1300/363-263,** or log on to www.customs.gov.au.

The duty-free allowance for **New Zealand** is NZ$700. Citizens over 17 can bring in 200 cigarettes, 50 cigars, or 250 grams of tobacco (or a mixture of all three if their combined weight doesn't exceed 250g); plus 4.5 liters of wine and beer, or 1.125 liters of liquor. New Zealand currency does not carry import or export restrictions. Fill out a certificate of export, listing the valuables you are taking out of the country; that way, you can bring them back without paying duty. Most questions are answered in a free pamphlet available at New Zealand consulates and Customs offices: *New Zealand Customs Guide for Travellers, Notice no. 4.* For more information, contact **New Zealand Customs Service,** the Customhouse, 17–21 Whitmore St., Box 2218, Wellington ((C) **04/473-6099** or 0800/428-786; www.customs.govt.nz).

4 Money

The currency is the **Bahamian dollar (B$1),** pegged to the U.S. dollar so that they're always equivalent. (In fact, U.S. dollars are accepted widely throughout The Bahamas.) There is no restriction on bringing foreign currency into The Bahamas. Most large hotels and stores accept traveler's checks, but you may have trouble using a personal check. It's a good idea to exchange enough money to cover airport incidentals and transportation to your hotel before you leave home.

You can change currencies at a local American Express ((C) **800/807-6233;** www.americanexpress.com) or Thomas Cook ((C) **800/223-7373;** www.thomascook.com) or at your bank.

Be sure to carry some small bills or loose change when traveling. Petty cash will come in handy for tipping and public transportation. Consider keeping the change separate from your larger bills, so that it's readily accessible and you'll be less of a target for theft.

What Things Cost in The Bahamas	US$/B$	UK£
Taxi from airport to Nassau's center	$20	£10.50
Local phone call	25¢	13p
Double room at Graycliff (deluxe)	$290	£152
Double room at Holiday Inn Junkanoo Beach (moderate)	$149	£78
Dinner for one at Chez Willie (expensive)	$60	£32
Dinner at Bahamian Kitchen (inexpensive)	$22	£11.50
Bottle of beer in a bar/hotel	$3–$3.95	£1.60–£2
Rolls of ASA 100 color film (36 exposures)	$6.50	£3.40
Movie ticket	$6	£3.20

ATMs

The easiest way to get cash away from home is from an ATM. The **Cirrus** (© 800/424-7787; www.mastercard.com) and **PLUS** (© 800/843-7587; www.visa.com) networks span the globe; look at the back of your bank card to see which network you're on, then call or check online for ATM locations at your destination. Know your personal identification number (PIN) and your daily withdrawal limit.

Keep in mind that many banks impose a fee every time a card is used at a different bank's ATM, and that fee can be higher for international transactions (up to $5 or more) than for domestic ones (where they're rarely more than $1.50). On top of this, the bank from which you withdraw cash may charge its own fee.

You can also get cash advances on your credit card at an ATM. Credit card companies do try to protect themselves from theft by limiting the funds someone can withdraw outside their home country, so call your credit card company before you leave home. And keep in mind that you'll pay interest from the moment of your withdrawal, even if you pay your monthly bills on time.

On New Providence Island and Paradise Island, there are plenty of ATMs, including one at the Nassau International Airport. There are far fewer ATMs on Grand Bahama Island (Freeport/Lucaya), but those that are here are strategically located—including ones at the airport and the casino (of course).

TRAVELER'S CHECKS

With 24-hour ATMs now available in most cities, traveler's checks are less necessary. However, if you don't want to pay ATM withdrawal fees, you might be better off with traveler's checks—provided that you don't mind showing identification every time you want to cash one. You can get traveler's checks at almost any bank.

American Express (© 800/221-7282) offers denominations of $20, $50, $100, $500, and for cardholders only $1,000. You'll pay a service charge ranging from 1% to 4%; Amex gold and platinum cardholders are exempt from the 1% fee.

Visa (© 800/732-1322) offers traveler's checks at Citibank locations nationwide, as well as at several other banks. The service charge ranges between 1.5% and 2%; checks come in denominations of $20, $50, $100, $500, and $1,000. AAA members can obtain Visa checks for a $9.95 fee (for checks up to $1,500) at most AAA offices or by calling © 866/339-3378.

MasterCard (© 800/223-9920) also offers traveler's checks.

If you choose to carry traveler's checks, keep a record of their serial numbers separate from your checks in the event that they are stolen or lost. You'll get a refund faster if you know the numbers.

CREDIT CARDS

Credit cards generally offer relatively good exchange rates, are a safe way to carry money, and provide a convenient record of all your expenses. You can also withdraw cash advances from credit cards at banks or ATMs, provided you know your PIN. If you've forgotten yours, or didn't even know you had one, call the number on the back of your credit card and ask the bank to send it to you. It usually takes 5 to 7 business days, though some banks will provide the number over the phone if you tell them your mother's maiden name or some other personal information. Keep in mind that when you use your credit card abroad, most banks assess a 2% fee above the 1% fee charged by Visa or MasterCard or American Express for currency conversion on credit charges. But credit cards still may be the smart way to go when you factor in things like exorbitant ATM fees and higher traveler's check exchange rates (and service fees).

5 When to Go

THE WEATHER

The temperature in The Bahamas averages between 75°F and 85°F (24°C–29°C) in both winter and summer, although it can get chilly in the early morning and at night. The Bahamian winter is usually like a perpetual late spring—naturally the high season for North Americans rushing to escape snow and ice. Summer brings broiling sun and humidity. Rain is likely in the summer and fall.

THE HURRICANE SEASON

The curse of Bahamian weather, the hurricane season, lasts (officially) from June 1 to November 30. But there is no cause for panic. More tropical cyclones pound the U.S. mainland than The Bahamas. Hurricanes are actually fairly infrequent here, and when one does come, satellite forecasts generally give adequate advance warning so that precautions can be taken.

If you're heading for The Bahamas during the hurricane season, you might want to visit the National Weather Service at www.nws.noaa.gov.

For an online 5-day forecast anytime, check the Weather Channel at www.weather.com (for free!) or call ℂ **900/WEATHER** (95¢ per min.).

Average Temperatures & Rainfall (in.) in The Bahamas

Note that these numbers are daily averages, so expect temperatures to climb significantly higher in the noonday sun and to cool off a good deal in the evening.

Month	Jan	Feb	Mar	Apr	May	June	July	Aug	Sept	Oct	Nov	Dec
Temp. °F	70	70	72	75	77	80	81	82	81	78	74	71
Temp. °C	21	21	22	24	25	27	27	28	27	26	23	22
Rainfall (in.)	1.9	1.6	1.4	1.9	4.8	9.2	6.1	6.3	7.5	8.3	2.3	1.5

THE "SEASON"

In The Bahamas, hotels charge their highest prices during the peak winter period from mid-December to mid-April, when visitors fleeing from cold north winds flock to the islands. Winter is the driest season.

If you plan to visit during the winter, try to make reservations at least 2 to 3 months in advance. And bear in mind that, at some hotels, it's impossible to book accommodations for Christmas and the month of February without even more lead time.

SAVING MONEY IN THE OFF SEASON

The Bahamas is a year-round destination. The islands' "off season" runs from late spring to late fall, when tolerable temperatures (see "The Weather," above) prevail throughout most of the region. Trade winds ensure comfortable days and nights, even in accommodations without air-conditioning. Although the noonday sun may raise temperatures to uncomfortable levels, cool breezes usually make the morning, late afternoon, and evening more pleasant here than in many parts of the U.S. mainland.

Dollar for dollar, you'll spend less money by renting a summer house or fully equipped unit in The Bahamas than you would on Cape Cod, Fire Island, Laguna Beach, or the coast of Maine.

The off season—roughly from mid-April to mid-December (rate schedules vary from hotel to hotel)—amounts to a summer sale. In most cases, hotel rates are slashed from 20% to a startling 60%. It's a bonanza for cost-conscious travelers, especially families who like to go on vacations together. In the chapters ahead, we'll spell out in dollars the specific amounts hotels charge during the off season.

6 Travel Insurance

TRAVEL INSURANCE AT A GLANCE

Check your existing insurance policies and credit card coverage before you buy travel insurance. You may already be covered for lost luggage, canceled tickets, or medical expenses. The cost of travel insurance varies widely, depending on the cost and length of your trip, your age, health, and the type of trip you're taking, but expect to pay between 5% and 8% of the vacation itself.

TRIP-CANCELLATION INSURANCE Trip-cancellation insurance helps you get your money back if you have to back out of a trip, if you have to go home early, or if your travel supplier goes bankrupt. Allowable reasons for cancellation can range from sickness to natural disasters to the State Department declaring your destination unsafe for travel. (Insurers usually won't cover vague fears, though, as many travelers discovered in Oct 2001 after canceling trips because they were wary of flying.) Trip-cancellation insurance is a good buy if you're getting tickets well in advance, but insurance policy details vary, so read the fine print—and especially make sure that your airline or cruise line is on the list of carriers covered in case of bankruptcy. A good resource is **"Travel Guard Alerts,"** a list of companies considered high-risk by Travel Guard International (see website below). Protect yourself further by paying for the insurance with a credit card—by law, consumers can get their money back on goods and services not received if they report the loss within 60 days after the charge is listed on their credit card statement.

Note: Many tour operators include insurance in the cost of the trip or can arrange insurance policies through a partnering provider, a convenient and often cost-effective way for the traveler to obtain insurance. Make sure the tour company is a reputable one, however: Some experts suggest you avoid buying insurance from the tour or cruise company you're traveling with, saying it's better to buy from a "third-party" insurer than to put all your money in one place.

For more information, contact one of the following recommended insurers: **Access America** (© 866/807-3982; www.accessamerica.com); **Travel Guard International** (© 800/826-4919; www.travelguard.com); **Travel Insured International** (© 800/243-3174; www.travelinsured.com); and **Travelex Insurance Services** (© 888/457-4602; www.travelex-insurance.com).

MEDICAL INSURANCE With the exception of certain HMOs and Medicare/Medicaid, most health insurance policies cover medical treatment—even hospital care—overseas. However, most out-of-country hospitals insist you pay your bills upfront, and then send you a refund after you've returned home and filed the necessary paperwork. In a worst-case scenario, that could include the high cost of an emergency evacuation. Check with your provider and if you require additional medical insurance, try **MEDEX Assistance** (© 410/453-6300; www.medexassist.com) or **Travel Assistance International** (© 800/821-2828; www.travelassistance.com); for general information on services, call the company's Worldwide Assistance Services, Inc. at © **800/777-8710;** www.worldwideassistance.com).

LOST-LUGGAGE INSURANCE On domestic flights, checked baggage is covered up to $2,500 per ticketed passenger. On international flights (including U.S. portions of international trips), baggage coverage is limited to approximately $9.07 per pound, up to approximately $635 per checked bag. If you plan to check items more valuable than the standard liability, see if your valuables are covered by your homeowner's policy, get baggage insurance as part of your comprehensive travel-insurance package, or buy Travel Guard's "Bag Trak" product. Don't buy insurance at the airport, as it's usually overpriced. Be sure to take any valuables or irreplaceable items with you in your carry-on luggage, as many valuables (including books, money, and electronics) aren't covered by airline policies. If your luggage is lost, immediately file a lost-luggage claim at the airport, detailing the luggage contents. For most airlines, you must report delayed, damaged, or lost baggage within 4 hours of arrival.

The airlines are required to deliver luggage, once found, directly to your house or destination free of charge.

7 Health & Safety

STAYING HEALTHY

Even on the remotest island, you'll find, if not a hospital, a local medicine man (or woman, in many cases). Many Bahamians are fond of herbal remedies. But you don't need to rely on these primitive treatments, as most resorts have either hospitals or clinics on-site.

The major health risk here is not tropical disease, as it is in some Caribbean islands, but rather the bad luck of ingesting a bad piece of shellfish, exotic fruit, or too many rum punches. If your body is not accustomed to some of these foods, or they haven't been cleaned properly, you may suffer diarrhea. If you tend to have digestive problems, then drink bottled water and avoid ice, unpasteurized milk, and uncooked food such as fresh salads. However, fresh food served in hotels is usually quite safe to eat.

The Bahamas has excellent medical facilities. Physicians and surgeons in private practice are readily available in Nassau, Cable Beach, and Freeport/Lucaya. Medical personnel hold satellite clinics periodically in small settlements, and there are about 35 other clinics, adding up to a total of approximately 50 health facilities throughout the outlying islands. (We've listed the names and telephone numbers of specific clinics in the individual island coverage that follows throughout this book.) If intensive or urgent care is required, patients are brought by the Emergency Flight Service to **Princess Margaret Hospital** (© 242/322-2861) in Nassau. Some of the big resort hotels have in-house physicians or can quickly secure one for you.

There is also a government-operated hospital, **Rand Memorial** (© 242/352-6735), in Freeport, and several government-operated clinics on Grand Bahama Island. Nassau and Freeport/Lucaya also have private hospitals.

Even if your interior plumbing is working fine, you face a danger of overexposure to the sun, which can be a real issue in The Bahamas. You must, of course, take the usual precautions you would anywhere against sunburn and sunstroke. Your time in the sun should be wisely limited for the first few days until you become accustomed to the more intense rays of the Bahamian sun. Also bring and use strong UVA/UVB sunblock products.

WHAT TO DO IF YOU GET SICK AWAY FROM HOME

In most cases, your existing health plan will provide the coverage you need, but you should check with your provider to be sure. If you're not covered, you may want to buy **travel medical insurance** (see the section on insurance above). Bring your insurance ID card with you wherever you travel.

If you suffer from a chronic illness, consult your doctor before your departure. For conditions like epilepsy, diabetes, or heart problems, wear a **MedicAlert Identification Tag** (© 888/633-4298; www.medicalert.org), which will immediately alert doctors to your condition and give them access to your records through MedicAlert's 24-hour hot line.

Pack **prescription medications** in your carry-on luggage, and carry prescription medications in their original containers, with pharmacy labels—otherwise they won't make it through airport security. Also bring along copies of your prescriptions in case you lose your pills or run out. Don't forget an extra pair of contact lenses or prescription glasses. Carry the generic name of prescription medicines, in case a local pharmacist is unfamiliar with the brand name.

Contact the **International Association for Medical Assistance to Travelers (IAMAT;** © **716/754-4883,** or in Canada 416/652-0137; www.iamat.org) for tips on travel and health concerns in The Bahamas. The United States **Centers for Disease Control and Prevention** (© **800/311-3435;** www.cdc.gov) provides up-to-date information on necessary vaccines and health hazards. If you get sick, consider asking your hotel concierge to recommend a local doctor—even his or her own. You can also try the emergency room at a local hospital; many have walk-in clinics for emergency cases that are not life threatening. You may not get immediate attention, but you won't pay the high price of an emergency room visit.

STAYING SAFE

Crime is increasing, and visitors should exercise caution and good judgment when visiting The Bahamas. While most criminal incidents take place in a part of Nassau not usually frequented by tourists (the "Over-the-Hill" area south of downtown), crime and violence has moved into more upscale tourist and residential areas.

In the last year the U.S. Embassy has received several reports of sexual assaults, including against teenage girls. Most assaults have been perpetrated against intoxicated young women, some of whom were reportedly drugged. To minimize the potential for sexual assault, the embassy recommends that young women stay in groups, consume alcohol in moderation, and not accept rides or drinks from strangers.

Travelers should avoid walking alone after dark or in isolated areas, and avoid placing themselves in situations where they are alone with strangers. Be cautious on deserted areas of beaches at all hours. Hotel guests should always lock their doors and should never leave valuables unattended, especially on beaches. Visitors should store passport/identity documents, airline tickets, credit cards, and extra cash in hotel safes. Avoid wearing expensive jewelry, particularly Rolex watches, which criminals have specifically targeted. Use only clearly marked taxis and make a note of the license plate number for your records.

The loss or theft of a passport overseas should be reported to the local police and the nearest embassy or consulate. A lost or stolen birth certificate and/or driver's license generally cannot be replaced outside the United States. U.S. citizens may refer to the Department of State's pamphlets, *A Safe Trip Abroad* and *Tips for Travelers to the Caribbean,* for ways to promote a trouble-free journey. The pamphlets are available by mail from the Superintendent of Documents, U.S. Government Printing Office, Washington, DC 20402, via the Internet at www.gpoaccess.gov/index.html, or via the Bureau of Consular Affairs home page at www.travel.state.gov.

8 Specialized Travel Resources

TRAVELERS WITH DISABILITIES

Because these islands are relatively flat, it's fairly easy to get around, even for persons with disabilities. To find an accessible hotel, call the **Bahamas Association for the Physically Disabled** (© 242/322-2393). This agency will also send a van to the airport to transport you to your hotel for a fee, and can provide ramps.

To obtain a free copy of *Air Transportation of Handicapped Persons,* published by the U.S. Department of Transportation, write to Free Advisory Circular No. AC12032, Distribution Unit, U.S. Department of Transportation, Publications Division, 3341Q 75 Ave., Landover, MD 20785 (© 301/322-4961; fax 301/386-5394; http://isddc.dot.gov). Only written requests are accepted.

Flying Wheels Travel (© 507/451-5005; fax 507/451-1685; www.flyingwheelstravel.com) offers escorted tours and cruises that emphasize sports and private tours in minivans with lifts. **Access-Able Travel Source** (© 303/232-2979; www.access-able.com) offers extensive access information and advice for traveling around the world with disabilities. **Accessible Journeys** (© **800/846-4537** or 610/521-0339; www.disabilitytravel.com) caters specifically to slow walkers and wheelchair travelers, and their families and friends.

Organizations that offer assistance to travelers with disabilities include the **MossRehab Hospital** (www.mossresourcenet.org), which provides a library of accessible travel resources online. The **SATH (Society for Accessible Travel and Hospitality; © 212/ 447-7284;** fax 212/725-8253; www.sath.org) offers a wealth of travel resources for all types of disabilities and informed recommendations on destinations, access guides, travel agents, tour operators, vehicle rentals, and companion services. Annual membership costs $45 for adults, $30 for seniors and students. The **American Foundation for the Blind** (AFB; © **800/232-5463;** www.afb.org) provides information on traveling with Seeing Eye dogs.

For more information targeted to travelers with disabilities, check out **iCan** (www.icanonline.net/channels/travel/index.cfm). You might also take a look at the quarterly magazine *Emerging Horizons* (www.emerginghorizons.com), which costs $15 annually, $20 outside the U.S.; and *Open World Magazine,* published by the Society for Accessible Travel and Hospitality (see above; subscription: $13 annually, $21 outside the U.S.).

TIPS FOR BRITISH TRAVELERS WITH DISABILITIES
Contact the Royal Association for Disability and Rehabilitation (RADAR), Unit 12, City Forum, 250 City Rd., London, EC1V 8AF (© **020/7250-3222;** fax 020/7250-0212; www.radar.org.uk).

GAY & LESBIAN TRAVEL

Think twice before choosing The Bahamas. Although many gay people visit or live here, the country has very strict anti-homosexual laws. Relations between homosexuals are subject to criminal sanctions carrying prison terms. If you would like to make visiting gay beaches, bars, or clubs part of your vacation, consider South Miami Beach, Key West, or Puerto Rico instead.

Of course, the big resorts welcome one and all, even if forced to do so. For many years, the all-inclusive Sandals Royal Bahamian on Cable Beach refused to accept same-sex couples and booked only heterosexual guests. However, rights groups in Canada and Great Britain lobbied successfully, and the Sandals people found they could no longer advertise their resorts, and their discriminatory policies, in those countries. As a result, Sandals capitulated and ended its previous ban. However, gay and lesbian couples looking for a carefree holiday should seriously consider if they want to spend their hard-earned dollars in a resort like Sandals that did not voluntarily end its ban against homosexuals until forced to do so by more liberal and far-sighted governments.

Single gays and gay couples should travel here with great discretion. If you're intent on visiting, check out the International Gay & Lesbian Travel Association (IGLTA; ✆ 800/448-8550 or 954/776-2626; fax 954/776-3303; www.iglta.com), which links travelers up with gay-friendly hoteliers, tour operators, and airline and cruiseline representatives. It offers monthly newsletters, marketing mailings, and a membership directory.

Above and Beyond Tours (✆ 800/397-2681; www.abovebeyondtours.com) is the exclusive gay and lesbian tour operator for United Airlines. **Now, Voyager** (✆ 800/255-6951; www.nowvoyager.com) is a well-known, gay-owned and -operated travel service. **Olivia Cruises & Resorts** (✆ 800/631-6277 or 415/962-5700; www.olivia.com) charters entire resorts and ships for exclusive lesbian vacations and offers smaller group experiences for both gay and lesbian travelers.

The following travel guides are available at most travel bookstores and gay and lesbian bookstores, or you can order them from the bookstore Giovanni's Room, 1145 Pine St., Philadelphia, PA 19107 (✆ 215/923-2960; www.giovannisroom.com): *Out and About* (✆ 800/929-2268; www.outandabout.com), which offers guidebooks and a newsletter ($20 a year for 10 issues) packed with solid information on the global gay and lesbian scene; *Spartacus International Gay Guide* (Bruno Gmünder Verlag; www.spartacusworld.com/gayguide) and *Odysseus: The International Gay Travel Planner* (Odysseus Enterprises Ltd.), both good, annual English-language guidebooks focused on gay men; the *Damron* guides (www.damron.com), with separate, annual books for gay men and lesbians; and *Gay Travel A to Z: The World of Gay & Lesbian Travel Options at Your Fingertips* by Marianne Ferrari (Ferrari International; Box 35575, Phoenix, AZ 85069), a good gay and lesbian guidebook series.

SENIOR TRAVEL

Anyone over the age of 50 can join **AARP** (formerly the American Association of Retired Persons), 601 E St. NW, Washington, DC 20049 (✆ 888/687-2277 or 202/434-2277; www.aarp.org). Members often get discounts on hotels, airfares, and car rentals. AARP offers members a wide range of benefits, including *AARP The Magazine* and a monthly newsletter.

Many reliable agencies and organizations target the 50-plus market. **Elderhostel** (© **877/426-8056;** www.elderhostel.org) arranges study programs for those aged 55 and over (and a spouse or companion of any age) in the U.S. and in more than 80 countries around the world. Most courses last 5 to 7 days in the U.S. (2–4 weeks abroad), and many include airfare, accommodations in university dormitories or modest inns, meals, and tuition. **ElderTreks** (© **800/741-7956;** www.eldertreks.com) offers small-group tours to off-the-beaten-path or adventure-travel locations, restricted to travelers age 50 and older.

Recommended publications offering travel resources and discounts for seniors include: the quarterly magazine *Travel 50 & Beyond* (www.travel50andbeyond.com); *Travel Unlimited: Uncommon Adventures for the Mature Traveler* (Avalon); *101 Tips for Mature Travelers,* available from Grand Circle Travel (© **800/221-2610** or 617/350-7500; www.gct.com); *The 50+ Traveler's Guidebook* (from St. Martin's Press); and *Unbelievably Good Deals and Great Adventures That You Absolutely Can't Get Unless You're Over 50* (from McGraw Hill), by Joann Rattner Heilman.

FAMILY TRAVEL

The Bahamas is one of the top family-vacation destinations in North America. The smallest toddlers can spend blissful hours on sandy beaches and in the shallow seawater or in swimming pools constructed with them in mind. Pursuits for older children range from boat rides to shell collecting to horseback riding, hiking, and dancing. Some resorts teach old-enough kids to swim, snorkel, or windsurf.

Look for our "Kids" icon, indicating attractions, restaurants, or hotels and resorts that are especially family friendly. See also "The Best Family Vacations," in chapter 1, for additional recommendations.

Familyhostel (© **800/733-9753;** www.learn.unh.edu/familyhostel) takes the whole family, including kids ages 8 to 15, on moderately priced domestic and international learning vacations. Lectures, field trips, and sightseeing are guided by a team of academics.

Recommended family travel Internet sites include **Family Travel Forum** (www.familytravelforum.com), a comprehensive site that offers customized trip planning; **Family Travel Network** (www. familytravelnetwork.com), an award-winning site that offers travel features, deals, and tips; **Traveling Internationally with Your Kids** (www.travelwithyourkids.com), a comprehensive site offering sound advice for long-distance and international travel with children; and **Family Travel Files** (www.thefamilytravelfiles.com), which offers an online magazine and a directory of off-the-beaten-path tours and tour operators for families.

AFRICAN-AMERICAN TRAVEL

Agencies and organizations that provide resources for black travelers include: **Rodgers Travel, Inc.** (© **800/825-1775** or 215/473-1775; www.rodgerstravel.com), a Philadelphia-based travel agency with an extensive menu of tours in destinations worldwide, including heritage and private group tours; and the **African-American Association of Innkeepers International** (© **877/422-5777**; www.african americaninns.com), which provides information on member B&Bs in the U.S., Canada, and the Caribbean.

Black Travel Online (www.blacktravelonline.com) posts news on upcoming events and includes links to articles and travel-booking sites. **Soul of America** (www.soulofamerica.com) is a more comprehensive website, with travel tips, event and family reunion postings, and sections on historically black beach resorts and active vacations.

9 Planning Your Trip Online

SURFING FOR AIRFARES

The "big three" online travel agencies, **Expedia.com** (www.expedia. com), **Travelocity** (www.travelocity.com), and **Orbitz** (www.orbitz. com), sell most of the air tickets bought on the Internet. (Canadian travelers should try expedia.ca and Travelocity.ca; U.K. residents can go for expedia.co.uk and opodo.co.uk.) Each has different business deals with the airlines and may offer different fares on the same flights, so it's wise to shop around. Expedia and Travelocity will also send you **e-mail notification** when a cheap fare becomes available to your favorite destination. Of the smaller travel agency websites, **SideStep** (www.sidestep.com) has gotten the best reviews from Frommer's authors. It's a browser add-on that purports to "search 140 sites at once," though in reality only beats competitors' fares as often as other sites do.

Also check **airline websites,** especially those of low-fare carriers, whose fares are often misreported or simply missing from travel agency websites. Even with major airlines, you can often shave a few bucks from a fare by booking directly through the airline and avoiding a travel agency's transaction fee. But you'll get most of these discounts only by booking online; even their phone agents know nothing about the cheapest fares. Great **last-minute deals** are available through free weekly e-mail services provided directly by the airlines. Most of these are announced on Tuesday or Wednesday and must be purchased online. Most are only valid for travel that weekend, but some can be booked weeks or months in advance. Sign up for weekly e-mail alerts at airline websites or check megasites that compile lists of last-minute specials, such as **SmarterTravel.com**. For last-minute trips, **site59.com** in the U.S. and **lastminute travel.com** in the U.S. and **lastminute.com** in Europe often have better air and hotel package deals than the major label sites. A website listing numerous bargain sites and airlines around the world is **www.itravelnet.com**.

If you're willing to give up some control over your flight details, use what is called an **"opaque" fare service** like **Priceline** (www.priceline.com; www.priceline.co.uk) or its smaller competitor **Hotwire** (www.hotwire.com). Both offer rock-bottom prices in exchange for travel on a "mystery airline" at a mysterious time of day, often with a mysterious change of planes en route. The mystery airlines are all major, well-known carriers—and the possibility of being sent from Philadelphia to Chicago via Tampa is remote; the airlines' routing computers have gotten a lot better than they used to be. But your chances of getting a 6am or 11pm flight are pretty high. Hotwire tells you flight prices before you buy; Priceline usually has better deals than Hotwire, but you have to play their "name our price" game. If you're new at this, the helpful folks at **BiddingForTravel** (www.biddingfortravel.com) do a good job of demystifying Priceline's prices and strategies. Priceline and Hotwire are great for flights within North America and between the U.S. and Europe. But for flights to other parts of the world, consolidators will almost always beat their fares. *Note:* In 2004 Priceline added nonopaque service to its roster. You now have the option to pick exact flights, times, and airlines from a list of offers—or opt to bid on opaque fares as before.

Frommers.com: The Complete Travel Resource

For an excellent travel-planning resource, we highly recommend **Frommers.com** (www.frommers.com), voted best travel site by *PC Magazine*. We're a little biased, of course, but we guarantee that you'll find indispensable travel tips, reviews, monthly vacation giveaways, and online-booking capabilities.

For much more about airfares and savvy air-travel tips and advice, pick up a copy of *Frommer's Fly Safe, Fly Smart* (Wiley Publishing, Inc.).

SURFING FOR HOTELS

Shopping online for hotels is a possibility in The Bahamas, although many small hotels and B&Bs don't show up on websites at all. Of the "big three" sites, **Expedia.com** may be the best choice, thanks to its long list of special deals. **Travelocity** (www.travelocity.com) runs a close second. Hotel specialist sites **hotels.com** and **quikbook. com** are also reliable. An excellent free program, **TravelAxe** (www.travelaxe.net), can help you search multiple hotel sites at once, even ones you may never have heard of.

Priceline and Hotwire are even better for hotels than for airfares; with both, you're allowed to pick the neighborhood and quality level of your hotel before offering your money. *Note:* Hotwire overrates its hotels by one star—what Hotwire calls a four-star is a three-star anywhere else.

SURFING FOR RENTAL CARS

For booking rental cars online, the best deals are usually found at rental-car company websites, although all the major online travel agencies also offer rental-car reservations services. Priceline and Hotwire work well for rental cars, too; the only "mystery" is which major rental company you get, and for most travelers the difference between Hertz, Avis, and Budget is negligible.

10 The 21st-Century Traveler

INTERNET ACCESS AWAY FROM HOME

Of course, using your own laptop—or PDA—gives you the most flexibility. But even without a computer, you can access your e-mail in The Bahamas, more likely at your hotel than at a cybercafe. **Call your hotel in advance** to see what your options are.

USING A CELLPHONE OUTSIDE THE U.S.

Take a look at your wireless provider's coverage map on its website or call the company directly to find out if your phone might work in The Bahamas. If not, two good wireless rental companies are **InTouch USA** (© 800/872-7626; www.intouchglobal.com) and **RoadPost** (www.roadpost.com; © 888/290-1606 or 905/272-5665). Give them your itinerary, and they'll tell you what wireless products you need. InTouch will also, for free, double-check whether your existing phone will work in The Bahamas; simply call © **703/222-7161** between 9am and 4pm Eastern Time, or go to http://intouch global.com/travel.htm.

11 Getting There: Flying to The Bahamas

Lying right off the east coast of Florida, the archipelago of The Bahamas is the easiest and most convenient foreign destination you can fly to unless you live close to the Canadian or Mexican borders.

Nassau is the busiest and most popular point of entry (this is where you'll fly if you're staying on Paradise Island). Freeport, on Grand Bahama, also has its own airport, which is served by flights from the U.S. mainland, too.

Flight time to Nassau from Miami is about 35 minutes; from New York, 2½ hours; from Atlanta, 2 hours and 5 minutes; from Philadelphia, 2 hours and 45 minutes; from Charlotte, 2 hours and 10 minutes; from central Florida, 1 hour and 10 minutes; and, from Toronto, 3 hours.

THE MAJOR AIRLINES

From the U.S. mainland, about a half-dozen carriers fly nonstop to the country's major point of entry and busiest airline hub, **Nassau International Airport** (© **242/377-7281**). Some also fly to the archipelago's second-most-populous city of Freeport.

American Airlines (© **800/433-7300;** www.aa.com), has several flights per day from Miami to Nassau as well as four daily flights from Fort Lauderdale to Nassau. In addition, the carrier flies three times daily from Miami to Freeport. It also offers three flights daily from Miami to Georgetown and one flight daily from Miami to Marsh Harbour.

Delta (© **800/221-1212;** www.delta.com) has several connections to The Bahamas, with service from Atlanta, Orlando, and New York's LaGuardia.

The national airline of The Bahamas, **Bahamasair** (© **800/222-4262;** www.bahamasair.com), flies to The Bahamas from Miami and Fort Lauderdale, landing at either Nassau (with seven nonstop flights daily) or Freeport (with two nonstop flights daily).

US Airways (© **800/428-4322;** www.usairways.com) offers daily direct flights to Nassau from Philadelphia and Charlotte, North Carolina.

Other carriers include **Continental Airlines** (© **800/525-0280;** www.continental.com), through its regional affiliate, Gulfstream International, has greatly expanded its link to The Bahamas through

South Florida. Continental operates flights between Fort Lauderdale and Andros Town on Andros, with four round-trip flights each week. The airline also offers daily service from Fort Lauderdale to both Georgetown and Governors Harbour. In addition, it maintains frequent links between Fort Lauderdale and Marsh Harbour, North Eleuthera, and Treasure Cay. **Twin Air** (② **954/359-8266**; www.flytwinair.com) flies from Fort Lauderdale three times a week to Rock Sound and Governor's Harbour and four times a week to North Eleuthera.

Air Canada (② **888/247-2262**; www.aircanada.com) is the only carrier offering scheduled service to Nassau from Canada. Direct flights from Toronto and Montreal leave daily; flights from Toronto and Montréal, as well as other Canadian cities, make connections in the U.S.

British travelers opt for transatlantic passage aboard **British Airways** (② **800/247-9297** in the U.S. or 0870/850-9850 in the U.K.; www.britishairways.com), which offers four weekly direct flights from London to Nassau. The airline also has at least one flight daily to Miami. From here, a staggering number of connections are available to Nassau and many other points within the archipelago on several carriers.

GETTING THROUGH THE AIRPORT

Generally, you'll be fine if you arrive at the airport **1 hour** before a domestic flight and **2 hours** before an international flight.

Bring a **current, government-issued photo ID** such as a driver's license or passport. Keep your ID at the ready to show at check-in, the security checkpoint, and sometimes even the gate. (Even children under 18 may need government-issued photo IDs for most international flights.)

Passengers with **e-tickets** can beat the ticket-counter lines by using airport **electronic kiosks** or even **online check-in** from your home computer. Online check-in involves logging on to your airlines' website, accessing your reservation, and printing out your boarding pass—and the airline may even offer you bonus miles to do so. If you're using a kiosk at the airport, bring the credit card you used to book the ticket or your frequent-flier card. Print out your boarding pass from the kiosk and simply proceed to the security checkpoint with your pass and a photo ID. If you're checking bags or looking to snag an exit-row seat, you will be able to do so using most airline kiosks. Even the smaller airlines are employing the kiosk system, but always call your airline to make sure these alternatives are available.

The Gulf of Mexico & the Caribbean

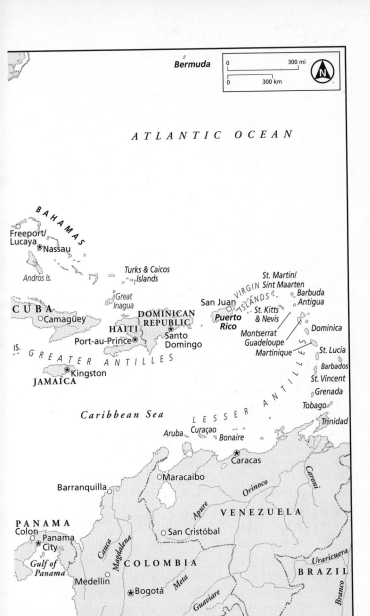

Bermuda

0   300 mi
0   300 km

N

ATLANTIC   OCEAN

BAHAMAS
Freeport/
Lucaya
Nassau
Andros Is.
Turks & Caicos
Islands
*Great
Inagua*
CUBA
Camagüey
**DOMINICAN
REPUBLIC**
HAITI
Port-au-Prince
Santo
Domingo
San Juan
*VIRGIN
ISLANDS*
St. Martin/
Sint Maarten
Barbuda
Antigua
*St. Kitts
& Nevis*
**Puerto
Rico**
Montserrat
Guadeloupe
Martinique
Dominica
St. Lucia
Barbados
St. Vincent
Grenada
Tobago
Trinidad
GREATER ANTILLES
IS.
Kingston
JAMAICA
Caribbean   Sea
LESSER   ANTILLES
Aruba
Curaçao
Bonaire
Caracas
Maracaibo
Barranquilla
Caroni
PANAMA
Colon
Panama
City
*Gulf of
Panama*
Cauca
Magdalena
COLOMBIA
Medellín
Bogotá
Meta
Guaviare
Apure
Orinoco
VENEZUELA
San Cristóbal
Uraricuera
BRAZIL
Branco

Curbside check-in is also a good way to avoid lines, although a few airlines still ban curbside check-in; call before you go.

Security lines are getting shorter than they were during 2001 and 2002, but long ones still remain. If you have trouble standing for long periods of time, tell an airline employee; the airline will provide a wheelchair. Speed up security by **not wearing metal objects** such as big belt buckles or clanky earrings. If you've got metallic body parts, a note from your doctor can prevent a long chat with the security screeners. Keep in mind that only **ticketed passengers** are allowed past security, except for folks escorting passengers with disabilities or children.

Federalization has stabilized **what you can carry on** and **what you can't.** The general rule is that sharp things are out, nail clippers are okay, and food and beverages must be passed through the X-ray machine—but that security screeners can't make you drink from your coffee cup. Bring food in your carry-on rather than checking it, as explosive-detection machines used on checked luggage have been known to mistake food (especially chocolate, for some reason) for bombs. Travelers in the U.S. are allowed one carry-on bag, plus a "personal item" such as a purse, briefcase, or laptop bag. You can stuff all sorts of things into a laptop bag; as long as it has a laptop in it, it's still considered a personal item. The Transportation Security Administration (TSA) has issued a list of restricted items; check its website (www.tsa.gov/public/index.jsp) for details.

The TSA has also recommended that you lock your checked baggage with TSA **"accepted and recognized" locks**. For more information, go to www.travelsentry.org and www.safeskielocks.com. Because TSA screeners can open and relock these locks, they can avoid damage to the lock or to your bag if a physical inspection is necessary. Alternatively, you might consider using plastic "zip ties," which can be bought at hardware stores and can be easily cut off.

FLYING FOR LESS: TIPS FOR GETTING THE BEST AIRFARE

Travelers who need to purchase tickets at the last minute, change their itinerary at a moment's notice, or fly one-way often get stuck paying the premium rate. Here are some ways to keep your airfare costs down.

- **Book long in advance, stay over Saturday night,** or **fly midweek** or **at less-trafficked hours**. If your schedule is flexible, say so, and ask if you can secure a cheaper fare by changing your flight plans.

- Keep an eye out in local newspapers for **promotional specials** or **fare wars,** when airlines lower prices on their most popular routes. Especially if you can travel in the off-months, you may snag a bargain.
- Search **the Internet** for cheap fares (see "Planning Your Trip Online").
- Look for **consolidators,** also known as bucket shops, which are sources for international tickets. Start by looking in Sunday newspaper travel sections. *Beware:* Bucket shop tickets are usually nonrefundable or rigged with stiff cancellation penalties, often as high as 50% to 75% of the ticket price, and some put you on charter airlines with questionable safety records. **FlyCheap** (© **800/FLY-CHEAP;** www.1800flycheap.com) is owned by package-holiday megalith MyTravel and so has especially good access to fares for sunny destinations. **Air Tickets Direct** (© **800/778-3447;** www.airticketsdirect.com) is based in Montreal and leverages the currently weak Canadian dollar for low fares; it'll also book trips to places that U.S. travel agents won't touch, such as Cuba.
- Join **frequent-flier clubs**. It's free, and you'll get the best choice of seats, faster response to phone inquiries, and prompter service if your luggage is stolen, your flight is canceled or delayed, or if you want to change your seat. Accrue enough miles, and you'll be rewarded with free flights and elite status. You don't need to fly to build frequent-flier miles—frequent-flier credit cards can provide thousands of miles for doing your everyday shopping.

12 Package Deals

Before you search for the lowest airfare on your own, you may want to consider booking your flight as part of a package deal—a way to travel independently but pay group rates.

A package tour is not an escorted tour, in which you're led around by a guide. Except by cruise ships visiting certain islands, the option of being escorted around six or so Bahamian islands on an escorted tour does not exist.

Often—and especially when booking popular destinations like The Bahamas—a package that includes airfare, hotel, and transportation to and from the airport will cost you less than just the hotel alone would have, had you booked plane tickets, hotels, and car rentals independently. Packages are sold in bulk to tour operators who resell them to the public at a cost that drastically undercuts standard rates.

It's important to spend a little time shopping around; just be sure to compare apples to apples, since the package offerings can vary. You can use the reviews and rack rates given in this book to evaluate whether a package is really a good deal.

Here are a few tips to help you tell one package from another, and figure out which one is right for you:

- **Read the fine print.** Hotel taxes? Airport transfers? Don't pay for a rental car you don't need. Before you commit to a package, know how much flexibility you have, say, if your child gets sick or your boss suddenly asks you to adjust your vacation schedule. Some packagers require ironclad commitments, whereas others charge only minimal fees for changes or cancellations.

- **Use your best judgment.** If a deal appears to be too good to be true, it probably is. Go with a reputable firm with a proven track record. When in doubt, ask your travel agent.

The best place to start your search is the travel section of your local Sunday newspaper. Also check the ads in the back of national travel magazines.

Vacation Together (© 877/444-4547; www.vacationtogether. com) allows you to search for and book packages offered by a number of tour operators and airlines. The **United States Tour Operators Association**'s website (© 212/599-6599; www.ustoa.com) has a search engine that allows you to look for operators that offer packages to a specific destination.

RECOMMENDED PACKAGE-TOUR OPERATORS

Liberty Travel (© 888/271-1584; www.libertytravel.com) is one of the biggest packagers in the Northeast, and it usually boasts a full-page ad in Sunday papers.

One good source of package deals is the airlines themselves. Most major airlines offer air/land packages, including **American Airlines Vacations** (© 800/321-2121; www.aavacations.com), **Delta Vacations** (© 800/221-6666; www.deltavacations.com), **US Airways Vacations** (© 800/455-0123; www.usairwaysvacations.com), and **Continental Airlines Vacations** (© 800/301-3800; www. covacations.com).

The biggest hotel chains and resorts also offer package deals. If you already know where you want to stay, call the resort itself and ask if it can offer land/air packages.

There's also **TourScan, Inc.,** 1051 Boston Post Rd., Darien, CT 06820 (© **800/962-2080** in the U.S.; www.tourscan.com), which researches the best value vacation at each hotel and condo.

For one-stop shopping on the Web, go to **www.vacation packager.com**, a search engine that will link you to many different package-tour operators offering Bahamas vacations, often with a company profile summarizing the company's basic booking and cancellation terms.

ALL-INCLUSIVE TOURS

Just-A-Vacation, Inc., 2910 Hamilton St., Hyattville, MD 20782 (© **800/683-6313;** www.justavacation.com) specializes in all-inclusive resorts on the islands of The Bahamas, plus other destinations in the Caribbean including Barbados, Jamaica, Aruba, St. Lucia, and Antigua.

Club Med (© **888/WEB-CLUB;** www.clubmed.com) has various all-inclusive options throughout the Caribbean and The Bahamas.

SPECIAL TOURS FOR FISHERMEN

Frontiers International (© **800/245-1950** or 724/935-1577; www.frontierstrvl.com) features fly- and spin-fishing tours of The Bahamas and is a specialist in saltwater-fishing destinations.

FOR BRITISH TRAVELERS

Package tours to The Bahamas can be booked through **Harlequin Worldwide Connoisseurs Collection,** 2 North Rd., South Ockendon, Essex RM15 6AZ (© **01708/850-300;** www.harlequin holidays.com). This agency offers both air and hotel packages not only to Nassau, but to most of the Out Islands as well. The company also specializes in scuba-diving and golf holidays.

Another specialist is **Kuoni Travel,** Kuoni House, Dorking, Surrey RH5 4AZ (© **01306/744-442;** www.kuoni.co.uk), which offers both land and air packages to The Bahamas, including such destinations as Nassau and Freeport, and to some places in the Out Islands. They also offer packages for self-catering villas on Paradise Island.

13 For the Cruise-Ship Traveler

Cruises to The Bahamas are usually either 3- or 4-day weekend getaways or weeklong itineraries in which the ship may stop at Nassau, Freeport, and/or one of several privately owned Bahamian islands for a day at the beach.

A brief summary on cruises is below, but for more detailed information on specific cruise lines that offer diversions in The Bahamas, consider picking up a copy of *Frommer's Cruises & Ports of Call 2006.*

Regardless of the ship you choose, your cruise will probably depart from the cruise capital of the world, Miami. A handful of vessels also depart for Bahamian waters from Port Everglades (adjacent to Fort Lauderdale), Port Canaveral, and, in rare instances, from New York. Many cruise-ship passengers combine a cruise with visits to Orlando's theme parks, Miami's South Beach, the Florida Everglades, or the Florida Keys and Key West.

Nearly all cabins aboard ships today have two twin beds that can be pushed together, plus storage space (of varying size), a shower and a toilet (ditto), and sometimes a TV showing a rotating stock of programs. If you want to keep costs to a minimum when booking, ask for one of the smaller, inside cabins (one without windows). If you like to be active all day and stay out late enjoying the ship's bars and nightclubs, you won't miss the sunshine anyway. On the other hand, ships offer suites today that have an amazing array of pampering options (including hot tubs on their own private verandas!).

Because they buy in such bulk, cruise lines typically offer some of the best deals on airfare to your port of embarkation, and also typically offer extension packages that allow pre- or post-cruise stays at a hotel or resort.

Getting around Freeport/Lucaya or Nassau is relatively easy, and the official shore excursions offered by most ships are dull and sometimes restrictive, so it's best to decide what you want to do (shopping, swimming, snorkeling, or gambling) and head off on your own during your stop at each port of call. You'll certainly have time to relax at the beach if you choose, or to enjoy watersports (the chapters that follow will give you details on what companies or outfitters to contact for equipment, so you needn't feel dependent on the cruise line for everything).

In Nassau, cruise ships anchor at piers along Prince George Wharf. Taxi drivers meet all arrivals and will transport you into the heart of Nassau, center of most shopping and sightseeing activities. Duty-free shops also lie just outside the dock area, but for that, you'd do better to go inside the city's commercial and historic core.

As you disembark, you'll find a tourist information office in a tall pink tower, where you can pick up maps of New Providence Island or of Nassau itself. One-hour walking tours are conducted from here if you'd like an overview of the city, with a guide pointing out historic monuments. Outside this office, an ATM will supply you with U.S. dollars if your cash is running low.

14 Getting Around

If your final destination is Paradise Island, Freeport, or Nassau (Cable Beach) and you plan to fly, you'll have little trouble in reaching your destination.

BY PLANE

The national airline of The Bahamas, **Bahamasair** (© 800/222-4262; www.bahamasair.com), serves 19 airports on 12 Bahamian islands.

BY RENTAL CAR

You don't really need to rent a car in The Bahamas, especially if you're coming for a few days of soaking in the sun at a resort's own beach. In Nassau and Freeport, you can easily rely on public transportation or taxis.

Most visitors need transportation only from the airport to their hotel; perhaps you can arrange an island tour later, and an expensive private car won't be necessary. Your hotel can always arrange a taxi for you if you want to venture out.

You may decide that you want a car to explore beyond the tourist areas of New Providence Island, and you're very likely to want one on Grand Bahama Island.

Just remember: Road rules are much the same as those in the U.S., but you *drive on the left.*

The major U.S. car-rental companies operate in The Bahamas, but not on all the remote islands. We always prefer to do business with one of the major firms if they're present because you can call ahead and reserve from home via a toll-free number; they tend to offer better-maintained vehicles; and it's easier to resolve any disputes after the fact. Call **Budget** (© 800/472-3325; www.budget.com), **Hertz** (© 800/654-3131; www.hertz.com), **Dollar** (© 800/800-3665; www.dollarcar.com), or **Avis** (© 800/331-1212; www.avis.com). Budget rents in Nassau and Paradise Island. Liability insurance is compulsory.

"Petrol" is easily available in Nassau and Freeport, though quite expensive. The major towns of the islands have service stations. You should have no problems on New Providence or Grand Bahama Island unless you start out with a nearly empty tank.

Visitors may drive with their home driver's license for up to 3 months. For longer stays, you'll need to secure a Bahamian driver's license.

As you emerge at one of the major airports, including those of Nassau (New Providence) and Freeport (Grand Bahama Island), you can pick up island maps that are pretty good for routine touring around those islands.

BY TAXI

Once you've reached your destination, you'll find that taxis are plentiful in the Nassau–Cable Beach–Paradise Island area and in the Freeport/Lucaya area on Grand Bahama Island. These cabs, for the most part, are metered—but they take cash only, no credit cards. See "Getting Around" in the chapters on each island that follow for further details.

15 Tips on Accommodations

The Bahamas offers a wide selection of accommodations, ranging from small private guesthouses to large luxury resorts. Hotels vary in size and facilities, from deluxe (offering room service, sports, swimming pools, and entertainment) to fairly simple inns.

There are package deals galore, and they are always cheaper than "rack rates." (A rack rate is what an individual pays if he or she literally walks in from the street. These are the rates we've listed in the chapters that follow, though you can almost always do better—especially at the big resorts.) It's sometimes good to go to a reliable travel agent to find out what, if anything, is available in the way of a land-and-air package before booking a particular accommodation.

There is no rigid classification of hotel properties in the islands. The word "deluxe" is often used (or misused) when "first class" might have been a more appropriate term. For that and other reasons, we've presented detailed descriptions of the properties so that you'll get an idea of what to expect. However, even in the deluxe and first-class resorts and hotels, don't expect top-rate service and efficiency. When you go to turn on the shower, sometimes you get water and sometimes you don't. You may even experience power failures.

The winter season in The Bahamas runs roughly from the middle of December to the middle of April, and hotels charge their highest

What the Hotel Symbols Mean

As you're shopping around for your hotel, you may see the following terms used:

- **AP (American Plan):** Includes three meals a day (sometimes called full board or full pension).
- **EP (European Plan):** Includes only the room—no meals.
- **CP (Continental Plan):** Includes continental breakfast of juice, coffee, bread, and jam.
- **MAP (Modified American Plan):** Sometimes called half board or half pension, this room rate includes breakfast and dinner (or lunch instead of dinner if you prefer).

prices during this peak period. Winter is generally the dry season in the islands, but there can be heavy rainfall regardless of the time of year. During the winter months, make reservations 2 months in advance if you can. You can't book early enough if you want to travel over Christmas or in February.

The off season in The Bahamas—roughly from mid-April to mid-December (although this varies from hotel to hotel)—amounts to a sale. In most cases, hotel rates are slashed a startling 20% to 60%. It's a bonanza for cost-conscious travelers, especially for families who can travel in the summer. Be prepared for very strong sun, though, plus a higher chance of rain. Also note that hurricane season runs through summer and fall.

MAP VS. AP, OR DO YOU WANT TO GO EP?

All Bahamian resorts offer a **European Plan (EP)** rate, which means that you pay for the price of a room. That leaves you free to dine around at night at various other resorts or restaurants without restriction. Another plan preferred by many is the **Continental Plan (CP),** which means you get a continental breakfast of juice, coffee, bread, and jam included in a set price. This plan is preferred by those who don't like to look around for a place to eat around breakfast time.

Another major option is the **Modified American Plan (MAP),** which includes breakfast and one main meal of the day, either lunch or dinner. The final choice is the **American Plan (AP),** which includes breakfast, lunch, and dinner. At certain resorts you will save money by booking in on either MAP or AP, because discounts are granted. If you dine a la carte often for lunch and dinner, your dining costs will be much higher than if you stay on the MAP or AP.

Dining at your hotel at night cuts down on transportation costs. Taxis especially are expensive. Nonetheless, if dining out and having many different culinary experiences is your idea of a vacation, and you're willing to pay the higher price, avoid AP plans or at least make sure the hotel where you're staying has more than one dining room.

One option is to ask if your hotel has a dine-around plan. You might still keep costs in check, but you can avoid a culinary rut by taking your meals in some other restaurants if your hotel has such a plan. Such plans are rare in The Bahamas, which does not specialize in all-inclusive resorts the way that Jamaica or some other islands do.

Before booking a room, check with a good travel agent or investigate on your own what you are likely to save by booking on a dining plan. Under certain circumstances in winter you might not have a choice if MAP is dictated as a requirement for staying there. It pays to investigate, of course.

THE RIGHT ROOM AT THE RIGHT PRICE

Ask detailed questions when booking a room. Specify your likes and dislikes. There are several logistics of getting the right room in a hotel. In general, back rooms cost less than oceanfront rooms, and lower rooms cost less than upper-floor units. Therefore, if budget is a major consideration with you, opt for the cheaper rooms. You won't have a great view, but you'll pay less and save your money for something else. Just make sure that it isn't next to the all-night drummers.

Of course, all first-class or deluxe resorts feature air-conditioning, but many Bahamian inns do not. Cooling might be by ceiling fans or, in more modest places, the breeze from an open window, which also brings the mosquitoes. If sleeping in a climate-controlled environment is important to your vacation, ascertain this in advance.

If you're being your own travel agent, it pays to shop around by calling the local number given for a hotel and its toll-free number if it has one. You can check online and call a travel agent to see where you can obtain the best price.

Another tip: Ask if you can get an upgrade or a free night's stay if you stay an extra few days. If you're traveling during the marginal periods between low and high season, you can sometimes delay your travel plans by a week or 10 days and get a substantial reduction. For example, a $300 room booked on April 12 might have been lowered to $180 by April 17, as mid-April marks the beginning of the low season in The Bahamas.

Tip for seniors: Ask if an AARP card will get you a discount.

Transfers from the airports or the cruise dock are included in some hotel bookings, most often in a package plan but usually not in ordinary bookings. This is true of first-class and deluxe resorts but rarely of medium-priced or budget accommodations. Always ascertain whether transfers (which can be expensive) are included.

When using the facilities at a resort, make sure that you know exactly what is free and what costs money. For example, swimming in the pool is nearly always free, but you might be charged for use of a tennis court. Nearly all watersports cost extra, unless you're booked on some special plan such as a scuba package. Some resorts seem to charge every time you breathe and might end up costing more than a deluxe hotel that includes most everything in the price.

Some hotels are right on the beach. Others involve transfers to the beach by taxi or bus, so factor in transportation costs, which can mount quickly if you stay 5 days to a week.

THE ALL-INCLUSIVES

A hugely popular option in Jamaica, the all-inclusive resort hotel concept finally has a foothold in The Bahamas. At most resorts, everything is included—sometimes even drinks. You get your room and all meals, plus entertainment and many watersports (although some cost extra). Some people find the cost of this all-inclusive holiday cheaper than if they'd paid individually for each item, and some simply appreciate knowing in advance what their final bill will be.

The first all-inclusive resort hotel in The Bahamas was **Club Med** (© 800/258-2633; www.clubmed.com) on Paradise Island. This is not a swinging-singles kind of place; it's popular with everybody, from honeymooners to families with kids along. There's another mammoth Club Med at Governor's Harbour on Eleuthera. Families with kids like it a lot here, and the resort also attracts scuba divers. There's a third branch in San Salvador, in the Southern Bahamas, which has more of a luxurious hideaway atmosphere.

The biggest all-inclusive of them all, **Sandals** (© 800/SANDALS; www.sandals.com), came to The Bahamas in 1995 on Cable Beach. This Jamaican company is now walking its sandals across the Caribbean, having established firm beachheads in Ocho Rios, Montego Bay, and Negril. The most famous of the all-inclusives (but not necessarily the best), it recently ended its ban against same-sex couples. See Chapter 3 for details.

RENTAL VILLAS & VACATION HOMES

You might rent a big villa, a good-size apartment in someone's condo, or even a small beach cottage (more accurately called a cabana).

Private apartments come with or without maid service (ask upfront exactly what to expect). This is more of a no-frills option than the villas and condos. The apartments may not be in buildings with swimming pools, and they may not have a front desk to help you.

Many cottages or cabanas ideally open onto a beach, although others may be clustered around a communal swimming pool. Most of them are fairly simple, containing no more than a plain bedroom plus a small kitchen and bathroom. In the peak winter season, reservations should be made at least 5 or 6 months in advance.

Hideaways International (© **888/843-4433** in the U.S. or 603/430-4433; www.hideaways.com) publishes *Hideaways Guide,* a 148-page pictorial directory of home rentals throughout the world, with full descriptions so you know what you're renting. Rentals range from cottages to staffed villas to whole islands! On most rentals you deal directly with owners. At condos and small resorts, Hideaways offers member discounts. Other services include specialty cruises, yacht charters, airline ticketing, car rentals, and hotel reservations. Annual membership costs $185.

Sometimes local tourist offices will also advise you on vacation-home rentals if you write or call them directly.

THE BAHAMIAN GUESTHOUSE

Many Bahamians stay at a guesthouse when traveling in their own islands. In The Bahamas, however, the term "guesthouse" can mean anything. Sometimes so-called guesthouses are really like simple motels built around swimming pools. Others are small individual cottages, with their own kitchenettes, constructed around a main building in which you'll often find a bar and restaurant serving local food.

FAST FACTS: The Bahamas

American Express Representing American Express in The Bahamas is **Destinatinos,** on Shirley Street (between Charlotte and Parliament sts.), Nassau (© **242/322-2931**). Hours are 9am to 5pm Monday through Friday. The travel department is also open Saturday 9am to 1pm. If you present a personal check and an Amex card, you can buy traveler's checks here.

Area Code The area code for The Bahamas is **242.**

ATMs See "Money," earlier in this chapter.

Business Hours In Nassau, Cable Beach, and Freeport/Lucaya, commercial banking hours are 9:30am to 3pm Monday through Thursday, 9:30am to 5pm on Friday. Most government offices are open Monday through Friday from 9am to 5pm, and most shops are open Monday through Saturday from 9am to 5pm.

Camera & Film Purchasing film in Nassau/Paradise Island or Freeport/Lucaya is relatively easy, if a little expensive.

Car Rentals See "Getting Around," earlier in this chapter. We do not recommend renting a car in The Bahamas.

Currency See "Money," earlier in this chapter.

Drug Laws Importing, possessing, or dealing unlawful drugs, including marijuana, is a serious offense in The Bahamas, with heavy penalties. Customs officers may at their discretion conduct body searches for drugs or other contraband goods.

Drugstores Nassau and Freeport are amply supplied with pharmacies (see individual listings).

Electricity Electricity is normally 120 volts, 60 cycles, AC. American appliances are fully compatible; British or European appliances will need both converters and adapters.

Embassies & Consulates The U.S. Embassy is on 42 Queen St., P.O. Box N-8197, Nassau (© **242/322-1181**), and the Canadian consulate is on Shirley Street Shopping Plaza, Nassau (© **242/393-2123**). The British High Commission is at Ansbacher House (3rd floor), East Street, Nassau (© **242/325-7471**).

Emergencies Throughout most of The Bahamas, the number to call for a medical, dental, or hospital emergency is © **911.** To report a fire, however, call © **411.**

Etiquette & Customs It is impolite anywhere to rush up to someone and demand that they supply you with directions to a place; Bahamians gently lead into conversations with a greeting and friendly comments before getting down to business.

Business in offices is conducted rather formally with exchange of business cards, elaborate handshakes, and the like. If you're doing business in The Bahamas, wear business clothes as you would to any office in America. Don't show up in resort wear or shorts for any formal meetings or functions.

When leaving the beach, it's recommended that men put on a shirt and pants, even a pair of jeans, before heading into a town. Women should wear a cover-up for their bathing suit, or else slip into a tropical dress or pants.

If you're planning to attend religious services, wear the best clothes you brought along. Bahamians believe in dressing up for their "Sunday-go-to meeting."

Regardless of how much you want to take a snapshot of an islander, it is extremely rude to photograph anyone without his or her permission.

Holidays Public holidays observed in The Bahamas are New Year's Day, Good Friday, Easter Sunday, Easter Monday, Whitmonday (7 weeks after Easter), Labour Day (the first Fri in June), Independence Day (July 10), Emancipation Day (the first Mon in Aug), Discovery Day (Oct 12), Christmas, and Boxing Day (the day after Christmas). When a holiday falls on Saturday or Sunday, stores and offices are usually closed on the following Monday.

Information See "Visitor Information," earlier in this chapter.

Internet Access Access is limited on the islands, but it can be obtained. **Cybercafe,** in The Mall at Marathon in Nassau (© **242/394-6254**), is open daily from 8:30am to 8pm, charging 15¢ per minute; there are four computers available. Web access is increasingly common at hotels in The Bahamas, you can usually access the Web. But if this issue is especially important to you, check with specific accommodations before booking.

Language In The Bahamas, locals speak English, but sometimes with a marked accent that provides the clue to their ancestry—African, Irish, or Scottish, for example.

Liquor Laws Liquor is sold in liquor stores and various convenience stores; it's readily available at all hours though not sold on Sundays. The legal drinking age is 18.

Lost & Found Be sure to tell all of your credit card companies the minute you discover your wallet has been lost or stolen and file a report at the nearest police precinct. Your credit card company or insurer may require a police report number or record of the loss. Most credit card companies have an emergency toll-free number to call if your card is lost or stolen; they may be able to wire you a cash advance immediately or deliver an emergency credit card in a day or two.

Visa's U.S. emergency number is ⓒ 800/847-2911. **American Express** cardholders and traveler's check holders should call ⓒ 800/221-7282. **MasterCard** holders should call ⓒ 800/307-7309. For other credit cards, call the toll-free number directory at ⓒ 800/555-1212.

If you need emergency cash over the weekend when all banks and American Express offices are closed, you can have money wired to you via **Western Union** (ⓒ 800/325-6000; www.westernunion.com).

Identity theft or fraud are potential complications of losing your wallet, especially if you've lost your driver's license along with your cash and credit cards. Notify the major credit-reporting bureaus immediately; placing a fraud alert on your records may protect you against liability for criminal activity. The three major U.S. credit-reporting agencies are **Equifax** (ⓒ 888/766-0008; www.equifax.com), **Experian** (ⓒ 888/397-3742; www.experian.com), and **TransUnion** (ⓒ 800/680-7289; www.transunion.com). Finally, if you've lost all forms of photo ID, call your airline and explain the situation; they might allow you to board the plane if you have a copy of your passport or birth certificate and a copy of the police report you've filed.

Mail & Postage Rates You'll need Bahamian (not U.S.) postage stamps to send postcards and letters. Most of the kiosks selling postcards also sell the stamps you'll need to mail them, so you probably won't need to visit the post office. Sending a postcard or an airmail letter (up to ½-oz. in weight) from The Bahamas to anywhere outside its borders (including the U.S., Canada, and the U.K.) costs 65¢, with another charge for each additional half ounce of weight.

Newspapers & Magazines Three newspapers are circulated in Nassau and Freeport: the *Nassau Guardian* (www.thenassau guardian.com), the *Tribune,* and the *Freeport News.* You can find such papers as the *New York Times, Wall Street Journal, USA Today, The Miami Herald, Times of London,* and *Daily Telegraph* at newsstands in your hotel and elsewhere in Nassau.

Passports Passport requirements vary according to your country of origin.

For Residents of the United States: Whether you're applying in person or by mail, you can download passport applications from the U.S. State Department website at **www.travel. state.gov.** For general information, call the **National Passport Agency** (ⓒ 202/647-0518). To find your regional passport office, either check the U.S. State Department website or call the **National Passport Information Center** (© 877/487-2778).

For Residents of Canada: Passport applications are available at travel agencies throughout Canada or from the central **Passport Office,** Department of Foreign Affairs and International Trade, Ottawa, ON K1A 0G3 (© **800/567-6868;** www.ppt.gc.ca).

For Residents of the United Kingdom: To pick up an application for a standard 10-year passport (5-year passport for children under 16), visit your nearest passport office, major post office, or travel agency or contact the **United Kingdom Passport Service** at © **0870/521-0410** or search its website at **www.ukpa.gov.uk**.

For Residents of Ireland: You can apply for a 10-year passport at the **Passport Office,** Setanta Centre, Molesworth Street, Dublin 2 (© **01/671-1633;** www.irlgov.ie/iveagh). Those under age 18 and over 65 must apply for a €12 3-year passport. You can also apply at 1A South Mall, Cork (© **021/272-525**) or at most main post offices.

For Residents of Australia: You can pick up an application from your local post office or any branch of Passports Australia, but you must schedule an interview at the passport office to present your application materials. Call the **Australian Passport Information Service** at © **131-232,** or visit the government website at **www.passports.gov.au**.

For Residents of New Zealand: You can pick up a passport application at any New Zealand Passports Office or download it from their website. Contact the **Passports Office** at © **0800/225-050** in New Zealand or 04/474-8100, or log on to **www.passports.govt.nz**.

Pets You'll have to get a valid import permit to bring any animal into The Bahamas. Application for such a permit must be made in writing, accompanied by a $10 processing fee and a $5 fax fee, to the **Director of Agriculture,** Department of Agriculture, P.O. Box N-3028, Nassau, The Bahamas (© **242/325-7413**), at least 4 weeks in advance.

Police Dial © **911.**

Safety When going to Nassau (New Providence), Cable Beach, Paradise Island, or Freeport/Lucaya, exercise the same caution you would if visiting Miami. Whatever you do, if people peddling drugs approach you, steer clear of them.

Women, especially, should take caution if walking alone on the streets of Nassau after dark, particularly if those streets appear to be deserted. Pickpockets (often foreigners) work the crowded casino floors of both Paradise Beach and Cable Beach. See that your wallet, money, and valuables are well secured.

If you're driving a rental car, always make sure your car door is locked, and never leave possessions in view in an automobile. Don't leave valuables such as cameras and purses lying unattended on the beach while you go for a swim. If you are traveling with valuables, especially jewelry, don't leave them unguarded in hotel rooms. Many of the larger hotels will provide safes. Keep your hotel room doors locked at all times.

Taxes Departure tax is $15 ($18 from Grand Bahama Island) for visitors ages 7 and up. A 6% tax is imposed on hotel bills; otherwise there is no sales tax in The Bahamas.

Telephone To call The Bahamas from the U.S. or Canada, dial 1-242 plus the seven-digit local number. From the U.K., dial 001-242 plus the local seven-digit number.

To make a direct international call from The Bahamas to the U.S. or Canada, dial 1 plus the area code and local number. To call other countries, dial 011 plus the country code (the U.K. is 44, for example), the area code (usually without its initial zero), and the local number.

For local calls within The Bahamas, simply dial the seven-digit number. To call from one island to another within The Bahamas, dial 1-242 and then the seven-digit local number.

Note that the old coin-operated phones are still prevalent and still swallow coins. Each local call costs 25¢; you can use either Bahamian or U.S. quarters. Those old phones, however, are gradually being replaced by phones that use calling cards (debit cards), similar in appearance to a credit card, that come in denominations of $5, $10, $20, and $50. They can be bought from any office of BATELCO (Bahamas Telephone Co.).

BATELCO's main branch is on Kennedy Drive, Nassau (© 242/302-7008), although a popular local branch lies in the commercial heart of Nassau, on East Street off Bay Street.

To get **directory assistance** within The Bahamas, dial © **916.** To reach an international or a domestic operator within The Bahamas, dial **0.** There is no distinction made in The Bahamas between the two types of operators.

To reach the major international services of **AT&T,** dial
🕾 **800/CALLATT,** or head for any phone with AT&T or USA DIRECT
marked on the side of the booth. Picking up the handset will
connect you with an AT&T operator. These phones are often
positioned beside cruise-ship docks to help passengers disem-
barking on shore leave for the day. **MCI** can be reached at
🕾 **800/888-8000.**

Time Eastern Standard Time is used throughout The
Bahamas, and daylight saving time is observed in the summer.

Tipping Many establishments add a service charge, but it's
customary to leave something extra if service has been especially fine. If you're not sure whether service has been
included in your bill, don't be shy—ask.

Bellboys and porters, at least in the expensive hotels,
expect a tip of $1 per bag. It's also customary to tip your maid
at least $2 per day—more if she or he has performed special
services such as getting a shirt or blouse laundered. Most service personnel, including taxi drivers, waiters, and the like,
expect 15% (20% in deluxe restaurants).

Tourist Offices See "Visitor Information," earlier in this chapter, and also specific island chapters.

Water Technically, tap water is drinkable throughout The
Bahamas. But we almost always opt for bottled. Resorts tend
to filter and chlorinate tap water more aggressively than other
establishments; elsewhere, bottled water is available at stores
and supermarkets, and tastes better than that from a tap.

Weddings The bride and groom must both be in The
Bahamas at the moment they apply for the $40 wedding
license here. If both are single and U.S. citizens, they must
obtain an affidavit to that effect from the U.S. Embassy in Nassau. The fee is $55 per person; you'll need to appear in person
with ID such as a passport (and, if applicable, proof of
divorce). If all of these requirements are met, you can then get
married after staying for 24 hours in The Bahamas. No blood
test is necessary. Contact the **Ministry of Tourism** at P.O. Box
N-3701, Nassau, The Bahamas (🕾 **888/NUPTIALS** or 242/356-
0435) for more details.

3

New Providence
(Nassau/Cable Beach)

One million visitors a year have cast their vote: They want to visit Nassau, adjoining Cable Beach, or Paradise Island (which is covered separately in chapter 4). This is the center of all the action: the best shopping, the best entertainment, the most historic attractions—plus some of the best beaches in The Bahamas.

The capital of The Bahamas, the historic city of Nassau is a 35-minute flight from Miami. Despite the development and the modern hotels, a laid-back tropical atmosphere still hangs over the city, and it still offers a good dose of colonial charm. The commercial and banking hub of The Bahamas, as well as a mecca for shoppers, Nassau lies on the north side of New Providence, which is 34km (21 miles) long and 11km (7 miles) wide at its greatest point.

Cable Beach, a stretch of sand just west of the city, is lined with luxury resorts—in fact, the Nassau/Cable Beach area has the largest tourist infrastructure in The Bahamas, though there's another concentration of luxury hotels on Paradise Island. (If you want to stay right on the sands, don't choose a hotel in downtown Nassau itself. Head for Cable Beach or Paradise Island. You can easily reach the beach from a base in Nassau, but it won't be right outside your window.)

When you're based in Nassau/Cable Beach, you have an array of watersports, golf, tennis, and plenty of duty-free shopping nearby—not to mention those fine, powdery beaches. In addition, the resorts, restaurants, and beaches of Paradise Island, discussed in the next chapter, are just a short distance away. (Paradise Island, which lies just opposite Nassau, is connected to New Providence Island by a toll bridge that costs $1 for cars, $2 for taxis, and is free for pedestrians; there's also frequent ferry and water-taxi service between Nassau and Paradise Island.)

As the sun goes down, Cable Beach and Paradise Island heat up, offering fine dining, glitzy casinos, cabaret shows, moonlight cruises, dance clubs, and romantic evening strolls. (We'd confine the evening stroll to Cable Beach or Paradise Island, and not the streets of downtown Nassau, which can be dangerous at night.)

The shops might draw a lot more business than the museums, but no city in The Bahamas is as rich in history as Nassau. You can take a "royal climb" up the Queen's Staircase to Fort Fincastle. These 66 steps lead to a fort said to have been cut in the sandstone cliffs by slaves in the 1790s. Other Nassau attractions include Ardastra Gardens, which feature 2 hectares (5 acres) of landscaping and more than 300 exotic birds, mammals, and reptiles. (Most popular are the trained pink flamingos that march for audiences daily to their trainer's commands.)

It's surprising that Nassau has retained its overlay of British colonial charm despite its proximity to Florida. It truly hasn't become Americanized; despite new development, traffic, and cruise-ship crowds, Nassau's a long way from becoming another Miami. Stately old homes and public buildings still stand proudly among the modern high-rises and bland government buildings. Tropical foliage lines streets where horse-drawn surreys still trot by, carrying visitors on leisurely tours. Police officers in white starched jackets and colorful pith helmets still direct traffic on the main streets as they have long done. It could almost be England—but for the weather, that is.

1 Orientation

ARRIVING

BY PLANE Planes land at **Nassau International Airport** (© 242/ 377-1759), which lies 13km (8 miles) west of Nassau by Lake Killarney.

No bus service goes from the airport to Cable Beach, Nassau, or Paradise Island. Your hotel may provide airport transfers if you've made arrangements in advance; these are often included in package deals. There are also any number of car-rental offices here if you plan to have a car while on New Providence Island (see "Getting Around," below), though we don't really think you need one.

If you don't have a lift arranged, take a taxi to your hotel. From the airport to the center of Nassau, expect to pay around $20; from the airport to Cable Beach, $15; from the airport to Paradise Island, $28 plus toll. Drivers expect to be tipped 15%, and some will remind you should you "forget." You don't need to stop at a currency exchange office before departing the airport: U.S. currency is fine for these (and any other) transactions.

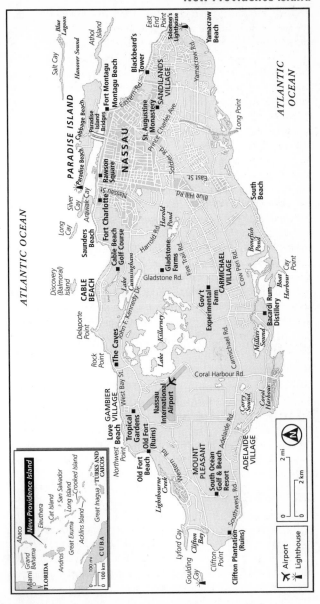

ATLANTIC OCEAN

ATLANTIC OCEAN

Salt Cay
Blue Lagoon
Hanover Sound
Athol Island

East End Point
Solomon's Lighthouse
Yamacraw Beach

Blackbeard's Tower
SANDILANDS VILLAGE
Yamacraw Rd.

PARADISE ISLAND
Fort Montagu
Montagu Beach
Cabbage Beach
Paradise Island Bridges
Eastern Rd.

St. Augustine Monastery
Prince Charles Ave.
Long Point

Paradise Beach
Rawson Square
NASSAU
Soldier Rd.

Silver Cay
Araiwak Cay
Nassau St.
East St.

Fort Charlotte
Blue Hill Rd.
South Beach

Long Cay
Saunders Beach
Cable Beach Golf Course
Harold Rd.
Harold Pond

Discovery (Balmoral) Island
CABLE BEACH
Gladstone Farms
Gladstone Rd.
CARMICHAEL VILLAGE
Bonefish Pond

Delaporte Point
Lake Cunningham
John F. Kennedy Dr.
Fire Trail Rd.
Cow Pen Rd.
Cay Point

Rock Point
The Caves
Lake Killarney
Gov't Experimental Farm
Carmichael Rd.
Boat Harbour
Bacardi Rum Distillery
Millars Sound

West Bay St.
Coral Harbour Rd.
Corry Sound

Northwest Point
Love
GAMBIER VILLAGE
Tropical Gardens
Old Fort (Ruins)
Nassau International Airport
Coral Harbour

Lighbourne Creek
Old Fort Beach
Western Rd.
MOUNT PLEASANT
Adelaide Rd.
ADELAIDE VILLAGE

Lyford Cay
Clifton Bay
South Ocean Golf & Beach Resort
Southwest Rd.

Goulding Cay
Clifton Point
Clifton Plantation (Ruins)

2 mi
0
2 km
0

N

✈ Airport
※ Lighthouse

FLORIDA
Miami
Grand Bahama
Abaco
Andros
New Providence Island
Eleuthera
Cat Island
San Salvador
Long Island
Great Exuma
Crooked Island
Acklins Island
Great Inagua
TURKS AND CAICOS
CUBA

0   100 mi
0   100 km

BY CRUISE SHIP   Nassau has spent millions of dollars expanding its port so that a number of cruise ships can come into port at once. Sounds great in theory. Practically speaking, however, facilities in Nassau, Cable Beach, and Paradise Island become extremely overcrowded as soon as the big boats dock. You'll have to stake out your space on the beach, and you will find shops and attractions overrun with visitors every day you're in port.

Cruise ships dock near Rawson Square, the heart of the city and the shopping area—and the best place to begin a tour of Nassau. Unless you want to go to one of the beach strips along Cable Beach or Paradise Island, you won't need a taxi. You can go on a shopping expedition near where you dock: The site of the Straw Market is nearby, at Market Plaza; Bay Street—the main shopping artery—is also close; and the Nassau International Bazaar is at the intersection of Woodes Rogers Walk and Charlotte Street.

The government has added **"Festival Place"** (© 242/322-7680) to the Prince George dock (where the cruise ships arrive). Festival Place is a multicolored structure worth visiting. This facility is open daily 8am to 5pm. It provides booths where you can find Reception Services (© 242/323-3182), tourist information, and merchants selling arts, crafts, and Bahamian candy. You can lounge and have a daiquiri while you listen to the live calypso entertainment, or even get your hair braided. You can ride a horse and surrey, or catch a water taxi.

VISITOR INFORMATION

The Bahamas Ministry of Tourism maintains a **tourist information booth** at the Nassau International Airport in the arrivals terminal (© 242/377-6806; www.bahamas.com). Hours are from 8:30am to 11pm daily.

Information can also be obtained from the Information Desk at the **Ministry of Tourism's Office,** Rawson Square (© 242/328-7810), which is open Monday to Friday 9am to 5pm.

THE LAY OF THE LAND

Most of the hotels in Nassau are city hotels and are not on the water. If you want to stay right on the sands, choose a hotel in Cable Beach (later in this chapter) or on Paradise Island (see chapter 4).

Rawson Square is the heart of Nassau, lying just a short walk from **Prince George Wharf,** where the big cruise ships, usually from Florida, berth. Here you'll see the Churchill Building, which contains the offices of the Bahamian prime minister along with other government ministries.

Busy **Bay Street,** the main shopping artery, begins on the south side of Rawson Square. This was the street of the infamous "Bay Street Boys," a group of rich, white Bahamians who once controlled all political and economic activity on New Providence.

On the opposite side of Rawson Square is **Parliament Square,** with a statue of a youthful Queen Victoria. Here are more government houses and the House of Assembly. These are Georgian and neo-Georgian buildings, some dating from the late 1700s.

The courthouse is separated by a little square from the **Nassau Public Library and Museum,** which opens onto Bank Lane. It was the former Nassau Gaol (jail). South of the library, across Shirley Street, are the remains of the **Royal Victoria Hotel,** which opened the year the American Civil War was launched (1861) and once hosted blockade runners and Confederate spies.

A walk down Parliament Street leads to the post office, and philatelists may want to stop in, since some Bahamian stamps are collector's items.

Going south, moving farther away from the water, Elizabeth Avenue takes you to the **Queen's Staircase,** one of the major landmarks of Nassau, leading to Bennet's Hill and Fort Fincastle.

If you return to Bay Street, you'll discover the tent of the **Straw Market,** a handcrafts emporium where you can buy all sorts of souvenirs. At the intersection of Charlotte Street is another major shopping emporium, the **Nassau International Bazaar.**

In Nassau, and especially in the rest of The Bahamas, you will seldom, if ever, find street numbers on hotels or other businesses. Sometimes in the more remote places, you won't even find street names. Get directions before heading somewhere in particular. Of course, you can always ask along the way, as most Bahamians tend to be very helpful.

2 Getting Around

BY TAXI

You can easily rely on taxis and skip renting a car. The rates for New Providence, including Nassau, are set by the government. Working meters are required in all taxis, although you will also find gypsy cabs without meters. When you get in, the fixed rate is $3, plus 35¢ for each additional .5km (⅓-mile). Each passenger over two pays an extra $3. Taxis can also be hired at the hourly rate of $45 for a five-passenger cab. Luggage is carried at a cost of 75¢ per piece, although the first two pieces are transported free. The radio-taxi call number is ☏ **242/323-4555.** It's also easy to get a taxi at the airport or at one of the big hotels.

BY CAR

You really don't need to rent a car. It's a lot easier to rely on taxis when you're ready to leave the beach and do a little exploring.

However, if you choose to drive (perhaps for a day of touring the whole island), some of the biggest U.S. car-rental companies maintain branches at the airport, downtown, and on Paradise Island. **Avis** (☏ **800/331-1212** or 242/377-7121; www.avis.com) operates at the airport, and also has branches at the cruise-ship docks at Bay Street and Cumberland Street, across from the British Colonial Hilton (☏ 242/326-6380). **Budget Rent-a-Car** (☏ **800/527-0700** or 242/377-9000; www.budgetrentacar.com) has a branch at the airport. **Dollar Rent-a-Car** (☏ **800/800-4000** or 242/377-7231; www.dollar.com) rents at the airport. **Hertz** (☏ **800/654-3131** or 242/377-8684; www.hertz.com) has an airport location.

Remember: Drive on the left!

BY JITNEY

The least-expensive means of transport is by jitney—medium-size buses that leave from the downtown Nassau area to outposts on New Providence. The fare is $1, and exact change, in coins or with a dollar bill, is required. The jitneys operate daily from 6:30am to 7pm. Some hotels on Paradise Island and Cable Beach run their own free jitney service. Buses to the Cable Beach area leave from the Navy Lion Road depot. Buses to the eastern area depart from the Frederick Street North depot, and buses to the malls leave from Fredrick Street North Depot.

BY BOAT

Water taxis operate daily from 9am to 6pm at 20-minute intervals between Paradise Island and Prince George Wharf at a round-trip cost of $6 per person. Ferry service runs from the end of Casuarina Drive on Paradise Island across the harbor to Rawson Square for a round-trip fare of $6 per person. The ferry operates daily from 9:30am to 4:15pm, with departures every half-hour from both sides of the harbor.

BY MOPED

Lots of visitors like to rent mopeds to explore the island. Unless you're an experienced moped rider, stay on quiet roads until you feel at ease. (Don't start out in all the congestion on Bay St.!) Many

Tips On Your Own Sturdy Feet

This is the only way to see Old Nassau, unless you rent a horse and carriage. All the major attractions and the principal stores are close enough to walk to. You can even walk to Cable Beach or Paradise Island, although it's a hike in the hot sun. Confine your walking to the daytime, and beware of pickpockets and purse snatchers. In the evening, avoid walking the streets of downtown Nassau, where muggings occur.

hotels have rentals on the premises. If yours doesn't, try **Knowles** (© 242/356-0741), at Festival Place, which rents mopeds for $45 per day. Included in the rental price are insurance and mandatory helmets for both drivers and passengers.

FAST FACTS: New Providence

American Express The local representative is **Destinations,** 303 Shirley St., between Charlotte and Parliament streets, Nassau (© 242/322-2931). Hours are Monday to Friday 9am to 5pm. The travel department is also open Saturday 9am to 1pm. If you present a personal check and an Amex card, you can buy traveler's checks here.

ATMs Major banks with ATMs in Nassau include the **Royal Bank of Canada** (© 242/322-2420), **Bank of Nova Scotia** (© 242/356-1517), and **Barclays** (© 242/356-8000). However, some accept cards only in the **Cirrus** network (© 800/424-7787), while others take only **PLUS** (© 800/843-7587). ATMs at both the Paradise Island and Cable Beach casinos dispense quick cash. You can also find ATMs at the airports.

Babysitting Hotel staff can help you hire an experienced sitter. Expect to pay around $10 to $15 an hour, plus $3 an hour for each additional child.

Climate See "When to Go," in chapter 2.

Complaints The government of The Bahamas is becoming more user friendly. If you have a complaint about any establishment, call the **Ministry of Tourist Complaint Unit** at © 242/356-0435.

Dentist Try the dental department of the **Princess Margaret Hospital** on Sands Road (℃ **242/322-2861**).

Doctor For the best service, use a staff member of the **Princess Margaret Hospital** on Sands Road (℃ **242/322-2861**).

Drugstores Try **Lowes Pharmacy,** Palm Dale (℃ **242/322-8594**), open Monday through Saturday from 8am to 6:30pm. They also have two branches: **Harbour Bay Shopping Center** (℃ **242/393-4813**), open Monday to Saturday 8am to 8:30pm and Sunday from 9am to 5pm; and **Town Center Mall** (℃ **242/325-6482**), open Monday to Saturday 10am to 9pm. Nassau has no late-night pharmacies.

Embassies & Consulates See "Fast Facts: The Bahamas," in chapter 2.

Emergencies For any major emergency, call ℃ **919.**

Eyeglass Repair The **Optique Shoppe,** 22 Parliament St. at the corner of Shirley Street (℃ **242/322-3910**), is convenient to the center of Nassau. Hours are Monday to Friday 9am to 5pm and on Saturday 9am to noon.

Hospitals The government-operated **Princess Margaret Hospital** on Sands Road (℃ **242/322-2861**) is one of the major hospitals in The Bahamas. The privately owned **Doctors Hospital,** 1 Collins Ave. (℃ **242/322-8411**), is the most modern private health care facility in the region.

Hot Lines For help or assistance of any kind, call ℃ **242/326-HELP.**

Information See "Visitor Information," above.

Internet Access Check out Cybercafe at **The Mall at Marathon** (℃ **242/394-6254**). Here you can get online from your own laptop or log on to one of the computers. The cost is 15 cents per minute. Some of the larger hotels also offer guests Internet access for a small fee.

Laundry & Dry Cleaning The **Laundromat Superwash** (℃ **242/323-4018**), at the corner of Nassau Street and Boyd Road, offers coin-operated machines; it's open 24 hours a day, 7 days a week. In the same building is the **New Oriental Dry Cleaner** (℃ **242/323-7249**). Another dry cleaner a short drive north of the center of town is the **Jiffy Quality Cleaner** (℃ **242/323-6771**) at the corner of Blue Hill Road and Cordeaux Avenue.

Newspapers & Magazines The *Tribune Daily* and *The Nassau Guardian*, both published in the morning, are the country's two competing daily newspapers. At your hotel and visitor information stations, you can find various helpful magazines, brochures, and booklets.

Photographic Needs The largest camera store in Nassau is **John Bull** (☎ **242/322-3328**), on Bay Street, 3 blocks west of Rawson Square.

Police Dial ☎ **911** or ☎ **919.**

Post Office The **Nassau General Post Office,** at the top of Parliament Street on East Hill Street (☎ **242/322-3344**), is open Monday through Friday from 9am to 5pm and on Saturday from 9am to 1pm at the Festival Place. Note that you can buy stamps from most postcard kiosks.

Safety Avoid walking in downtown Nassau at night, where there are sometimes robberies and muggings. (Most tourists are never affected, but better safe than sorry.) Cable Beach and Paradise Island are safer places to be in the evening.

Taxes Each visitor leaving from New Providence pays a $15 departure tax. There is no sales tax, though there is a 6% hotel tax.

3 Where to Stay

In the hotel descriptions that follow, we've listed regular room prices or "rack rates," but these are simply for ease of comparison. They are likely to be accurate for smaller properties, but you can almost always do better at the larger hotels and resorts. *Note:* Read the section "Packages for the Independent Traveler" in chapter 2 before you book a hotel separately from your airfare, and if you do book yourself, always inquire about honeymoon specials, golf packages, summer weeks, and other discounts. In many cases, too, a travel agent can get you a package deal that would be cheaper than these official rates.

Hotels add a 6% "resort levy" tax to your rate. Sometimes this is quoted as part of the price; at other times, it's added to your final bill. When you are quoted a rate, always ask if the tax is included. Many hotels also add a 15% service charge to your bill. Ask about these charges in advance so you won't be shocked when you receive the final tab.

Where to Stay in Nassau

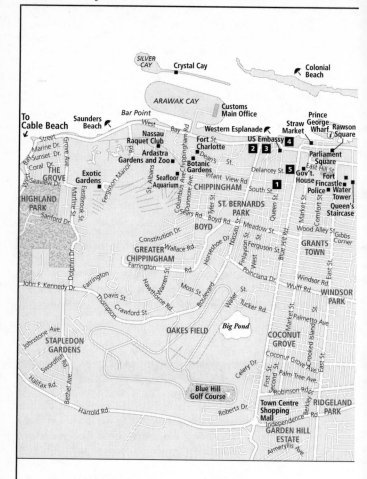

British Colonial Hilton **4**

Buena Vista Hotel **1**

El Greco Hotel **3**

Graycliff **5**

Holiday Inn Junkanoo Beach **2**

Nassau Harbour Club **6**

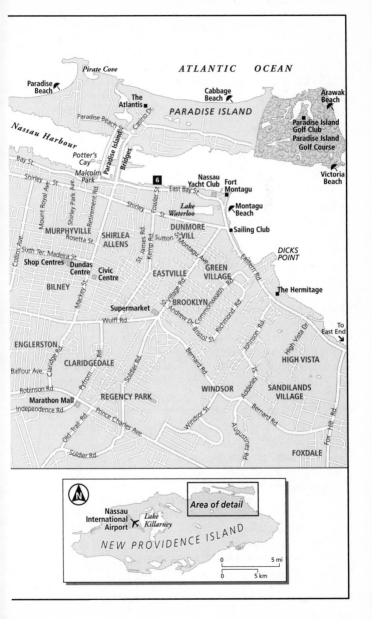

Pirate Cove

Paradise Beach

The Atlantis

ATLANTIC OCEAN

Cabbage Beach

PARADISE ISLAND

Arawak Beach

Paradise Beach Dr

Casino Dr

Nassau Harbour

Paradise Island Bridges

Potter's Cay

Bay St

Shirley St

Malcolm Park

Mount Royal Ave

Shirley Park Ave

Retirement Rd.

Fowler St.

Shirley

6

East Bay St

Nassau Yacht Club

Fort Montagu

Paradise Island Golf Club

Paradise Island Golf Course

Victoria Beach

Lake Waterloo

Montagu Beach

MURPHYVILLE

Rosetta St.

SHIRLEA ALLENS

St. James Rd.

Kemp Rd.

Sutton

Montagu Ave.

DUNMORE S..VILL

Sailing Club

DICKS POINT

Collins Ave.

Sixth Ter. Madeira St.

Shop Centres

Dundas Centre

Civic Centre

EASTVILLE

St. Village Rd.

GREEN VILLAGE

Eastern Rd.

The Hermitage

BILNEY

Mackey St.

Supermarket

Wulff Rd.

Andrew Dr.

Commonwealth Rd.

BROOKLYN

Bristol St.

Richmond Rd.

Johnson Rd.

High Vista Dr.

To East End

ENGLERSTON

Claridge Rd.

CLARIDGEDALE

Balfour Ave.

Robinson Rd.

Marathon Mall

Independence Rd.

Pyfrom Rd.

Soldier Rd.

REGENCY PARK

Prince Charles Ave.

Soldier Rd.

Bernard Rd.

WINDSOR

Windsor St.

Adderley St.

Augustine Rd.

HIGH VISTA

SANDILANDS VILLAGE

Bernard Rd.

Fox Hill Rd.

FOXDALE

N

Nassau International Airport

Lake Killarney

Area of detail

NEW PROVIDENCE ISLAND

0   5 mi

0   5 km

Taxes and service are not included in the rates listed below. We'll lead off with a selection of hotels within the heart of Nassau, followed by accommodations in Cable Beach. Most visitors prefer to stay at Cable Beach since the resorts here are right on the sand. But you can stay in Nassau and commute to the beaches at Cable Beach or Paradise Island; it's cheaper but less convenient. Those who prefer the ambience of Old Nassau's historic district and being near the best shops may decide to stay in town.

NASSAU
EXPENSIVE

British Colonial Hilton ★★   In the restored British Colonial Hilton, there's a palpable air of the long-ago days when The Bahamas was firmly within the political and social orbit of Britain. This landmark seven-story hotel has seen its share of ups and downs over the years. Plush and glamorous when it was built in 1900, it burned to the ground in 1920, and was rebuilt 3 years later before deteriorating into a flophouse. Between 1996 and 1999, a Canadian entrepreneur poured $68 million into its restoration.

Don't expect the glitz and glitter of Cable Beach or Paradise Island here—the Hilton is after business travelers rather than the casino crowd. It also lacks the aristocratic credentials of Graycliff (see below). Nonetheless, it's a dignified and friendly, but rather sedate, hotel with a discreetly upscale decor (no Disney-style themes or gimmicks). Bedrooms are a bit on the small side, but capped with rich crown moldings and accessorized with tile or stone-sheathed

---

Fun Fact   **In Suite Double O, a "License to Kill"**

In both *Thunderball* and *Never Say Never Again,* James Bond, or secret agent 007, was served shaken martinis at the British Colonial. To commemorate that historic event, the Hilton-owned property now has a "Double-O" suite filled with Bond memorabilia, including posters, books, CDs, movie stills, and all the best Bond flicks, including *Goldfinger* and *Live and Let Die.* Guests can take a Bond book from the suite, perhaps *Tomorrow Never Dies,* and curl up on a chaise lounge at the beach. The suite is a one-bedroom unit with living room and ocean views. When you get tired of the movie Bond, you might be able to stroll over to the next chair and meet the real Bond—Sean Connery is often at his island home on nearby Lyford Cay.

---

bathrooms with shower/tub combinations. The staff, incidentally, is superbly trained and motivated; we've found them upbeat and hard-working. There's a small beach a few steps away, but it's not very appealing (it's on the channel separating New Providence from Paradise Island, with no "cleansing" wave action at all).

1 Bay St. (P.O. Box N-7148), Nassau, The Bahamas. © 800/HILTONS or 242/322-3301. Fax 242/302-9009. www.hilton.com. 291 units. Winter $205–$325 double, $435–$2,000 suite; off season $190–$210 double, $440–$900 suite. AE, DC, DISC, MC, V. Bus: 10. **Amenities:** 2 restaurants; 2 bars; outdoor pool; health club; full-service spa; Jacuzzi; tour desk; business center; secretarial service; limited room service; babysitting; laundry service; dry cleaning. *In room:* A/C, TV, dataport, mini-bar, coffeemaker, hair dryer, iron, safe, trouser press.

Graycliff ✿   Now in a kind of nostalgic decay, Graycliff remains the grande dame of downtown Nassau hotels even though her tiara is a bit tarnished and her age showing. In spite of its drawbacks, this place still has its devotees, especially among older readers. Originally an 18th-century private home and an example of Georgian colonial architecture, it's now an intimate inn, with an old-fashioned atmosphere. Even though the inn isn't on the beach, people who can afford to stay anywhere often choose Graycliff because it epitomizes the old-world style and grace that evokes Nassau back in the days when the Duke and Duchess of Windsor were in residence. Churchill, of course, can no longer be seen paddling around in the swimming pool with a cigar in his mouth, and the Beatles are long gone, but the three-story Graycliff continues without the visiting celebs, who today head for Paradise Island. Beach lovers usually go by taxi to either nearby Goodman's Bay or to the Western Esplanade Beach, nearly adjacent to Arawak Cay. The bigger British Colonial Hilton is Graycliff's main competitor; they both have a rather staid, deliberately unflashy ambience.

The historic garden rooms in the main house, are large and individually decorated with antiques, though the better units are the more modern garden rooms. The Yellow Bird, Hibiscus, and Pool cottages are ideal choices, but the most luxurious accommodation of all is the Mandarino Suite, with Asian decor, a king-size bed, an oversize bathroom, and a private balcony overlooking the swimming pool. Bathrooms are spacious, with shower/tub combinations, deluxe toiletries, and robes.

8–12 W. Hill St. (P.O. Box N-10246), Nassau, The Bahamas. © 800/688-0076 or 242/322-2796. Fax 242/326-6110. www.graycliff.com. 18 units. Winter $290–$400 double, $400 cottage; off season $200 double, $310 cottage. AE, MC, V. Bus: 10 or 21A. **Amenities:** 2 restaurants; 2 bars; 3 outdoor pools; spa; Jacuzzi; sauna; limited room service; massage; babysitting; laundry service; dry cleaning. *In room:* A/C, TV, dataport, minibar, hair dryer, iron, safe.

MODERATE

Holiday Inn Junkanoo Beach *(Value)*   West of downtown Nassau, this hotel overlooks Junkanoo Beach. Although not as fine as Cable Beach, Junkanoo is also a safe beach with tranquil waters, white sands, and a lot of shells; the hotel offers lounge chairs on the beach but no waiter service for drinks. This place is a good value for those who don't want to pay the higher prices charged by the more deluxe hotels along Cable Beach. All the motel-style bedrooms have a view of either the beach or Nassau Harbour, and they come with extras you don't always find in a moderately priced choice, such as alarm clocks, two-line phones, and a working desk. All come with well-maintained bathrooms containing shower/tub combinations.

The on-site Bay Street Grille is not reason enough to stay here, although you can dine outside in a tropical courtyard overlooking the pool. The West Coast Bar and Grill is another dining option.

W. Bay St. (P.O. Box SS-19055), Nassau, The Bahamas. © 800/465-4329 or 242/366-2561. Fax 242/323-1408. www.holiday-inn.com. 183 units. Winter $238–$245 double, $403 suite; off season $260–$269 double, $403 suite. AE, DISC, MC, V. Bus: 10 or 17. **Amenities:** Restaurants; bar; 2 outdoor pools; health club; spa; salon; tour desk; 24-hr. room service; laundry service; dry cleaning; nonsmoking rooms; Internet cafe; rooms for those w/limited mobility. *In room:* A/C, TV, dataport, fridge, coffeemaker, hair dryer, iron, safe.

INEXPENSIVE

Buena Vista Hotel   Although this place really revolves around its restaurant (p. 72), it rents a few spacious bedrooms upstairs. It's a good bargain if you don't mind the lack of resort-style facilities. The building, with a pale pink facade, started out a century ago as a private home, and stands about 1km (⅔-mile) west of downtown Nassau. Expect a pastel decor, with a tasteful mix of antiques and reproductions. Each room comes with a small bathroom containing a shower/tub combination; staff might be a bit distracted because of the demands of the busy restaurant downstairs.

Delancy and Augusta sts. (P.O. Box N-564), Nassau, The Bahamas. © 242/322-2811. Fax 242/322-5881. www.buenavista-restaurant.com. 5 units. Mid-Apr to mid-Dec $70 double; mid-Dec to mid-Apr $100 double. AE, MC, V. Bus: 16. **Amenities:** Restaurant; limited room service. *In room:* A/C, TV, fridge, coffeemaker, iron.

El Greco Hotel   Across the street from Lighthouse Beach, and a short walk from the shops and restaurants of Bay Street, El Greco is a well-managed bargain choice that attracts many European travelers. The Greek owners and staff genuinely seem to care about their guests—in fact, the two-story hotel seems more like a small European B&B than your typical Bahamian hotel.

The midsize rooms aren't that exciting, but they're clean and comfortable, with decent beds and small tile bathrooms, containing shower/tub combinations. Bedrooms have a bright decor—a sort of Mediterranean motif, each with two ceiling fans and carpeted floors. Accommodations are built around a courtyard that contains statues crafted in the Italian baroque style, draped with lots of bougainvillea. A restaurant isn't on-site, but you can walk to many places nearby for meals.

W. Bay St. (P.O. Box N-4187), Nassau, The Bahamas. ℂ 242/325-1121. Fax 242/325-1124. www.bahamasnet.com. 27 units. Winter $109 double, $150 suite; off season $79 double, $125 suite. AE, MC, V. Free parking. Bus: 10. **Amenities:** Restaurant (dinner only); bar; pool; limited room service; babysitting. *In room:* A/C, TV.

Nassau Harbour Club Hotel & Marina   Don't expect lush and sprawling gardens, or much peace and privacy here—this hotel is in the heart of Nassau's action and is usually overrun in March and early April with college kids on spring break. A compound of two-story pink buildings from the early 1960s arranged like a horseshoe around a concrete terrace, it occupies a bustling strip of land between busy Bay Street and the edge of the channel that separates New Providence from Paradise Island. From your room, you'll have views of yachts and boats moored at a nearby marina, and easy access to the shops, bars, and restaurants of downtown Nassau and within the Harbour Bay Shopping Centre. Throughout, it's down-to-earth and just a bit funky. Bedrooms are simple and small but comfortable and equipped with bathrooms containing shower/tub combinations. However, they are a little worn and located near the animated hubbub of the busy bar.

E. Bay St. (P.O. Box SS-5755), Nassau, The Bahamas. ℂ **242/393-0771.** Fax 242/393-5393. 50 units. Winter $90–$130 double, $140 suite; off season $80–$110 double, $110 suite. Extra person $25 per day. AE, MC, V. Free parking. Bus: 11 or 19. **Amenities:** Restaurant; bar; outdoor pool. *In room:* A/C, TV, fridge.

CABLE BEACH

The glittering shoreline of Cable Beach, located west of Nassau, is topped only by Paradise Island (see chapter 4). It has loyal fans, many of whom think Paradise Island is too snobbish. Cable Beach has for years attracted visitors with its broad stretches of beachfront, a wide array of sports facilities, and great nightlife, including casino action. Deluxe or first-class resorts, two of which are all-inclusive, line the shoreline.

VERY EXPENSIVE

Breezes Bahamas 👍   SuperClubs, which competes successfully with Sandals (see below), spent $125 million transforming a tired old relic, the Ambassador Beach Hotel, into this all-inclusive resort. The nearby Sandals is more imposing, elegant, stylish, and upscale, with better amenities and views. Rowdier and more raucous, and located on a prime 450m (1,476-ft.) beachfront along Cable Beach, Breezes attracts a more middle-of-the-road crowd; it's unpretentious and more affordable (though it ain't exactly cheap, and we think it's rather overpriced for what it is). This U-shaped beachfront resort has two wings of rooms plus a main clubhouse facing a large pool area. Except between March and May, when no one under 19 is admitted, both couples and single travelers over 15 are accepted here. Everything is included—the room, meals, snacks, unlimited wine (not the finest) with lunch and dinner, even premium brand liquor at the bars, plus activities and airport transfers.

The refurbished hotel rooms contain pastel-painted wooden furniture with Formica tops, and a working air-conditioning system. Rooms, however, are not as luxurious as those at Sandals. Tiled bathrooms are medium-size but well equipped with a shower and bathtub.

Diners can sample unremarkable international fare at the food court, although the Italian restaurant serves a better dinner. A beachside grill and snacks are available throughout the day. Entertainment includes a high-energy disco, a piano bar, and a nightclub. Karaoke is inevitable, but the professional Junkanoo live shows, which are presented every Saturday night, are better, and local bands often perform. The social centerpiece is a sometimes-overcrowded terrace with a swimming pool.

P.O. Box CB-13049, Cable Beach, Nassau, The Bahamas. ✆ **800/GO-SUPER** or 242/327-5356. Fax 242/327-5155. www.superclubs.com. 400 units. Winter $297–$540 double, $775 suite; off season $292–$513 double, $680 suite. Rates include all meals, drinks, tips, airport transfers, and most activities. AE, DISC, MC, V. Free parking. Bus: 10. No children under 15 year-round; no one under 19 Mar–May. **Amenities:** 4 restaurants; 4 bars; 2 outdoor pools; 2 tennis courts; health club; watersports equipment; laundry service; nonsmoking rooms; rooms for those w/ limited mobility. *In room:* A/C, TV, coffeemaker, hair dryer, iron, safe.

Sandals Royal Bahamian Hotel 👍👍👍   This is the most upscale Sandals resort in the world. It's shockingly expensive, though you can often get special promotional rates that make it more reasonable. It originated as a very posh hotel, the Balmoral Beach, in the 1940s. In 1996, the Jamaica-based Sandals chain poured $20 million into

Where to Stay & Dine in Cable Beach

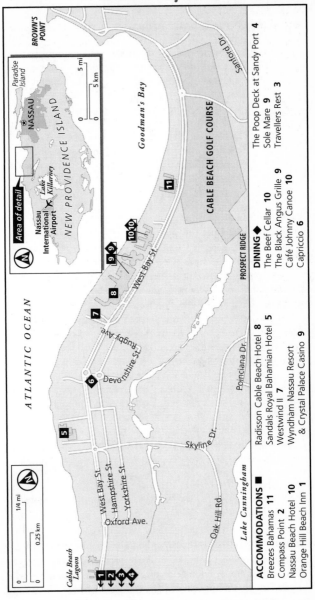

ACCOMMODATIONS ■
Breezes Bahamas **11**
Compass Point **2**
Nassau Beach Hotel **10**
Orange Hill Beach Inn **1**

Radisson Cable Beach Hotel **8**
Sandals Royal Bahamian Hotel **5**
Westwind II **7**
Wyndham Nassau Resort
& Crystal Palace Casino **9**

DINING ◆
The Beef Cellar **10**
The Black Angus Grille **9**
Café Johnny Canoe **10**
Capriccio **6**

The Poop Deck at Sandy Port **4**
Sole Mare **9**
Travellers Rest **3**

65

Moments   Junkanoo Festivals

No Bahamian celebration is as raucous as the Junkanoo (which is also the name of the music associated with this festival). The special rituals originated during the colonial days of slavery, when African-born newcomers could legally drink and enjoy themselves only on certain strictly predetermined days of the year. In its celebration, Junkanoo closely resembles Carnaval in Rio and Mardi Gras in New Orleans. Its major difference lies in the costumes and the timing (the major Junkanoo celebrations occur the day after Christmas, a reminder of the medieval English celebration of Boxing Day on Dec 26, and New Year's Day).

In the old days, Junkanoo costumes were crafted from crepe paper, often in primary colors, stretched over wire frames. (One sinister offshoot of the celebrations was that the Junkanoo costumes and masks were used to conceal the identity of anyone seeking vengeance on a white or on another slave.) Locals have more money to spend on costumes and Junkanoo festivals today than they did in decades past. Today, the finest costumes can cost up to $10,000 and are sometimes sponsored by local bazaars, lotteries, and charity auctions, though everyday folks from all walks of Bahamian life join in, too, usually with their own homemade costumes, many of which are sensual or humorous. The best time and place to observe Junkanoo is New Year's Day in Nassau, when throngs of cavorting, music-making, and costumed figures prance through the streets. Find yourself a good viewing position on Bay Street. Less elaborate celebrations take place in major towns on the other islands, including Freeport.

renovating and expanding this property on a sandy beach a short walk west of the more glittery megahotels of Cable Beach. Everywhere, you'll find manicured gardens, rich cove moldings, hidden courtyards tastefully accentuated with sculptures, and many of the trappings of Edwardian England in the tropics.

A favorite for honeymoon getaways, Sandals offers well-furnished and often elegant rooms, all classified as suites. Some are in the Manor House, while others are in outlying villas. The villas are

The Art of the Massage

The Ultra Spa at Sandals Royal Bahamian Resort & Spa in Nassau has repeatedly made the top 10 list of spa resorts in the *Condé Nast Traveler* reader's choice survey. The decor features walls and floors of Italian Satumia stone, rich mahogany doors and a collection of pre-Raphaelite prints in gilded frames. One service offered, Massage Duet, allows couples to learn the art of massage from a professional so they can practice on each other in the comfort of one's hotel room.

preferred because they have romantic, secluded settings and easy access to nearby plunge pools. Some units have Jacuzzis and private pools, and some of the bathrooms are enormous. The bedrooms have thick cove moldings, formal English furniture, and shower/tub combination bathrooms loaded with perfumed soaps and cosmetics. The rooms that face the ocean offer small, curved terraces with ornate iron railings and views of an offshore sand spit, Sandals Key.

For a long time, only heterosexual guests were allowed at this resort. Recently, the British and Canadian governments said they wouldn't allow Sandals to advertise its resorts if it continued discriminatory policies against same-sex couples. In 2004, Sandals capitulated and ended the ban. Today gay couples are allowed in as guests.

Bahamian and international fare is offered in generous portions in the property's restaurants. In addition to spectacular buffets, the options include white-glove service and continental dishes in the Baccarat Dining Room. The two latest additions include Kimono's, offering Japanese cuisine, and Casanova, specializing in Italian fare. Other choices are The Royal Café for southwestern grilled specialties, and Spices, for upscale buffets at breakfast, lunch, and dinner. The pool here is one of the most appealing on Nassau, with touches of both Vegas and ancient Rome (outdoor murals and replicas of ancient Roman columns jutting skyward above the water). Complimentary shuttle bus service goes to the casino and nightlife options at the nearby Crystal Palace complex, plus concierge service is offered in suites and upper-tier doubles.

W. Bay St. (P.O. Box CB-13005), Cable Beach, Nassau, The Bahamas. © **800/SANDALS** or 242/327-6400. Fax 242/327-6961. www.sandals.com. 405 units. Winter $4,760–$8,820 per couple for 7 days ($1,620–$3,000 per couple for 2 days); off season $4,470–$8,590 per couple for 7 days ($1,520–$2,920 per couple for 2 days). Rates include all meals, drinks, and activities. AE, DISC, MC, V. Free parking.

Bus: 10. Couples only; no children or singles allowed. **Amenities:** 8 restaurants; 9 bars; 6 outdoor pools; 2 tennis courts; health club; full-service spa; watersports equipment; nonsmoking rooms; rooms for those w/limited mobility. *In room:* A/C, TV, coffeemaker, hair dryer, iron, safe.

EXPENSIVE

Radisson Cable Beach Hotel 🐕 *(Kids)* Right in the middle of Cable Beach (its best asset) this high-rise is connected by a shopping arcade to the Crystal Palace Casino. The nearby Wyndham Nassau Marriott Resort is glitzier and has better facilities, but the Radisson is still one of the most desirable choices for families, as it has the best children's programs in the area, and because many of its bedrooms contain two double beds, suitable for a family of four. The nine-story property has an Aztec-inspired facade of sharp angles and strong horizontal lines, built in a horseshoe-shaped curve around a landscaped beachfront garden. You'll think of Vegas when you see the rows of fountains in front, the acres of marble sheathing inside, and the four-story lobby with towering windows. Big enough to get lost in, but with plenty of intimate nooks, the hotel offers an almost endless array of things to do. Note, however, that readers frequently complain of staff attitude and slow service at this sprawling resort.

Bedrooms are modern and comfortable if rather standard, with big windows that open onto views of the garden or the beach. Units are equipped with one king-size bed or two doubles, along with phones with voice mail, plus tiled combination bathrooms (tub and shower).

The hotel contains six restaurants, the most glamorous of which is the Amici, serving a traditional Italian cuisine in a two-story garden setting. You can also spice up your evening at Islands, which sometimes has karaoke and other entertainment. We try to avoid the overpriced Avocado's or Bimini's, both of which have poor service and an uninspired cuisine. The Mini-Market Grill serves Caribbean/continental breakfast and lunch buffets, and the Forge is a steak-and-seafood restaurant where guests are seated around a tabletop grill to prepare their own steaks, seafood, or chicken. Beach parties and revues are often staged.

W. Bay St. (P.O. Box N-4914), Cable Beach, Nassau, The Bahamas. © **800/333-3333** or 242/327-6000. Fax 242/327-6987. www.radisson-cablebeach.com. 685 units. Winter $175–$250 double; off season $150–$250 double; year-round $550–$950 suite. AE, DISC, MC, V. Free parking. Bus: 10. **Amenities:** 6 restaurants; 3 bars; 3 outdoor pools; 5 tennis courts; gym; kid's camp (ages 4–12); shopping arcade; salon; limited room service; babysitting; laundry service; dry cleaning; rooms for those w/limited mobility. *In room:* A/C, TV, dataport, coffeemaker, hair dryer, iron, safe.

Wyndham Nassau Resort & Crystal Palace Casino *Overrated* *Kids*
This big, flashy megaresort on the lovely sands of Cable Beach is so vast and all-encompassing that some of its guests never venture into Nassau during their stay on the island. The complex incorporates five high-rise towers, a futuristic central core, and a cluster of gardens and beachfront gazebos—all linked by arcades, underground passages, and minipavilions. Guest rooms come in several different price brackets ranging from standard island view to ocean vista, each with private balconies. If you're a big spender, corner suites with lots of space are the way to go, complete with wraparound balconies and king-sized beds looking out onto the water through floor-to-ceiling glass. Combination bathrooms (shower/tub) most often come with dressing areas and dual basins. We continue to get complaints from readers who found their bedrooms disappointing. Yet other readers have praised the accommodations. If at all possible, it's better to look at your room before checking in. The hotel seems to be in some sort of chaotic flux, so proceed carefully before making it your choice for a vacation.

Aside from a massive casino, the largest in The Bahamas, the complex contains a wide array of dining and drinking facilities. Two of its restaurants, Black Angus Grille for succulent steaks and other American fare, and Sole Mare with a gourmet Italian cuisine, are among the finest in New Providence. Even if you're not a guest of the hotel, you might want to avail yourself of the drinking and dining options or the casino action here.

W. Bay St. (P.O. Box N-8306), Cable Beach, Nassau, The Bahamas. © 800/222-7466 or 242/327-6200. Fax 242/327-5227. www.wyndhamnassauresort.com. 850 units. Winter $179–$250 double, $250–$500 suite; off season $149–$169 double, $220–$230 suite. AE, DC, DISC, MC, V. Free self-parking, valet parking $5. Bus: 10. **Amenities:** 8 restaurants; 3 bars; outdoor pool; nearby golf course; 10 tennis courts; health club; Jacuzzi; sauna; children's programs (4–12); business center; 24-hr. room service; babysitting; laundry service; dry cleaning; nonsmoking rooms; rooms for those w/limited mobility. *In room:* A/C, TV, dataport (in some), minibar, coffeemaker, hair dryer, iron, safe.

MODERATE

Nassau Beach Hotel *Kids*   This place has been somewhat overshadowed by the glitzy properties a short walk away, but a crowd of loyal fans—often families—comes every year, enjoying a 900m (2,952-ft.) white-sand beach. Guests here avoid the carnival at such neighboring megaresorts as the Wyndham Nassau Resort. A good value, the Nassau Beach is a conservative, moderately priced choice with a lively but restrained atmosphere.

Family-Friendly Hotels

Camp Junkanoo at the Radisson Cable Beach (p. 68) provides a supervised program for children 4 to 12 at no additional cost. Activities include swimming, treasure hunts, and nature walks. Kids Klub at the Wyndham Nassau Resort offers supervised activities in the hotels own beachfront clubhouse, the Kids Klub Pavilion, for children aged 4 to 12. Activities range from scavenger hunts to nature exploration to beach games to Sega and Nintendo.

The hotel was built in the 1940s, with three separate wings in a beige-and-white twin-towered design, and it features modified Georgian detailing and tile- and marble-covered floors. Today, the place has been enhanced by fresh landscaping and touches that include ceiling fans and mahogany, English-inspired furniture. Each of the midsize accommodations contains summery rattan pieces, comfortable beds, and a marble bathroom with a tub/shower combination.

On-site are five restaurants (including the Beef Cellar, which is reviewed under "Where to Dine"), plus entertainment in the evening (including live bands and dancing). It's also near the Crystal Palace Casino.

W. Bay St. (P.O. Box N-7756), Cable Beach, Nassau, The Bahamas. © **888/627-7282** or 242/327-7711. Fax 242/327-8829. www.nassaubeachhotel.com. 400 units. $95–$150 double; $250–$300 1-bedroom suite, $350–$400 2-bedroom suite. AE, DISC, MC, V. Free parking. Bus: 10. **Amenities:** 5 restaurants; 3 bars; 2 pools; 6 tennis courts; health club; watersports equipment/rentals; babysitting; laundry service; nonsmoking rooms; Internet cafe; rooms for those w/limited mobility. *In room:* A/C, TV, hair dryer, iron, safe.

Westwind II *(Kids)* Set on the western edge of Cable Beach's hotel strip, 9.5km (6 miles) from the center of Nassau, the Westwind II is a cluster of two-story buildings that contain two-bedroom, two-bathroom timeshare units, each with a full kitchen (there's a grocery store nearby). The size and facilities of these units make them ideal for traveling families. These units are available to the public whenever they're not otherwise occupied by investors. All the diversions of the megahotels are close by and easily reached, but in the complex itself, you can enjoy a low-key, quiet atmosphere and privacy. (A masonry wall separates the compound from the traffic of W. Bay St. and the hotels and vacant lots that flank it.) Each unit has a pleasant decor that includes white tiled floors, rattan furniture, bathrooms with shower/tub combinations, and either a balcony or a terrace. Since units are identical, price differences depend on whether the units face the beach, the pool, or the garden. The manicured grounds feature palms, flowering hibiscus shrubs, and seasonal flower beds. Don't stay here if you expect any of the luxuries or facilities of the nearby Nassau Beach Hotel (see above). Westwind II is more for do-it-yourself types.

W. Bay St. (P.O. Box CB-11006), Cable Beach, Nassau, The Bahamas. © **866/369-5921** or 242/327-7019. Fax 242/327-7529. www.westwindii.com. 54 units. Nov–Apr $1,579–$1,825 per week for up to 4 people; May–Oct $1,282–$1,400 per week for up to 4 people. MC, V. Bus: 10. **Amenities:** Bar; 2 pools; 2 tennis courts; babysitting; coin-operated laundry; rooms for those w/limited mobility. *In room:* A/C, TV, kitchen, fridge, coffeemaker, iron.

WEST OF CABLE BEACH

Compass Point ⭐⭐ *(Finds)* Charming, personalized, and casually upscale, this is an alternative to the megahotels of Cable Beach, which lie about 9.5km (6 miles) to the east. Think British colonial hip, with guests straight out of Soho (either London or New York) and a smattering of music-industry types. The place isn't as snobby as Graycliff, but for those who want an intimate inn and like the vibrant Bahamian colors, there is no other place like it on the island. Scattered over .8 hectares (2 acres) of some of the most expensive terrain in The Bahamas, the property lies beside one of the few sandy coves along the island's northwest coast, about 20 minutes from downtown Nassau and near a great snorkeling beach. The beach is very small, a sandy crescent that virtually disappears at high tide.

Each unit is a private, fully detached "hut" or cottage painted in pulsating, vivid colors. Everything larger than a studio has a kitchenette. Designed for privacy, all the units have exposed rafters, high ceilings with fans, and windows facing ocean breezes, and they have all been renovated, the furnishings replaced, the bathrooms and kitchens redone, and an air-conditioning system installed. Some of the huts are raised on stilts.

W. Bay St. (P.O. Box CB13842), Gambier, Love Beach, New Providence, The Bahamas. © **800/633-3284** or 242/327-4500. Fax 242/327-2407. www.compasspoint bahamas.com. 18 units. Winter $245 cabana, $305–$390 1-bedroom cottage, $470 2-bedroom cottage; off-season rates 20% lower. AE, MC, V. Free parking. Bus: Western Bus. **Amenities:** Bar; outdoor pool; limited room service; babysitting; laundry service; dry cleaning. *In room:* A/C, TV, minibar, coffeemaker, hair dryer, iron, safe.

Orange Hill Beach Inn ⭐ *(Finds)* This hotel, set on 1.4 landscaped hillside hectares (3½ acres), lies about 13km (8 miles) west of Nassau and 1.5km (1 mile) east of Love Beach, which has great snorkeling. It's perfect for those who want to escape the crowds and stay in a quieter part of New Providence Island; it's easy to catch a cab or jitney to Cable Beach or downtown Nassau. The welcoming owners, Judy and Danny Lowe, an Irish-Bahamian partnership, jokingly refer to their operation as "Fawlty Towers Nassau."

This place was built as a private home in the 1920s and became a hotel in 1979 after the Lowes added more rooms and a swimming pool. Rooms and apartments come in a variety of sizes, although most are small. The bathrooms, likewise, are small but well maintained. Each has a balcony or patio, and a few apartments are equipped with kitchenettes. Many of the guests are European, especially in summer. It has been renovated with updated furniture in the rooms, as well as upgrading the bathroom units.

On-site is a bar serving sandwiches and salads throughout the day, and a restaurant that offers simple but good dinners. Diving excursions to the rich marine fauna of New Providence's southwestern coast are among the most popular activities here.

W. Bay St., just west of Blake Rd. (P.O. Box N-8583), Nassau, The Bahamas. (© 888/399-3698 or 242/327-7157. Fax 242/327-5186. www.orangehill.com. 32 units. Winter $119–$130 double, $164 apt; off season $102–$117 double, $117–$140 apt. MC, V. Free parking. Bus: Western Bus. **Amenities:** Restaurant; bar; outdoor pool; laundry service and coin-operated laundry; rooms for those w/limited mobility. *In room:* A/C, TV, kitchenette (in some).

4 Where to Dine

NASSAU

Nassau restaurants open and close often. Even if reservations aren't required, it's a good idea to call first just to see that a place is still functioning. European and American cuisines are relatively easy to find in Nassau. Surprisingly, it used to be difficult to find Bahamian cuisine, but in recent years, more places have begun to offer authentic island fare.

VERY EXPENSIVE

Buena Vista ⋆ CONTINENTAL/BAHAMIAN/SEAFOOD
Although not quite up there with Graycliff, this restaurant is definitely a runner-up in Nassau's culinary sweepstakes. It's a block west of Government House (Delancy St. is opposite the cathedral close off St. Francis Xavier, and only a short distance from Bay St.). It opened back in the 1940s in a colonial mansion set on 2 hectares (5 acres) of tropical foliage. Traditional elegance and fine preparations have always characterized this place.

You're likely to be shown to the main dining room, unless you request the cozy and intimate Victoria Room or, even better, the Garden Patio, which has a greenhouse setting and a ceiling skylight. The chef scours Nassau's markets to collect the freshest and finest ingredients, which he puts together in menus bursting with flavor and full of originality. Look for impromptu daily specials such as breaded veal chop or Long Island duckling. Besides the nouvelle cuisine here, you'll also find respect for tradition. The rack of lamb Provençale is a classic, but you might want to try instead some of the lighter veal dishes. The cream of garlic soup has plenty of flavor but never overpowers. Instead of wildly fanciful desserts, Buena Vista sticks to the classics—say, cherries jubilee or baked Alaska flambé au cognac. Service is deft, efficient, and polite. Calypso coffee finishes the meal off nicely as you listen to soft piano music.

Delancy and Meeting sts. ℭ **242/322-2811.** www.buenavista-restaurant.com. Reservations recommended. Main courses $28–$40; fixed-price dinner $38–$48. AE, MC, V. Mon–Sat 7–9:30pm.

Chez Willie 𝆏𝆏 FRENCH/BAHAMIAN

Elegant and romantic in aura, Chez Willie is a hot dinner reservation along Bay Street, luring visitors to Nassau in the evening. (*Note:* Most people arrive at the restaurant by taxi in lieu of wandering the deserted streets, which can be a bit dangerous at night.)

Jackets are preferred for men, and you can dine alfresco, listening to live piano music. Somehow this place recaptures some of the grandeur of Nassau in its cafe society days. In this relaxing atmosphere, you are likely to meet the host Willie Armstrong himself. You'll recognize him by his bow tie with jeweled clip, kissing the hand of female guests. In the courtyard is a fountain and regal statuary.

The food is exquisite. Launch into your repast by trying the stone crab claws with a Dijon mustard sauce or perhaps a fresh Bahamian tuna and crab mousse in a light sauce. Much of the fare here is familiar but beautifully prepared with first-rate ingredients. Main courses range from lobster thermidor to sautéed Dover sole in a tarragon-and-tomato-laced sauce. We often opt for the broiled seafood platter in a sauce made with fresh herbs. The chef's special is grouper in puff pastry with crabmeat, served with a coconut cream sauce. Special dinners for two, taking an hour, feature beef Wellington, a delicate chateaubriand, or roast rack of lamb.

W. Bay St. ℭ **242/322-5364.** Reservations required. Jacket preferred for men. Main courses $30–$52; fixed-price menu for 2 $60–$100 per person. AE, DISC, MC, V. Daily 6:30–10pm.

Where to Dine in Nassau

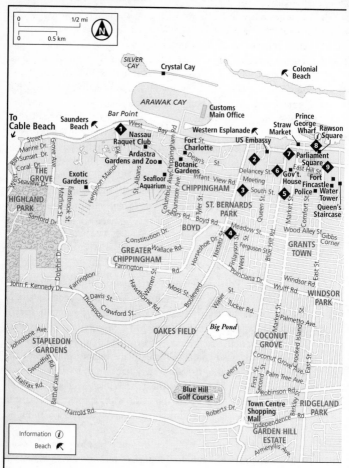

Bahamian Kitchen **8**

Buena Vista **3**

Café Matisse **9**

Café Skans **1**

Chez Willie **2**

Conch Fritters Bar & Grill **7**

Crocodiles Waterfront Bar & Grill **10**

Double Dragon **12**

East Villa Restaurant and Lounge **13**

Gaylord's **11**

Graycliff **6**

Palm Tree **5**

Poop Deck **14**

Shoal Restaurant and Lounge **4**

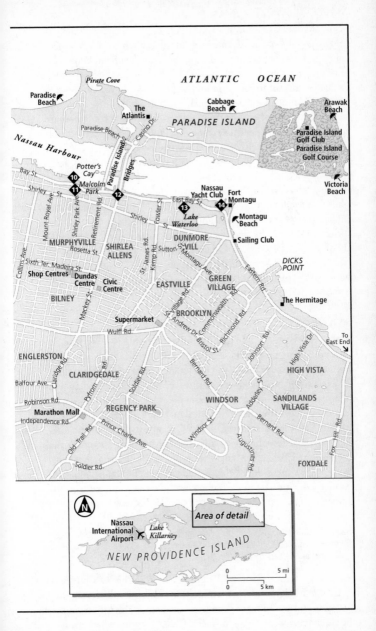

Graycliff ⚓ CONTINENTAL   Part of the Graycliff hotel, an antiques-filled colonial mansion located opposite Government House, this restaurant is the domain of connoisseur and bon vivant Enrico Garzaroli. The chefs use local Bahamian products whenever available and turn them into an old-fashioned, heavy cuisine that still has a lot of appeal for tradition-minded visitors, many of whom return here year after year. Young diners with more contemporary palates might head elsewhere, though, as the food has fallen off a bit of late. The chefs, neither completely traditional nor regional, produce such dishes as grouper soup in puff pastry, and plump, juicy pheasant cooked with pineapples grown on Eleuthera. Lobster is another specialty, half in beurre blanc and the other sided with a sauce prepared with the head of the lobster. Other standard dishes include escargots, foie gras, and *tournedos d'agneau* (lamb). The pricey wine list is the finest in the country, with more than 180,000 bottles. The collection of Cuban cigars here—almost 90 types—is said to be the most varied in the world.

W. Hill St. ☎ 242/322-2796. Reservations required. Jacket advised for men. Main courses lunch $20–$30, dinner $38–$52. AE, DISC, MC, V. Mon–Fri noon–3pm; daily 6:30–10pm. Bus: 10.

MODERATE

Café Matisse ⚓ INTERNATIONAL/ITALIAN   Set directly behind Parliament House, in a peach building that was built a century ago as a private home, this restaurant is on everybody's short list of downtown Nassau favorites. It serves well-prepared Italian and international cuisine to businesspeople, workers from nearby government offices, and all kinds of deal makers. There are dining areas within an enclosed courtyard, as well as on two floors of the interior, which is decorated with colorful Matisse prints. It's run by the sophisticated Bahamian-Italian team of Greg and Gabriella Curry, who prepare menu items that include an enticing cannelloni with lobster sauce; mixed grill of seafood; grilled rack of lamb with grilled tomatoes; a perfect filet mignon in a green-pepper sauce; and a zesty curried shrimp with rice. There are also meal-size pizzas.

Bank Lane at Bay St., just north of Parliament Sq. ☎ 242/356-7012. Reservations recommended. Main courses lunch $14–$20, dinner $16–$35. AE, MC, V. Tues–Sat noon–3pm and 6–10pm. Bus: 17 or 21.

East Villa Restaurant and Lounge CHINESE/CONTINENTAL   You might imagine yourself in Hong Kong during the 1980s in this well-designed modern house across the road from the headquarters of the Nassau Yacht Club. It's somewhat upscale, sometimes attracting rich Florida yachters to its dimly lit precincts, where aquariums bubble in a simple but tasteful contemporary setting. Zesty Szechwan flavors appear on the menu, but there are less spicy Cantonese alternatives, including sweet-and-sour chicken and steamed vegetables with cashews and water chestnuts. Lobster tail in the spicy Chinese style is one of our favorites. Dishes can be ordered mild, medium, or zesty hot.

E. Bay St. (©) **242/393-3377**. Reservations required. Lunch $8–$16; main courses $10–$38. AE, MC, V. Sun–Fri noon–3pm; daily 6–10pm. Bus: 11 or 19.

Gaylord's NORTHERN INDIAN   The Indian owners of this restaurant arrived in The Bahamas via Kenya and then England, and they are wryly amused at their success in "bringing India to The Bahamas." Within a room lined with Indian art and artifacts, you'll dine on a wide range of savory and zesty Punjabi, tandoori, and curried dishes. Some of the best choices are the lamb selections, although such concessions to local culture as curried or tandoori-style conch have also begun cropping up on the menu. If you don't know what to order, consider a tandoori mixed platter, which might satisfy two of you with a side dish or two. Any of the *korma* dishes, which combine lamb, chicken, beef, or vegetables in a creamy curry sauce, are very successful. Takeout meals are also available.

Dowdeswell St. at Bay St. (©) **242/356-3004**. Reservations recommended. Main courses $15–$50; vegetarian dinner $25. AE, MC, V. Mon–Fri noon–3pm; daily 6:30–11pm. Bus: 10 or 17.

Poop Deck BAHAMIAN/SEAFOOD   This is a favorite with yachters and others who find a perch on the second-floor, open-air terrace, which overlooks the harbor and Paradise Island. If you like dining with a view, you won't find a better place than this in the heart of Nassau. At lunch, you can order conch chowder (perfectly seasoned) or a juicy beef burger. The waiters are friendly, the crowd is convivial, and the festivities continue into the evening with lots of drinking and good cheer. Native grouper fingers served with peas 'n' rice is the Bahamian soul food dish on the menu. Two of the best seafood selections are the fresh lobster and the stuffed mushrooms with crabmeat. The creamy homemade lasagna with crisp garlic bread is another fine choice.

Nassau Yacht Haven Marina, E. Bay St. (©) **242/393-8175**. Reservations recommended. Lunch $15–$30; main courses $25–$52. AE, MC, V. Daily noon–4:30pm and 5–10:30pm. Bus: 10, 19, or 23.

Shoal Restaurant and Lounge BAHAMIAN   Many of our good friends in Nassau swear that this is the best joint for authentic local food. We're not entirely convinced this is true, but we rank it near the top. The place is a beehive of activity on Saturday mornings, when seemingly half of Nassau shows up for the chef's specialty, boiled fish and johnnycake. This may or may not be your fantasy, but to a Bahamian it's like pot liquor and turnip greens with cornbread to a Southerner. Far removed from the well-trodden tourist path, this restaurant is a real favorite of residents. After all, where else can you get a good bowl of okra soup these days? Naturally, conch chowder is the preferred opener. Many diners follow the chowder with more conch, "cracked" this time. But you can also order some unusual dishes such as Bahamian-style mutton using native spices and herbs. The seafood platter—with lobster, shrimp, and fried grouper—is more international in appeal. Peas 'n' rice accompanies everything. The restaurant even offers to transport you to and from the restaurant from your hotel free of charge.

Nassau St. ℂ 242/323-4400. Main courses $9–$38. AE, DISC, MC, V. Daily 7:30am–10:30pm.

INEXPENSIVE

Bahamian Kitchen *Value* *Kids* BAHAMIAN   Next to Trinity Church, this is one of the best places for good Bahamian food at modest prices. Down-home dishes, full of local flavor, include lobster Bahamian style, fried red snapper, conch salad, stewed fish, curried chicken, okra soup, and pea soup and dumplings. Most dishes are served with peas 'n' rice. You can order such old-fashioned Bahamian fare as stewed fish and corned beef and grits, all served with johnnycake. If you'd like to introduce your kids to Bahamian cuisine, this is an ideal choice. There's takeout service if you're planning a picnic.

Trinity Place, off Market St. ℂ 242/325-0702. Lunch $6–$13; main courses $9–$23. AE, MC, V. Mon–Sat 11am–10pm. Bus: 10.

Café Skans *Value* INTERNATIONAL   This is a straightforward, Formica-clad diner with an open kitchen, offering flavorful food that's served without fanfare in generous portions. It's next door to the Straw Market site, attracting local residents and office workers from the government buildings nearby. Menu items include Bahamian fried or barbecued chicken; bean soup with dumplings; souvlakia or gyros in pita bread; and burgers, steaks, and various kinds of seafood platters. This is where workaday Nassau comes for breakfast.

Bay St., adjacent to the Straw Market. ℂ 242/322-2486. Reservations required. Breakfast $4–$9; sandwiches $6–$19; main-course platters $6–$25. MC, V. Mon–Fri 8am–5pm; Sat–Sun 8am–6pm.

Conch Fritters Bar & Grill BAHAMIAN/INTERNATIONAL
A true local hangout with real island atmosphere, this light-hearted restaurant changes its focus several times throughout the day. Lunches and dinners are high-volume, high-turnover affairs mitigated only by attentive staff who seem genuinely concerned about the well-being of their guests. Live music is presented every day except Monday from 7pm until closing, when the place transforms again into something of a singles bar. Food choices are rather standard but still quite good, including cracked conch, fried shrimp, grilled salmon, six different versions of chicken, blackened rib-eye steak, burgers, and sandwiches. Specialty drinks from the active bar include a Goombay Smash.

Marlborough St. (across from the British Colonial Hilton). ⓒ **242/323-8801.** Burgers, sandwiches, and platters $10–$40. AE, MC, V. Daily 10am–11:30pm.

Crocodiles Waterfront Bar & Grill INTERNATIONAL/BAHAMIAN   One of the most appealing, funky bar/restaurants in Nassau lies about a 2-minute walk from the Nassau side of the Paradise Island Bridge, with a view over the water. Set on a deck that's partially protected with thatched parasols but mostly open to the sky and a view of the channel, it's completely casual. (You'll recognize the place by the hundreds of stenciled crocodiles happily cavorting on the wall that separates the place from the dense traffic of E. Bay St.) After one of the rum concoctions from the bar, you might get into the swing of things. If you're hungry, order up cracked or grilled conch, a grilled 10-ounce sirloin steak, teriyaki-marinated tuna, grilled lobster tail, Bahamian-style fried chicken, crab cakes, or the standard but creamy lasagna. A particularly good sandwich choice is blackened mahi-mahi. There's a lounge on the premises with frequent live entertainment.

E. Bay St. ⓒ **242/323-3341.** Main courses $11–$33. AE, DISC, MC, V. Daily 11am–midnight. Bus: 10 or 17.

Double Dragon CANTONESE/SZECHWAN   The chefs hail from the province of Canton in mainland China, and that's the inspiration for most of the food here. If you've ever really wondered about the differences between Cantonese and Szechwan cuisine, a quick look at the menu here will highlight them. Lobster, chicken, or beef, for example, can be prepared Cantonese style, with a mild black-bean or ginger sauce; or in spicier Szechwan formats of red peppers, chiles, and garlic. Honey-garlic chicken and orange-flavored shrimp are always popular and succulent. Overall, this place is a fine choice if you're eager for a change from grouper and burgers.

Bridge Plaza Commons, Mackey St. ✆ **242/393-5718**. Main courses $8–$22. AE, DISC, MC, V. Mon–Thurs noon–10pm; Fri noon–11pm; Sat 4–11pm; Sun 5–10pm. Bus: 10.

Palm Tree ✿ *Value* BAHAMIAN/AMERICAN   This restaurant occupies the homestead of a Bahamian matriarch, Lydia Russell, who died in the 1980s. This place is set within a white-and-green-colored stucco house in the heart of Nassau. Inside, you'll find lots of exposed wood, a color scheme of white and black, and lots of local paintings inspired by Junkanoo. Menu items are as down-home as you can get (cracked conch, baked pork chops, fried or steamed grouper, minced or broiled lobster, and baked chicken) and are served with two of at least seven side dishes like potato salad, creamed corn, beets, coleslaw, macaroni and cheese, peas 'n' rice, or fried plantains.

Corner of Market and Cockburn sts. ✆ **242/322-4201**. Main courses $6–$10. No credit cards. Mon–Sat 8am–10pm. Bus: 8.

CABLE BEACH
VERY EXPENSIVE

The Black Angus Grille ✿ INTERNATIONAL/STEAKS/SEAFOOD   This is your best bet for dining if you're testing your luck at the Crystal Palace Casino nearby (and you may need to win to pay the hefty bill here). The Rotisserie in the Sheraton Grand Resort Paradise Island has the edge and is also more reasonably priced, but this is a close runner-up. Serving some of the best beef and steaks along Cable Beach, it's the favorite of hundreds of casino goers. Set one floor above the gambling tables, it has a boldly geometric decor of brightly colored tile work and comfortable banquettes.

Although steaks are frozen and flown in from the mainland, they are well prepared—succulent, juicy, and cooked to your specifications. The filet mignon is especially delectable, although the T-bone always seems to have more flavor. Prime rib is a nightly feature. The kitchen also prepares a number of sumptuous seafood platters, and Bahamian lobster tails here are fresh and flavorful.

In the Wyndham Nassau Resort & Crystal Palace Casino, W. Bay St. ✆ **242/327-6200**. Reservations recommended. Main courses $35–$60. AE, DC, DISC, MC, V. Daily 6–11pm. Bus: 10.

Sole Mare ✿✿ NORTHERN ITALIAN   This is our top choice for elegant dining along Cable Beach, and it also serves the best Northern Italian cuisine along the beach strip. The chefs are well trained and inventive. A filet of whatever fresh fish is available that day appears on the menu and is the keynote of many a delectable meal here. Many of the other ingredients have to be imported from the mainland, but the chefs still work their magic with them. Our lobster tail stuffed with crabmeat was a splendid choice, as was our dining partner's veal scaloppine sautéed with fresh mushrooms. Veal also appears rather delectably sautéed with endive, a dish you might enjoy in an upmarket tavern in northern Italy. The dessert soufflés are excellent, especially when served with the vanilla sauce.

In the Wyndham Nassau Resort & Crystal Palace Casino, W. Bay St. ℂ 242/327-6200. Reservations required. Main courses $35–$70. AE, DC, DISC, MC, V. Thurs–Sat 3–11pm (hours may vary, call ahead). Bus: 10.

EXPENSIVE

The Beef Cellar ℛ STEAKS/SEAFOOD   If you like steak, look no farther than Cable Beach and its Nassau Beach Hotel. The steaks here are juicy, succulent, and tender—and cooked just as you like. Located downstairs from the hotel's lobby, within a short walk of the casino at the neighboring Wyndham Nassau Resort, the Beef Cellar features a warmly masculine decor of exposed stone and leather, two-fisted drinks, and tables that have individual charcoal grills for diners who prefer to grill their own steaks. The seafood platters are also superb, including shrimp kabob and grilled salmon in a dill sauce. The prices here are more reasonable than those at the Black Angus Grille in the Wyndham Resort.

In the Nassau Beach Hotel. ℂ 242/327-7711. Main courses $20–$40. AE, DC, MC, V. Daily 6:30–10pm.

Provence ℛ MEDITERRANEAN   The best dishes in Nassau that feature the sunny cuisine of Provence in France are showcased here with the chef's self-styled *cuisine du soleil.* Lying near the end of West Bay Street, Provence prepares many dishes with superb simplicity—Atlantic salmon with citrus butter, for example—so as not to mar the natural flavor. Other dishes are heavily spiced such as the rib-eye steak in a fire-breathing pepper sauce. Although lacking certain key ingredients (such as hogfish), the chefs also turn out a delightful bouillabaisse evocative of the type served in Marseille. Daily seafood specials are featured—our favorite being the pan-seared sea bass, or else you might order the filet of black grouper.

Old Town Sandyport. ℂ 242/327-0985. Reservations required. Main courses $27–$40. AE, DISC, MC, V. Mon–Sat 11:30am–3pm and 6–10:30pm.

MODERATE

Capriccio ITALIAN/INTERNATIONAL   Set beside a prominent roundabout, about .5km (⅓-mile) west of the megahotels of
Cable Beach, this restaurant lies within a grandly Italian building
with Corinthian columns and an outdoor terrace. Inside, it's a lot
less formal, outfitted like a luncheonette, but with lots of exposed
granite, busy espresso machines, and kindly Bahamian staff who
have been trained in their understanding of Italian culinary nuance.
At lunch you get pretty ordinary fare such as fresh salads, sandwiches, and a few hot platters like cracked conch. But the cooks
shine at night, offering dishes such as chicken breast with sage and
wine sauce, spaghetti with pesto and pine nuts, and seafood platters.

W. Bay St. ✆ 242/327-8547. Reservations recommended. Lunch items $6–$17;
dinner main courses $15–$28. MC, V. Mon–Sat 11am–10pm; Sun 5–10pm.

The Poop Deck at Sandy Port INTERNATIONAL/SEAFOOD
This is the largest and most imposing restaurant west of Cable
Beach, convenient for the owners of the many upscale villas and
condos that surround it. It's set within a pink concrete building
that's highly visible from West Bay Street—but despite its impressive exterior, it's a bit sterile-looking on the inside. This simple
island restaurant evolved from a roughneck bar that occupied this
site during the early 1970s. Lunch is usually devoted to well-prepared burgers, pastas, sandwiches, and salads. Dinners are more substantial, featuring filet mignon, surf and turf (seafood and steak
combo), cracked conch, and fried shrimp caught off the Bahamian
Long Island. The house drink is a Bacardi splish-splash, containing
Bacardi Select, Nassau Royal Liqueur, pineapple juice, cream, and
sugar-cane syrup.

Poop Deck Dr., off W. Bay St. ✆ 242/327-DECK. Reservations recommended. Main
courses lunch $10–$30, dinner $19–$60. AE, DISC, MC, V. Tues–Sun noon–10:30pm.

INEXPENSIVE

Café Johnny Canoe *Kids* INTERNATIONAL/BAHAMIAN
There's absolutely nothing stylish about this place (it was originally
a Howard Johnson's), but because of its good value and cheerful
staff, it's almost always filled with satisfied families. Within a yellow-
painted interior that's accented with Junkanoo memorabilia, you
can order filling portions of diner-style food with a Bahamian twist:
cracked conch and lobster, grilled mahi-mahi, grouper fingers with
tartar sauce, homemade soups, and fried fish. Sandwiches always
come with one side order; platters always come with two. The place
is named after the legend of a Bahamian slave who escaped in the

canoe of a Junkanoo band. There's live Junkanoo music, accented with goatskin drums and synchronized cowbells, on Friday nights.

In the Nassau Beach Hotel, W. Bay St. ✆ **242/327-3373**. Breakfast $6–$14; salads, sandwiches, and lunch and dinner platters $12–$30. AE, DISC, MC, V. Daily 7:30am–11pm.

WEST OF CABLE BEACH

Travellers Rest ☽ *Value* BAHAMIAN/SEAFOOD   Set in an isolated spot about 2.5km (1½ miles) west of the megahotels of Cable Beach, this restaurant feels far away from it all. Its owners will make you feel like you're dining on a remote Out Island. Travellers Rest is set in a cozy cement-sided house that stands in a grove of sea-grape and palm trees facing the ocean. It was established by Winnipeg-born Joan Hannah in 1972, and since then has fed ordinary as well as famous folks like Stevie Wonder, Gladys Knight, spy novelist Robert Ludlum, Julio Iglesias, Eric Clapton, and Rosa Parks. You can dine outside, but if it's rainy (highly unlikely), you can go inside the tavern with its small bar decorated with local paintings. Many diners use the white-sand beach across from the restaurant to get here; others pull up in their own boats. In this laid-back atmosphere, you can feast on well-prepared grouper fingers, barbecue ribs, curried chicken, steamed or cracked conch, or minced crawfish, and finish perhaps with guava cake, the best on the island. The conch salad served on the weekends is said to increase virility in men.

W. Bay St., near Gambier (14km/8¾ miles west of the center of Nassau). ✆ **242/327-7633**. Main courses lunch $7.50–$25, dinner $14–$28. AE, MC, V. Daily noon–11pm. Bus: Western Bus.

5 Beaches, Watersports & Other Outdoor Pursuits

One of the great sports centers of the world, Nassau and the islands that surround it are marvelous places for swimming, sunning, snorkeling, scuba diving, boating, water-skiing, and deep-sea fishing, as well as tennis and golf.

You can learn more about most of the available activities by calling **The Bahamas Sports Tourist Office** (✆ **800/32-SPORT** or 954/236-9292) from anywhere in the continental United States. Call Monday through Friday from 9am to 5pm, EST. Or, write the center at 1200 South Pine Island Rd., Suite 750, Plantation, FL 33324.

HITTING THE BEACH

In the Bahamas, as in Puerto Rico, the issue about public access to beaches is a hot and controversial subject. Recognizing this, the government has made efforts to intersperse public beaches with easy access between more private beaches where access may be impeded. Although megaresorts discourage nonresidents from easy access to their individual beaches, there are so many public beaches on New Providence Island and Paradise Island that all a beach lover has to do is stop his or her car (or else walk) to many of the unmarked, unnamed beaches that flank the edge of these islands.

The average visitor will not have a problem with beaches because most people stay in one of the large beachfront resorts where the ocean meets the sand right outside of the hotel.

For those hoping to explore more of the coast, here are the "no problem, man" beaches—the ones that are absolutely accessible to the public:

Cable Beach 🏖🏖 No particular beach is actually called Cable Beach, yet this is the most popular beachfront on New Providence Island. Instead of an actual beach, Cable Beach is the name given to a string of resorts and beaches that lie in the center of New Providence's northern coast, attracting the most visitors. This beachfront offers 6.5km (4 miles) of soft white sand, with many different types of food, restaurants, snack bars, and watersports offered by the hotels lining the waterfront. Calypso music floats to the sand from hotel pool patios where vacationers play musical chairs and see how low they can limbo. Vendors wend their way between sunblock-slathered bodies. Some sell armloads of shell jewelry, T-shirts, beach cover-ups, and fresh coconuts for sipping the sweet "water" straight from the shell. Others offer their hair-braiding services or sign up visitors for water-skiing, jet skiing, and banana boat rides. Kiosks advertise parasailing, scuba-diving, and snorkeling trips, as well as party cruises to offshore islands. Waters can be rough and reefy, then calm and clear a little farther along the shore. There are no public toilets here, because guests of the resorts use their hotel facilities. If you're not a guest of the hotel, or not a customer, you are not supposed to use the facilities. Cable Beach resorts begin 4.8km (3 miles) west of downtown Nassau. Even though resorts line much of this long swath of beach, there are various sections where public access is available without crossing through private hotel grounds.

Caves Beach On the north shore, past the Cable Beach Hotel properties, Caves Beach is 11km (7 miles) southwest of Nassau. It stands near Rock Point, right before the turnoff along Blake Road that leads to the airport. Since visitors often don't know of this

---

Finds **A Beach for Lovers**

Continuing west along West Bay Street, you reach **Love Beach,** across from Sea Gardens, a good stretch of sand lying east of Northwest Point. Love Beach, although not big, is a special favorite with lovers. The snorkeling is superb, too. It's technically private, though no one bothers visitors who come, and locals fervently hope it won't ever become overrun like Cable Beach.

---

place, it's a good spot to escape the hordes. It's also a good beach with soft sands. There are no toilets or changing facilities.

Delaporte Beach   Just west of the busiest section of Cable Beach, Delaporte Beach is a public access beach where you can also escape the crowds. It opens onto clear waters and boasts white sands, although it has no facilities, including toilets. Nonetheless, it's an option.

Goodman's Bay   This public beach lies east of Cable Beach on the way toward the center of Nassau. Goodman's Bay and Saunders Beach (see below) often host local fund-raising cookouts, where vendors sell fish, chicken, conch, peas 'n' rice, or macaroni and cheese. People swim and socialize to blaring reggae and calypso music. To find out when one of these beach parties is happening, ask the staff at your hotel or pick up a local newspaper. A playground is here, along with toilet facilities.

Old Fort Beach ⟨⟨   We often head here to escape the crowds on weekdays, a 15-minute drive west of the Nassau International Airport (take W. Bay St. toward Lyford Cay). This lovely sandy beach opens onto the turquoise waters of Old Fort Bay near the western part of New Providence. The least developed of the island's beaches, it attracts many homeowners from swanky Lyford Cay nearby. In winter, the beach can be quite windy, but in summer it's as calm as the Caribbean Sea.

Saunders Beach   East of Cable Beach, this is where many islanders go on the weekends. To reach it, take West Bay Street from Nassau in the direction of Coral Island. This beach lies across from Fort Charlotte, just west of Arawak Cay. Like Goodman's Bay (see above) it often hosts local fund-raising cookouts open to the public. These can be a lot of fun. There are no public facilities.

Western Esplanade If you're staying at a hotel in downtown Nassau, such as the British Colonial, this one (also known as Junkanoo Beach) is a good beach to patronize close to town. On this narrow strip of sand convenient to Nassau, you'll find toilets, changing facilities, and a snack bar.

BIKING

A half-day bicycle tour with **Bahamas Outdoors Ltd.** (*ⓒ* **242/362-2772;** about $60) can take you on a 5km (3-mile) bike ride along some scenic forest and shoreline trails in the Coral Harbour area on the southwestern coast of New Providence. You pass along a trail that has mangrove creeks and pine forests as a scenic backdrop and can take time off for a kayak trip to a shallow for snorkeling. Some of the major hotels on Paradise Beach and Cable Beach rent bikes to their guests. You can bike along Cable Beach or the beachfront at Paradise Island, but Nassau traffic is too congested.

BOAT CRUISES

Cruises from the harbors around New Providence Island are offered by a number of operators, with trips ranging from daytime voyages for snorkeling, picnicking, sunning, and swimming, to sunset and moonlight cruises.

   Barefoot Sailing Cruises, Bay Shore Marina (*ⓒ* **242/393-0820;** www.barefootsailingcruises.com) runs the *Wind Dance,* which leaves for all-day cruises from this dock, offering many sailing and snorkeling possibilities. This is your best bet if you're seeking a more romantic cruise and don't want 100 people aboard. The cruises usually stop at Rose Island, which is a charming, picture-perfect spot, with an uncrowded white sandy beach and palm trees. You can also sail on a ketch, the 16m (52-ft.) *Riding High,* which is bigger than the 12m (39-ft.) *Wind Dance.* Cruise options are plentiful, ranging from a half-day of sailing, snorkeling, and exploring ($55), to a full day ($89), to private dinner cruises of 3 moonlit hours ($650 for two people). If the cruise becomes a party, $500 is charged for the first two guests, then $65 for each additional person.

   Flying Cloud, Paradise Island West Dock (*ⓒ* **242/363-4430**), features catamaran cruises carrying 50 people on day and sunset trips. It's a good bet for people who want a more intimate cruise and shy away from the heavy volume carried aboard Majestic Tours catamarans (see below). Snorkeling equipment is provided free. Monday to Saturday half-day charters cost $50 per person; a 2½-hour sunset cruise goes for $50. Evening bookings are on Monday, Wednesday, and Friday. A 5-hour cruise leaves on Sunday at 10am that costs $65 per person.

Majestic Tours Ltd., Hillside Manor (© **242/322-2606**), will book 3-hour cruises on two of the biggest catamarans in the Atlantic, offering views of the water, sun, sand, and outlying reefs. This is the biggest and most professionally run of the cruise boats, and it's an affordable option; but we find that there are just too many other passengers aboard. The *Yellow Bird* is suitable for up to 250 passengers. It departs from Prince George's Dock; ask for the exact departure point when you make your reservation. The cost is $18 per adult, $9 for children under 10, and snorkeling equipment is $10 extra. The outfitter has also added another boat, the *Robinson Crusoe,* holding 350 passengers. On Wednesday, Friday, and Sunday, there are cruises from 10am to 4:30pm, costing $45 for adults and half price for children 11 and under. Sunset dinner cruises from 7 to 10pm on Tuesday and Friday cost $50 per adult, again half price for children.

FISHING

May to August are the best months for the oceanic bonito and the blackfin tuna; June and July for blue marlin; and November through February for the wahoo found in reefy areas.

Arrangements can be made at any of the big hotels, but unfortunately, there's a hefty price tag. Prices are usually $350 for a half-day boat rental for parties of two to six, or $700 for a full day's fishing.

One of the most reliable companies, **Born Free Charters** (© **242/393-4144**), offers a fleet of 3 vessels that can seat six comfortably; they can be rented for a half-day ($450–$600) or a full day ($900–$1,200). Each additional person is charged $50 depending on boat size. Fishing choices are plentiful: You can troll for wahoo, tuna, and marlin in the deep sea, or cast in the shallows for snapper, grouper, and yellowtail. Anchoring and bottom-fishing are calmer options. We recommend this charter because Born Free offers so many types of fishing and gives you a lot of leeway regarding where you want to fish and how much time you want to spend.

Occasionally, a boat owner will configure him- or herself and their boat as a venue for deep-sea fishing, and unless you're dealing with a genuinely experienced guide, your fishing trip may or may not be a success. Two of the most consistently reliable deep-sea fishermen are the father-son team of John and Teddy Pratt, who maintain 11m (36-ft.) and 13m (43-ft.) boats, either of which is available for full- or half-day deep-sea fishing excursions. Both boats dock every night at the island's largest marina, the 150-slip **Nassau Yacht Haven,** on East Bay Street (© **242/393-8173**), where a member of the staff will direct you toward either of the two boats. Alternatively, you can call © **242/422-0364** to speak to one of the men directly. It takes about 20 minutes of boat travel to reach an offshore point where dolphin and wahoo may or may not be biting, depending on a raft of complicated seasonable factors. These trips need to be booked weeks in advance.

GOLF

Some of the best golfing in The Bahamas is found in Nassau. The following courses are open to the public, not just to guests of the hotels that operate the properties.

Radisson Cable Beach Golf Course ✪✪ on West Bay Road, Cable Beach (© **242/327-6000**), is a spectacular 18-hole, 7,040-yard, par-72 championship golf course that's better than ever. The redesign of the course features a reshaping of the course's fairways, repositioning of greens, and the creation of new hazards and water-lined holes through two-thirds of the course. Better year-round playing conditions have been assured by the addition of a salt-tolerant grass known as paspalum that is greener, firmer and more upright, withstanding the salty breezes and tropical climate while offering a premium putting surface. The development was overseen by veteran designer and consultant Fred M. Settle, Jr., of International Golf Design, Inc. The Cable Beach course is under the management of the Radisson Cable Beach Hotel, but it's often used by guests of the other hotels nearby. Greens fees are $105 for residents of The Bahamas and for people staying at the Radisson, $135 to $150 for all other players. Carts are included.

HORSEBACK RIDING

Happy Trails Stables, Coral Harbour, on the southwest shore (© **242/362-1820;** www.windsorequestriancentre.com), offers a 90-minute horseback trail ride for $95, including free transportation to and from your hotel. Riders must weigh less than 200 pounds. The stables are signposted from the Nassau International Airport, which is 3km (2 miles) away. Children must be 12 or older, and reservations are required, especially during the holiday season.

SNORKELING, SCUBA DIVING & UNDERWATER WALKS

There's great snorkeling off most of the beaches on New Providence, especially **Love Beach.** Most any of the hotels and resorts will rent or loan you snorkeling equipment. Several of the companies mentioned above under "Boat Cruises" also offer snorkel trips, as does Bahamas Divers, below.

Our favorite sight for snorkeling is **Goulding Cay,** lying off the western tip of New Providence. Underwater you'll find a virtual field of hard corals, especially the elegant elkhorn. The clear waters here and the shallow coral heads make it ideal for filmmakers. In fact, it's been featured in many films, ranging from a number of 007 movies to *20,000 Leagues Under the Sea.* More elkhorn coral awaits you to the south at **Southwest Reef,** which also has some stunning star coral found in water less than 2.4m (8 ft.) deep in many places. To the north is the curiously named **Fish Hotel,** which is not much on coral but is graced with large schools of fish, especially red snapper, jacks, and grunts.

There are more dive sites around New Providence than you can see in one visit, so we've included a few of our favorites. **Shark Wall** is the most intriguing, which is a diving excursion 16km (10 miles) off the coast; others include the **Rose Island Reefs,** the **Southwest Reef,** the **Razorback,** and **Booby Rock Reef.** Dive outfitters can also lead you to many old shipwrecks off the coast, along with caves and cliffs. Wrecks include *Mahoney* and *Alcora,* plus the wreck used in the James Bond film, *Never Say Never Again.* Divers also explore the airplane propeller used in another Bond film, *Thunderball.* All dive outfitters feature one or more of these sites.

Bahamas Divers, East Bay Street (© **242/393-5644**), has packages that range from a half-day of snorkeling at offshore reefs for $30 per person, to a half-day scuba trip with preliminary pool instruction for beginners for $89 for two tanks or $55 for one tank; other equipment is an additional cost. Half-day excursions for certified divers to deeper outlying reefs, drop-offs, and blue holes can be arranged.

Participants receive free transportation from their hotel to the boats. Children must be 10 or older, and reservations are required, especially during the holiday season.

Hartley's Undersea Walk , East Bay Street (© **242/393-8234**), offers an exciting and educational experience. They take you out from Nassau Harbour aboard the yacht *Pied Piper.* During the 3½-hour cruise, you take a boat ride out to a reef. After donning a lead and glass helmet, you descend a ladder into 4 to 5 meters (12–15 ft.) of water. Air is pumped into the helmet through a long tube. You can keep your glasses on or your contact lenses in, because your face and hair stay completely dry. For about 25 minutes, you walk through a garden of tropical fish, sponges, and other undersea life.

Entire families can go on this safe adventure, which costs $125 (no reduced child's fare). You don't even have to be able to swim. Two trips run per day, at 9:30am and 1:30pm, Tuesday through Saturday. Arrive 30 minutes before departures, and make reservations 5 to 10 days in advance. Free transportation is available to and from your hotel.

Stuart Cove's Dive Bahamas, Southwest Bay Street, South Ocean (P.O. Box CB13137, Nassau; ℂ **800/879-9832** in the U.S. or 242/362-4171), is about 10 minutes from top dive sites, including the coral reefs, wrecks, and an underwater airplane structure used in filming James Bond thrillers. Divers on expeditions here are taken to the island's most thrilling underwater site, the wreck of the *Caribe Breeze,* depicted in the film, *Open Water.* The staff here feeds reef sharks some 15m (49 ft.) below the surface, and, from a position of safety, snorkelers above can see the show down below. The Porpoise Pen Reefs, named for Flipper, and steep sea walls are also on the diving agenda. A two-tank dive in the morning costs $88, or an all-day program goes for $135. All prices for boat dives include tanks, weights, and belts. An open-water certification course starts at $695. Bring along two friends, and the price drops to $495 per person. Escorted boat snorkeling trips cost $48; children under 12 are $24. A special feature is a series of shark-dive experiences priced from $135. In one outing, Caribbean reef sharks swim among the guests. In one dive, called Shark Arena, divers kneel down while a dive master feeds the sharks off a long pole. Another experience, the Shark Buoy in 1,800m (5,904 ft.) of ocean, involves a dive among silky-skinned sharks at about 9m (30 ft.). They swim among the divers while the dive master feeds them.

The outfitter has generated much excitement with its introduction of yellow "submarines," actually jet bikes called Scenic Underwater Bubbles. An air-fed bubble covers your head as these self-contained and battery-powered jet bikes propel you through an underwater wonderland. The subs are popular with nondivers, and they're viewed as safe for kids as well (that is, those older than 12). An underwater armada is escorted along to view the reefs, all for a cost of $99. The whole experience, from pickup at your hotel or cruise ship to return, takes about 3 hours.

TENNIS

Courts are available at some hotels. Guests usually play free or for a nominal fee, whereas visitors are charged.

Most of the courts at Cable Beach are under the auspices of the **Radisson Cable Beach Hotel,** West Bay Street (✆ **242/327-6000**). Residents of Radisson play free until sunset. Non-Radisson guests pay $10 per person per hour.

Another hotel offering tennis courts is the **Nassau Beach Hotel,** West Bay Street and Cable Beach (✆ **242/327-7711**), with six Flexipave night-lit courts. Guests play for free between 9am to 5pm (after 5pm $7 per hr.) and nonguests play for $7 per hour.

6 Seeing the Sights

Most of Nassau can be explored on foot, beginning at Rawson Square in the center. Here is where Bahamian fishers unload a variety of produce and fish—crates of mangoes, oranges, tomatoes, and limes, plus lots of crimson-lipped conch. To experience this slice of Bahamian life, go any morning Monday through Saturday before noon.

THE TOP ATTRACTIONS

Ardastra Gardens ⍟   The main attraction of the Ardastra Gardens, almost 2 hectares (5 acres) of lush tropical planting about 1.5km (1 mile) west of downtown Nassau near Fort Charlotte, is the parading flock of **pink flamingos.** The Caribbean flamingo, national bird of The Bahamas, had almost disappeared by the early 1940s but was brought back to significant numbers through the efforts of the National Trust. They now flourish in the rookery on Great Inagua. A flock of these exotic feathered creatures has been trained to march in drill formation, responding to the drillmaster's commands with long-legged precision and discipline. A flock of marching flamingos perform daily at 10:30am, 2:10pm, and 4:10pm.

Other exotic wildlife at the gardens include boa constrictors (very tame), kinkajous (honey bears) from Central and South America, green-winged macaws, peacocks and peahens, blue-and-yellow macaws, capuchin monkeys, iguanas, ring-tailed lemurs, red-ruff lemurs, margays, brown-headed tamarins (monkeys), and a crocodile. There are also numerous waterfowl to be seen in Swan Lake, including black swans from Australia and several species of wild ducks. Parrot feedings are at 11am, 1:30pm, and 3:30pm.

You can get a good look at Ardastra's flora by walking along the signposted paths. Many of the more interesting and exotic trees bear plaques with their names.

Chippingham Rd. ℂ **242/323-5806.** www.ardastra.com. Admission $12 adults, $6 children 4–12 years old, under 4 free. Daily 9am–4:30pm. Bus: 10.

National Art Gallery of The Bahamas ⭐   At long last this archipelago nation has a national showcase to display its talented artists. In a restored historic building in the center of Nassau, the gallery showcases Bahamian art, past and present. Bahamian art as an entity has existed for only 50 years. Museum curators claim that the present collection is only the nucleus of a long-range strategy to beef up the present number of works. Most of the paintings on exhibit are divided into a historical and a contemporary collection. Pioneering Bahamian artists are honored, as are younger and more modern painters. Perhaps in the realm of primitive or even native art, many of the paintings are quite sophisticated, especially Amos Ferguson's *Snowbirds*. He used house paint on cardboard to create a remarkable portrait.

Villa Doyle, West Hill St. ℂ **242/328-5800.** www.nagb.org.bs. Admission $3 adults, $2 seniors and students, $1 children 14 and under. Tues–Sat 11am–4pm.

Finds **Hanging Out at Potter's Cay**

The liveliest place in Nassau during the day is Potter's Cay, a native market that thrives beneath the Paradise Island Bridge. (While here, be sure to spend some time watching the mail boats leaving and coming to this quay.)

From the Out Islands, fishing boats and heavily laden sloops arrive early in the morning to unload the day's catch. These boats carry spiny lobster, grouper, fresh crab, jack, mackerel, and other fish. You'll see chefs finding inspiration here for the day's menu.

You'll also find vendors selling freshly harvested vegetables, including the fiery hot peppers so beloved by locals, along with paw-paws (papaya), stalks of bananas, fresh herbs, various root vegetables, tomatoes, and squash along with an array of luscious exotic fruits. *Here's a tip:* Many of these vendors have a wicked sense of humor and will offer you a taste of the tamarind fruit, claiming it's the "sweetest taste on God's earth." Invariably tricked visitors spit it out. The taste is horrendously offensive.

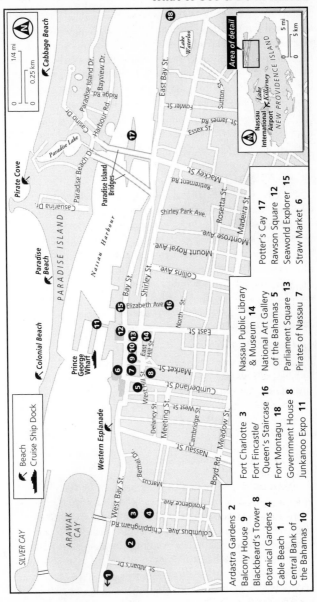

Ardastra Gardens **2**
Balcony House **9**
Blackbeard's Tower **8**
Botanical Gardens **4**
Cable Beach **1**
Central Bank of
the Bahamas **10**

Fort Charlotte **3**
Fort Fincastle/
Queen's Staircase **16**
Fort Montagu **18**
Government House **8**
Junkanoo Expo **11**

Nassau Public Library
& Museum **14**
National Art Gallery
of the Bahamas **5**
Parliament Square **13**
Pirates of Nassau **7**

Potter's Cay **17**
Rawson Square **12**
Seaworld Explorer **15**
Straw Market **6**

Seaworld Explorer ☙ If you are curious about life below the waves but aren't a strong swimmer, hop aboard this submarine, which holds about 45 passengers. Tours last 90 minutes and include 55 minutes of actual underwater travel at depths of about 3.5m (11 ft.) below the waves. Big windows allow big views of a protected ecology zone offshore from the Paradise Island Airport. About 20 minutes are devoted to an above-water tour of landmarks on either side of the channel that separates Nassau from Paradise Island.

Deveaux St. Docks. ✆ **242/356-2548**. Reservations required. Tours $37 adults, $19 children ages 2–12. Tours Thurs–Sun 11:30am year-round; additional departure at 1:30pm Dec–June.

MORE ATTRACTIONS

Balcony House The original design of this landmark house is a transplant of late-18th-century southeast American architecture. The pink, two-story structure is named for its overhanging and much photographed balcony. Restored in the 1990s, the House has been returned to its original design, recapturing a historic period. The mahogany staircase inside was thought to have been salvaged from a wrecked ship in the 1800s. You visit the house on a guided tour.

Trinity Place and Market St. ✆ **242/302-2621**. Free admission, but donation advised. Mon–Wed and Fri 10am–4:30pm; Thurs 10am–1pm.

Blackbeard's Tower These crumbling remains of a watchtower are said to have been used by the infamous pirate Edward Teach in the 17th century. The ruins are only mildly interesting—there isn't much trace of buccaneering. What's interesting is the view: With a little imagination, you can see Blackbeard peering out from here at unsuspecting ships. Blackbeard also purportedly lived here, but this is hardly well documented.

Yamacraw Hill Rd. (8km/5 miles east of Fort Montagu). No phone. Free admission. Daily 24 hr. Reachable by jitney.

Botanical Gardens More than 600 species of tropical flora are found in this 7.2 hectare (18-acre) park, located within a former rock quarry near Fort Charlotte. The garden features vine-draped arbors, two freshwater ponds with lilies, water plants, tropical fish, and a small cactus garden. After viewing them, you can take a leisurely walk along one of the trails.

Chippingham Rd. No phone. Admission $3 adults, $1.50 children under 12. Mon–Fri 8am–4pm; Sat–Sun 9am–4pm. Bus: 10 or 17.

Central Bank of The Bahamas The nerve center that governs the archipelago's financial transactions is also the venue for a year-round exhibition of paintings that represent some of the emerging new artistic talent of the island. The cornerstone of the building itself was laid by Prince Charles on July 9, 1973, when the country became independent from Britain. His mother, in February of 1975, officially inaugurated the bank.

Trinity Place and Frederick St. *©* **242/322-2193.** Free admission. Mon–Fri 9:30am–4:30pm.

Fort Charlotte Begun in 1787, Fort Charlotte is the largest of Nassau's three major defenses, built with plenty of dungeons. It used to command the western harbor. Named after King George III's consort, it was built by Gov. Lord Dunmore, who was also the last royal governor of New York and Virginia. Its 42 cannons never fired a shot, at least not at an invader (only seven cannons remain on-site). Within the complex are underground passages, which can be viewed on free tours. Tour guides at the fort are free but are very happy to accept a tip.

Off W. Bay St. on Chippingham Rd. *©* **242/325-9186.** Free admission. Daily 8am–4pm. Bus: 10.

Fort Fincastle Reached by climbing the Queen's Staircase, this fort was constructed in 1793 by Lord Dunmore, the royal governor. You can take an elevator ride to the top and walk on the observation floor (a 38m-/125-ft.-high water tower and lighthouse) for a panoramic view of the harbor. The tower is the highest point on New Providence. The so-called bow of this fort is patterned like a paddle-wheel steamer, the kind used on the Mississippi; it was built to defend Nassau against a possible invasion, though no shot was ever fired.

Although the ruins of the fort hardly compete with the view, you can walk around on your own. Be wary, however, of the very persistent young men who will try to show you the way here. They'll try to hustle you, but you really don't need a guide to see some old cannons on your own.

Elizabeth Ave. No phone. Free admission to fort; tickets to water tower $1. Mon–Sat 8am–5pm. Bus: 10 or 17.

Fort Montagu Built in 1741, this fort—the oldest one on the island—stands guard at the eastern entrance to the harbor of Nassau. The Americans captured it in 1776 during the War of Independence.

Less interesting than Fort Charlotte and Fort Fincastle, the ruins of this place are mainly for fort buffs. Many visitors find the nearby park, with well-maintained lawns and plenty of shade, more interesting than the fort itself. Vendors often peddle local handcrafts in this park, so you can combine a look at a ruined fort with a shopping expedition if you're so inclined.

Eastern Rd. Free admission. No regular hours. Bus: 10 or 17.

Junkanoo Expo   This museum is dedicated to Junkanoo—the colorful, musical, and surreal festival that takes place on December 26 when Nassau explodes into a riot of sounds, festivities, celebrations, and masks. It is the Bahamian equivalent of the famous Mardi Gras in New Orleans. If you can't visit Nassau for Junkanoo, this exhibition is the next best thing. You can see the lavish costumes and floats, which the revelers use during this annual celebration. The bright colors and costume designs are impressive if for no other reason than the sheer size of the costumes themselves. Some of the costumes are nearly as big as one of the small parade floats, but they are worn and carried by one person. The Expo has been installed in an old customs warehouse at the entrance to the Nassau wharf. The Expo also includes a souvenir boutique with Junkanoo paintings and a variety of Junkanoo handcrafts.

Prince George Wharf, Festival Place. ⓒ 242/323-3182. Free admission. Daily 9am–5pm.

Pirates of Nassau (Kids)   This museum, which opened in 2003, celebrates the dubious "golden age of piracy" (1690–1720). Nassau was once a bustling and robust town where pirates grew rich from plundered gold and other goods robbed at sea. Known as a paradise for pirates, it attracted various rogues and the wild women who flooded into the port to entertain them—for a price, of course. The museum recreates those bawdy, lusty days in a series of exhibits illustrating pirate lore. You can walk through the belly of a pirate ship (the *Revenge*) as you hear "pirates" plan their next attack. You can smell the dampness of a dungeon, and you'll even hear the final prayer of an ill-fated victim before he walks the gangplank. It's fairly cheesy, but fun for kids. Exhibits also tell the saga of Captain Woodes Rogers, who was sent by the English crown to suppress pirates in The Bahamas and the Caribbean.

Marlborough and George sts. ⓒ 242/356-3759. Admission $12 adults, $6 children 3–18, free for children 2 and under. Mon–Sat 9am–6pm; Sun 9am–12:30pm. Bus: 10.

7 Shopping

Nassau shopping is now more upscale than in decades past. Swanky jewelers and a burgeoning fashion scene have appeared. There are still plenty of T-shirts claiming that "It's Better in The Bahamas," but in contrast you can also find platinum watches and diamond jewelry.

The range of goods is staggering; in the midst of all the junk souvenirs, you'll find an increasing array of china, crystal, or watches from such names as Bally, Herend, Lalique, Baccarat, and Ferragamo.

But can you really save money on prices stateside? The answer is "yes" on some items, "no" on others. To figure on what's a bargain and what's not, you've got to know the price of everything back in your hometown, turning yourself into a sort of human calculator about prices.

Don't try to bargain with the salespeople in Nassau stores as you would do with merchants at the local market. The price asked in the shops is the price you must pay, but you won't be pressed to make a purchase. The salespeople here are courteous and helpful in most cases.

There are no import duties on 11 categories of luxury goods, including china, crystal, fine linens, jewelry, leather goods, photographic equipment, watches, fragrances, and other merchandise. Antiques, of course, are exempt from import duty worldwide. But even though prices are "duty-free," you can still end up spending more on an item in The Bahamas than you would back in your hometown. It's a tricky situation.

If you're contemplating a major purchase, such as a good Swiss watch or some expensive perfume, it's best to do some research in your hometown discount outlets before making a serious purchase in The Bahamas. While the alleged 30% to 50% discount off stateside prices might apply in some cases, it's not true in most cases. Certain cameras and electronic equipment, we have discovered, are listed in The Bahamas at, say, 20% or more below the manufacturer's "suggested retail price." That sounds good, except the manufacturer's suggested price might be a lot higher than what you'd pay in your hometown. You aren't getting the discount you think you are. Some shoppers even take along department-store catalogs from the States to determine if they are indeed getting a bargain.

A lot of price-fixing seems to be going on in Nassau. For example, a bottle of Chanel is likely to sell for pretty much the same price regardless of the store.

How much you can take back home depends on your country of origin. For more details, plus Customs requirements for some other countries, refer to "Entry Requirements & Customs," in chapter 2.

The principal shopping areas are **Bay Street** and its side streets downtown, as well as the shops in the arcades of hotels. Not many street numbers are used along Bay Street; just look for store signs.

ANTIQUES

Marlborough Antiques   This store carries the type of antiques you'd expect to find in a shop in London: antique books, antique maps and engravings, English silver (both sterling and plate), and unusual table settings (fish knives and so on). Among the most appealing objects is the store's collection of antique photographs of the islands. Also displayed are works by Bahamian artists Brent Malone, Davide White, and Maxwell Taylor. Corner of Queen and Marlborough sts. ✆ 242/328-0502.

ART

Kennedy Gallery   Although many locals come here for custom framing, the gallery also sells original artwork by well-known Bahamian artists, including limited-edition prints, handcrafts, pottery, and sculpture. Parliament St. ✆ 242/325-7662.

CIGARS

Remember, U.S. citizens are prohibited from bringing Cuban cigars back home because of the trade embargo. If you buy them, you're supposed to enjoy them in The Bahamas.

Tropique International Smoke Shop   Many cigar aficionados come here to indulge their passion for Cubans, which are handpicked and imported by Bahamian merchants. The staff at this outlet trained in Havana, so they know their cigars. In Wyndham Nassau Resort & Crystal Palace Casino, W. Bay St. ✆ 242/327-7292.

CRYSTAL, CHINA & GEMS

Solomon's Mines   Evoking the title of a 1950s MGM flick, this is one grand shopping adventure. This flagship store, with many branches, is one of the largest duty-free retailers in either The Bahamas or the Caribbean, a tradition since 1908. Entering the store is like a shopping trip to London or Paris; the amount of merchandise is staggering, from a $50,000 Patek Philippe watch to one of the largest collections of Herend china in the West. Most retail price tags on watches, china, jewelry, crystal, Herend, Baccarat,

Ferragamo, Bally, Lalique, and other names are discounted 15% to 30%—and some of the merchandise and oddities here are not available in the States, such as their stunning collection of African diamonds. The selection of Italian, French, and American fragrances and skin-care products are the best in the archipelago. Bay St. © 242/356-6920. Charlotte and Bay sts. © 242/325-7554.

FASHION

Barry's Limited   One of Nassau's more formal and elegant clothing stores, this shop sells garments made from lamb's wool and English cashmere. Elegant sportswear (including Korean-made guayabera shirts) and blazers are sold here. Most of the clothes are for men, but women often stop in for the stylish cuff links, studs, and other accessories. Bay and George sts. © 242/322-3118.

Bonneville Bones   The name alone will intrigue, but it hardly describes what's inside. This is the best men's store we've found in Nassau. You can find everything here, from standard T-shirts and designer jeans to elegant casual clothing, including suits. Bay St. © 242/328-0804.

Cole's of Nassau   This boutique offers the most extensive selection of designer fashions in Nassau. Women can be outfitted in everything from swimwear to formal gowns, from sportswear to hosiery. Cole's also sells gift items, sterling-silver designer and costume jewelry, hats, shoes, bags, scarves, and belts. Parliament St. © 242/322-8393.

Fendi   This is Nassau's only outlet for the well-crafted Italian-inspired accessories endorsed by this famous leather-goods company. With handbags, luggage, shoes, watches, wallets, and portfolios to choose from, the selection may well solve some of your gift-giving quandaries. Charlotte St. at Bay St. © 242/322-6300.

HANDICRAFTS

Sea Grape Boutique   This is the finest gift shop on New Providence, with an inventory of exotic decorative items that you'll probably find fascinating. It includes jewelry crafted from fossilized coral, sometimes with sharks' teeth embedded inside, and clothing that's well suited to the sometimes-steamy climate of The Bahamas. There's a second branch of this outfit, Sea Grape Too, in the Radisson Hotel's Mall, on Cable Beach (© 242/327-5113). W. Bay St. (next to Travelers Restaurant). © 242/327-1308.

JEWELRY

Colombian Emeralds   Famous around the Caribbean, this international outlet is not limited to emeralds, although its selection of that stone is the best in The Bahamas. You'll find an impressive display of diamonds, as well as other precious gems. The gold jewelry here sells for about half the price it does Stateside, and many of the gems are discounted 20% to 30%. Ask about their "cyber-shopping" program. Bay St. (C) **242/326-1661.**

John Bull   The jewelry department here offers classic selections from Tiffany & Co.; cultured pearls from Mikimoto; the creations of David Yurman, Carrera y Carrera, Greek and Roman coin jewelry; and Spanish gold and silver pieces. It's the best name in the business. The store also features a wide selection of watches, cameras, perfumes, cosmetics, leather goods, and accessories. It is one of the best places in The Bahamas to buy a Gucci or Cartier watch. Bay St. (C) **242/322-4253.**

MARKETS

The **Nassau International Bazaar** consists of some 30 shops selling international goods in a new arcade. A pleasant place for browsing, the $1.8-million complex sells goods from around the globe. The bazaar runs from Bay Street down to the waterfront (near the Prince George Wharf). With cobbled alleyways and garreted storefronts, the area looks like a European village.

Prince George Plaza, Bay Street, is popular with cruise-ship passengers. Many fine shops (Gucci, for example) are found here. When you get tired of shopping, you can dine at the open-air rooftop restaurant that overlooks Bay Street.

A fire on September 2, 2001, destroyed most of the infrastructure of **Nassau's Straw Market,** along with virtually all of its merchandise. Since then, the Straw Market has occupied a tent on Bay Street, opposite the intersection of Bay Street with George Street, about 2 blocks from its original premises. Hours of the Straw Market are daily from 7am to around 8pm, although each individual vendor (there are around 200 of them) sets his or her own hours. Merchandise is what it's always been: Hats, weavings, baskets, valises, all woven from reeds, straw, and grasses.

PERFUMES & COSMETICS

Nassau has several good perfume outlets, notably **John Bull** and **Little Switzerland,** which also stock a lot of nonperfume merchandise.

The Beauty Spot   The largest cosmetic shop in The Bahamas, this outlet sells duty-free cosmetics by Lancôme, Chanel, YSL, Elizabeth Arden, Estée Lauder, Clinique, Christian Dior, and Biotherm, among others. It also operates facial salons. Bay and Frederick sts. *©* **242/322-5930.**

The Perfume Bar   This little gem has exclusive rights to market Boucheron, and it also stocks the Clarins line (though not exclusively). Bay St. *©* **242/322-7216.**

The Perfume Shop   In the heart of Nassau, within walking distance of the cruise ships, the Perfume Shop offers duty-free savings on world-famous perfumes. Treat yourself to a flacon of Eternity, Giorgio, Poison, Lalique, Shalimar, or Chanel. Those are just a few of the scents for women. For men, the selection includes Drakkar Noir, Polo, and Obsession. Corner of Bay and Frederick sts. *©* **242/322-2375.**

8 New Providence After Dark

Gone are the days when tuxedo-clad gentlemen and elegantly gowned ladies drank and danced the night away at such famous nightclubs as the Yellow Bird and the Big Bamboo. You can still find dancing, along with limbo and calypso, but for most visitors, the major attraction is gambling.

Cultural entertainment in Nassau is limited, however. The chief center for this is the **Dundas Center for the Performing Arts,** which sometimes stages ballets, plays, or musicals. Call *©* **242/393-3728** to see if a production is planned at the time of your visit.

ROLLING THE DICE

As another option, you can easily head over to Paradise Island and drop into the massive, spectacular casino in the Atlantis resort. See chapter 4.

Wyndham Nassau Resort & Crystal Palace Casino   This dazzling casino—the only one on New Providence Island—is now run by Wyndham Nassau Resort. Although some experienced gamblers claim you get better odds in Vegas, the Crystal Palace stacks up well against the major casinos of the Caribbean. The 3,252-sq.-m (35,000-sq.-ft.) casino is filled with flashing lights, and the gaming room features hundreds of slot machines, blackjack tables, roulette wheels, craps tables, a baccarat table, and a big six. W. Bay St., Cable Beach. *©* **242/327-6200.**

THE CLUB & MUSIC SCENE

Club Waterloo   They've seen it all over the years at the Club Waterloo, located in an old colonial mansion set beside a narrow saltwater estuary known as Lake Waterloo. To qualify for the $5 cover charge, you can purchase a visitors' pass from most taxi drivers, which will get you inside the door. If you're not registered at a hotel, the cover charge is $20 Wednesday to Sunday, going up to $30 on Friday and Saturday. But despite these high prices, you'll get the feeling that very few people actually pay full price: It's management's way of screening out the bad drunks. The main bar is open nightly from 4pm to 4am, and the Shooters Sports bar is open from midnight to 4am. You'll also find an open-air pool bar, and a Bacardi Bar, which specializes in its namesake. The crowd tends to be an eclectic mix of locals, Europeans, and American vacationers, both singles and couples. E. Bay St. ✆ 242/393-7324. Cover $5–$30, including 1 or 2 drinks.

King & Knights Native Calypso Show   This is the only folkloric Bahamian show on New Providence. Its linchpin is Eric Gibson ("King Eric"), a talented musician and calypso artist from Acklins Island. He has functioned as the semiofficial ambassador of Bahamian goodwill, conducting concert tours throughout North America, Europe, and Australia. A musical staple here since the late 1950s, his act includes a half-dozen musicians, four or five dancers, a "calypsonian" who might double as a comedian, and a limbo contortionist. The shows are a little short (only 90 min.), but end with a sequence that emulates the Junkanoo festival. If you opt for a dinner here, you can schedule it for whenever you want, before, during, or after the show. Shows are Monday to Saturday at 8:30pm. In the Nassau Beach Hotel, Cable Beach. ✆ 242/327-7711. Reservations recommended. Cover charge $25, dinner and show $45.

The Zoo   Set midway between Cable Beach and the western periphery of Nassau, this is the largest and best-known nightspot of its kind on New Providence. It's housed on two floors of what was once a warehouse, with five bars, an indoor/outdoor restaurant (Zoo Cafe), and a sometimes-crowded dance floor that attracts mainly an under-30 crowd. Each of the five bars has a different theme, including an underwater theme, a jungle theme, and a *Gilligan's Island* theme. The sports bar is complete with pool tables and wide-screen broadcasts. The most raucous area of the complex is on the street level, where a young crowd congregates to drink and dance. If you're looking for a respite from the brouhaha below, climb a flight of stairs to the "VIP Lounge," which offers stiff drinks and the chance for conversation. Most of the complex is open Tuesday to Sunday 8am to 3am. W. Bay St. at Saunders Beach. ✆ **242/322-7195.** Cover $10–$25.

VEGAS-STYLE SHOWS

Rain Forest Theater This 800-seat theater (previously known as the Palace Theater) is a major nightlife attraction. Fake palm trees on each side and lots of glitz set the scene for the Las Vegas–style extravaganzas and Caribbean revues that are presented on its stage. Shows are presented every Monday, Wednesday, and Friday, at 8:30pm. The show is complimentary, however there is a 1-drink minimum. In the Crystal Palace Casino, W. Bay St., Cable Beach. ✆ **242/327-6200.**

THE BAR SCENE

Charlie's on the Beach/Cocktails 7 Dreams The focus within this sparsely decorated club is local gossip, calypso and reggae music, and stiff drinks, all of which can combine into a high-energy night out in Nassau. The setting is a simple warehouselike structure a few blocks west of the British Colonial Hilton, though management warns that during some particularly active weekends (including spring break), the entire venue might move, short-term, to a larger, and as yet undetermined, location. Open only Wednesday and Friday to Sunday 9pm to 4am. W. Bay St. near Long Wharf Beach. ✆ **242/328-3745.** Cover $10–$30.

Crocodiles Waterfront Bar & Grill Look for the hundreds of crocodiles stenciled into the wall that shields this watering hole from busy East Bay Street, and venture into the funky bar for a rum drink. There's a relaxed vibe on the deck, which offers a bit of shade under thatched parasols. You can order moderately priced steak, seafood, or sandwiches (see the full review under "Where to Dine," earlier in this chapter). Both the restaurant and bar are open daily 11am to midnight. E. Bay St. (a 2-min. walk from the Nassau side of the Paradise Island Bridge). ✆ **242/323-3341.**

The Drop Off Every harbor town has a rowdy, raucous, and sudsy dive with whiffs of spilled beer and ample doses of iodine from the nearby sea, and in Nassau, this is it. Most of its clients are either local residents, or workers aboard one of the fishing and cargo boats that bob at anchor in nearby Nassau Harbor. The setting is a cavernous room lined with murals of underwater life, all within a cellar that's usually several degrees cooler than the baking sidewalks outside. There's disco music some evenings after 11pm, and a short list of two-fisted platters that includes grilled or fried snapper or grouper, steaks, burgers, and sandwiches. Call for hours. E. Bay St. at East St. © 242/322-3444.

Out Island Bar/The Beach Bar These bars, both within the same hotel, are used primarily by its guests, but are open to all, attracting everybody from newlyweds to those who married when Eisenhower was in office. The more central of the two is the Out Island Bar, set adjacent to the lobby and outfitted in a breezy wicker and rattan theme that goes well with the party-colored drinks that are its specialty. If you want a view, head for The Beach Bar, which is thatch-covered and set directly on the sands of one of the best beaches in the area. Call for hours. In the Nassau Beach Hotel, Cable Beach. © 242/327-7711.

4

Paradise Island

Paradise Island—just 180m (590 ft.) off the north shore of Nassau—boasts gorgeous beaches and beautiful foliage, including brilliant red hibiscus and a grove of casuarina trees sweeping down to form a tropical arcade.

Now the priciest piece of real estate in The Bahamas, this island once served as a farm for Nassau and was known as Hog Island. Now, the centerpiece of Paradise Island is the mammoth Atlantis Paradise Island Resort & Casino, which has become a nightlife mecca and a sightseeing attraction in its own right.

For those who want top hotels, casino action, Vegas-type revues, fabulous beaches, and a posh address, Paradise Island is the place. It's now sleeker and more upscale than Cable Beach, its closest rival, and Freeport/Lucaya. True, Paradise Island is overbuilt and overly commercialized, but its natural beauty still makes it a choice vacation spot, perfect for a quick 3- or 4-day getaway.

Paradise Island is treated as a separate entity in this guide, but it is actually part of New Providence, connected by a bridge. You can travel between the two on foot, by boat, or by car. So you can stay in Nassau or Cable Beach and come over to enjoy the beaches, restaurants, attractions, and casino on Paradise Island. You can also stay on Paradise Island and easily go into Nassau for a day of sightseeing and shopping. So view this section as a companion to chapter 3, where you can find more information on transportation, nearby sights, and sports and recreation choices.

1 Orientation

ARRIVING

Most visitors to Paradise Island arrive in Nassau and commute to Paradise Island by ground transport. However, **Chalks International Airways** (℃ **800/424-2557,** or 242/363-3114; www.chalks oceanairways.com) flies daily from Fort Lauderdale International Airport directly into Paradise. There are about five flights on weekdays, rising to around eight flights on Saturday and Sunday. The airplanes are Grumman G-73T; each aircraft carries up to 17 passengers. The airline's headquarters are at 704 SW 34th St., Fort Lauderdale, FL 33315.

When you arrive at the **Nassau International Airport** (see chapter 3 for information on flying into Nassau), you won't find bus service to take you to Paradise Island. Many package deals will provide hotel transfers from the airport. Otherwise, if you're not renting a car, you'll need to take a taxi. Taxis in Nassau are metered and take cash only, no credit cards. It will usually cost you $30 to go by cab from the airport to your hotel. The driver will also ask you to pay the one-way $1 bridge toll (this charge will be added onto your metered fare at the end).

VISITOR INFORMATION

Paradise Island does not have a tourist office, so refer to the tourist facilities in downtown Nassau (see "Orientation," at the beginning of chapter 3). The concierge or the guest services staff at your hotel can also give you information about the local attractions.

ISLAND LAYOUT

Paradise Island's finest beaches lie on the Atlantic (northern) coastline; the docks, wharves, and marinas are located on the southern side. Most of the island's largest and glossiest hotels and restaurants, as well as the famous casino and a lagoon with carefully landscaped borders, lie west and north of the roundabout. The area east of the roundabout is less congested, with only a handful of smaller hotels, a golf course, the Versailles Gardens, the Cloister, the airport, and many of the island's privately owned villas.

2 Getting Around

You don't need to rent a car. Most visitors walk around Paradise Island's most densely developed sections and hire a taxi for the occasional longer haul. For information on renting a car, refer to "By Rental Car," on p. 37 in chapter 2.

The most popular way to reach nearby Nassau is to **walk across the toll bridge.** There is no charge for pedestrians.

If you want to tour Paradise Island or New Providence by **taxi,** you can make arrangements with either the taxi driver or the hotel reception desk. Taxis wait at the entrances to all the major hotels. The going hourly rate is about $60 in cars or small vans.

If you are without a car and don't want to take a taxi or walk, you can take a **ferry to Nassau.** The ferry to Nassau leaves from the dock on Casino Drive every half-hour, and the 10-minute ride costs $3 one-way. Quicker and easier than a taxi, the ferry deposits you right at Bay Street. Daily service is from 9:30am to 4:15pm.

Water taxis also operate between Paradise Island and Prince George Wharf in Nassau. They depart daily from 8:30am to 6pm at 20-minute intervals. Round-trip fare is $6 per person.

If you are a guest at one of the properties of Atlantis Paradise Island Resort & Casino, you can take a complimentary tour of the island, leaving daily at noon.

Unlike New Providence, no public buses are allowed on Paradise Island.

3 Where to Stay

In the off season (mid-Apr to mid-Dec), prices are slashed by at least 20%—and perhaps a lot more, though the weather isn't as ideal. But because Paradise Island's summer business has increased dramatically, you'll never see some of the 60% reductions that you might find at a cheaper property in the Greater Nassau area. Paradise Island doesn't have to lower its rates to attract summer business. For inexpensive accommodations, refer to the recommendations on New Providence Island (see chapter 3). Paradise Island ain't cheap!

VERY EXPENSIVE

Atlantis Paradise Island Resort & Casino *★★★* *Kids*   This megaresort of The Bahamas is *massive,* opening onto a long stretch of white-sand beach with a sheltered marina. Think Vegas in the Tropics, with a fairly interesting ancient mythology theme thrown in, and you'll get the picture. The advantage is that you'll never be bored; the downside is that it's sprawling, and the service just can't keep up with the number of guests here. The Atlantis is a

---

Tips **Coming Attractions**

Atlantis's next phase of development includes a 600-room all-suite luxury hotel, to be situated west of the Royal Towers; a 400-unit condo hotel; additional water-themed attractions, including a dolphin encounter; and 9,290 sq. m (100,000 sq. ft.) of additional group and meeting facilities. Nobu, a world-renowned Japanese restaurant headed by namesake chef Nobu Matsuhisa and funded by partner Robert DeNiro, is expected to be open at the Atlantis by Christmas 2006.

Where to Stay & Dine in Paradise Island

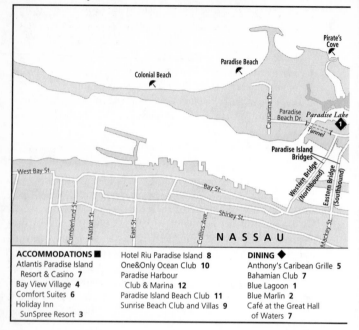

ACCOMMODATIONS ■
Atlantis Paradise Island
  Resort & Casino **7**
Bay View Village **4**
Comfort Suites **6**
Holiday Inn
  SunSpree Resort **3**

Hotel Riu Paradise Island **8**
One&Only Ocean Club **10**
Paradise Harbour
  Club & Marina **12**
Paradise Island Beach Club **11**
Sunrise Beach Club and Villas **9**

DINING ◆
Anthony's Caribean Grille **5**
Bahamian Club **7**
Blue Lagoon **1**
Blue Marlin **2**
Café at the Great Hall
  of Waters **7**

self-contained "water world," with the Lost Continent of Atlantis as its theme. It's a great choice for a family vacation, since kids love all the facilities and gimmicks, and the children's program is outstanding. Singles and young couples who want a lot of action like it, too, though some people find it too over-the-top and impersonal. The Atlantis proudly offers so many sports, dining, and entertainment options that many guests never set foot off the property during their entire vacation.

A soaring "Royal Tower"—one of the tallest buildings in The Bahamas—is replete with decorative sea horses, winged dragons, and megasize conch shells sprouting from cornices and rooflines. The casino and entertainment complex lie in an area over the watery depths of a lagoon. The best and most plush accommodations are in the Royal Tower. (Rooms in the Royal Tower's Imperial Club have a personal concierge and upgraded amenities.) But even in the older, less expensive sections, rooms have a comfortable tropical decor. Every unit sports a balcony or terrace with water views, individually controlled air-conditioning, in-room movies, and voice mail and

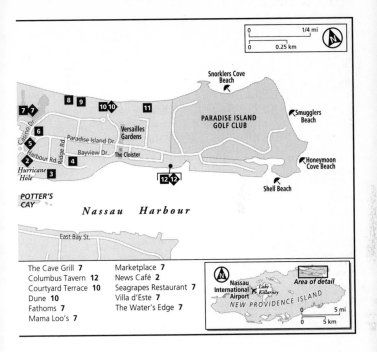

The Cave Grill **7**	Marketplace **7**
Columbus Tavern **12**	News Café **2**
Courtyard Terrace **10**	Seagrapes Restaurant **7**
Dune **10**	Villa d'Este **7**
Fathoms **7**	The Water's Edge **7**
Mama Loo's **7**	

modem access, plus roomy bathrooms with tubs and showers. The most deluxe accommodation is the Bridge Suite, renting for $25,000 a day and sometimes occupied by Michael Jordan while hosting his celebrity invitational at the on-site golf course.

Any old hotel might sport tropical gardens, but the Atlantis goes one better by featuring the world's largest collection of outdoor open-air marine habitats, each of them aesthetically stunning. A few of these were conceived for snorkelers and swimmers, but most were designed so guests could observe the marine life from catwalks above and from glassed-in underwater viewing tunnels. Even folks who don't stay here—including thousands of cruise-ship passengers—come to check out these 11 distinctly different exhibition lagoons containing millions of gallons of water and at least 200 species of tropical fish. They include a shark tank, a stingray lagoon, and separate holding tanks for lobsters, piranhas, and underwater exotica. Swimmers can meander along an underwater snorkeling trail (Paradise Lagoon) and explore a five-story, Disney-style replica of a Mayan temple complete with 18m (59-ft.) water slides.

The focal point of this extravagance is the massive **Paradise Island Casino,** the best-designed casino in The Bahamas. There are 13 bars, nightclubs, and lounges, including a cigar bar (see "Paradise Island After Dark," later in this chapter). There are also 17 restaurants, some reviewed under "Where to Dine," below; expect to pay a lot to dine in most of them.

Casino Dr. (P.O. Box N-4777), Paradise Island, The Bahamas. ✆ **800/ATLANTIS** or 242/363-3957. Fax 242/363-6300. www.atlantis.com. 2,349 units. Winter $360–$720 double, from $810 suite; off season $285–$565 double, from $685 suite. Package deals available. AE, DC, DISC, MC, V. Free self-parking, valet parking $5 a day. **Amenities:** 17 restaurants; 18 lounges and clubs; 11 pools; golf course; 10 tennis courts; health club; spa; sauna; watersports equipment/rentals; children's programs (5–12); salon; 24-hr. room service; massage; babysitting; laundry service; dry cleaning; nonsmoking rooms; rooms for those w/limited mobility. *In room:* A/C, TV, dataport, minibar, fridge, hair dryer, iron, safe.

One&Only Ocean Club ✮✮✮   This resort is the most exclusive address on Paradise Island, with sky-high prices that match the pampering service (the best in The Bahamas) and refined ambience. The white-sand beach that lies adjacent to the hotel is the finest in the Nassau/Paradise Island area. This is also one of the best-developed tennis resorts in The Bahamas. In 1999, the property began undergoing a major expansion and renovation. A favorite honeymoon spot, it's more upscale than the megahotel Atlantis, which is really a fun family resort. Guests can revel in the casino and nightlife activities of Atlantis nearby, and then retire to this more tranquil, secluded, and intimate retreat.

The tasteful and spacious rooms are plushly comfortable with king-size beds, gilt-framed mirrors, and dark-wood armoires. The marble bathrooms in the suites are massive, and each contains a bidet, twin basins, and both a tub and shower.

The real heart and soul of the resort lies in the surrounding gardens, which were designed by the island's former owner, Huntington Hartford. This resort, in fact, was once his private home. Formal gardens surround a French cloister set on 14 hectares (35 acres) of manicured lawns. The 12th-century carvings of the Cloister are visible at the crest of a hill, across a stretch of terraced waterfalls, fountains, a stone gazebo, and rose gardens. Larger-than-life statues dot the vine-covered niches on either side of the gardens. Begin your tour of the gardens at the large swimming pool, which feeds a series of reflecting pools that stretch out toward the cloister. A new addition is the child-friendly family pool, replete with aqua toys and a waterfall.

Arguably the best dining on Paradise Island can be found at the resort's Dune restaurant, creation of culinary legend Jean-Georges Vongerichten. In addition, a pair of fountains illuminates the Courtyard Terrace at night. See "Where to Dine" later in this chapter for a review of both restaurants. Another option is a beachfront restaurant and bar, where you can dine under cover but still in the open air.

Ocean Club Dr. (P.O. Box N-4777), Paradise Island, The Bahamas. © **800/321-3000** or 242/363-2501. Fax 242/363-2424. www.oneandonlyresorts.com. 106 units, 3 private villas. Winter $725–$1,025 double, $1,280–$2,000 suite, $5,000–$6,000 villa; off season $475–$760 double, $775–$1,400 suite, $4,500–$5,500 villa. AE, MC, V. Free parking. **Amenities:** 3 restaurants; 4 bars; 2 pools; golf course; 6 tennis courts; health club; spa; steam room; shuttle to Atlantis casino; 24-hr. room service; babysitting; laundry service; dry cleaning; nonsmoking rooms. *In room:* A/C, TV, dataport, kitchenette (in some), minibar, hair dryer, iron, safe, butler service.

EXPENSIVE

Holiday Inn SunSpree Resort ☆ *Kids*   This older, 12-floor property adjacent to the waters of Nassau Harbour opens onto a marina with very little beach, but a good-sized swimming pool. It was rescued from oblivion in the late 1990s when a Florida-based investment group, Driftwood Ventures, renovated it. This group turned it into an all-inclusive resort, which lies just a short stroll away from the popular Atlantis and all its attractions. Bedrooms are midsize with twin or king-size beds, plus well-maintained private bathrooms with tub and shower combinations. The decor is comfortable, airy and sunny, and outfitted with tropically inspired colors and upholstery. All third-floor rooms and select units on the fourth floor are designated for nonsmokers only. The food served at the restaurants is palatable but needs much improvement, and service is very slow, so be duly warned. However, there are nightly live shows to spice up the lackluster gourmet, including fire dancing and Bahamian bands.

Harbour Dr. (P.O. Box SS-6249), Paradise Island, The Bahamas. © **800/HOLIDAY** or 242/363-2561. Fax 242/363-3803. www.paradiseislandbahama.com. 246 units. Winter $320–$437 double, $537 suite; off season $269–$374 double, $474 suite. Rates are all-inclusive. AE, DC, DISC, MC, V. **Amenities:** 3 restaurants; 2 bars; pool; 2 tennis courts; health club; Jacuzzi; watersports equipment/rental; children's programs; car rental; massage; nonsmoking rooms; rooms for those w/limited mobility. *In room:* A/C, TV, dataport, fridge, beverage maker, hair dryer, iron, safe.

Hotel Riu Paradise Island ☆ *Kids*   Opening onto a 5km (3-mile) stretch of sandy beach, this is the newest addition to the beachfront. In December 2004, the Riu Hotels chain refurbished the old

Sheraton Grand here into an all-inclusive megaresort. Among the renovations was the enlargement of the pool, the addition of a restaurant, and general room enhancement. This 14-story ecru high-rise offers some of the most comfortably appointed bedrooms on Paradise Island. It's more understated than the Atlantis, a lot cheaper, and more user friendly and manageable in terms of size and layout. Your kids would be happier with all the spectacular events at the Atlantis, but the Riu is a viable runner-up for the family trade. Guests can leave the shelter of the poolside terrace and settle almost immediately onto one of the waterside chaise lounges at the beach. The hotel is within walking distance of the casino, restaurants, and nightlife facilities of the Atlantis Paradise Island Resort & Casino properties.

Welcoming drinks are served while you relax on comfortable chairs in the lobby bar amid palm trees and tropical foliage. All the spacious accommodations here are deluxe and tastefully decorated, and equipped with medium-size bathrooms containing tub/shower combos. Many have spacious balconies that afford sweeping water views or luxurious terraces.

For an extra charge, you can skip the all-inclusive dinner fare and dine at Tengoku, a Japanese-themed restaurant. Other choices available to jaded buffet-goers include Atlantic Restaurant—serving some of Paradise Island's finest steaks and featuring a nonsmoking section, plus a terrace—and Sir Alexander, which is Riu's gourmet a la carte restaurant featuring highly refined, mainly continental gourmet cuisine with first-rate ingredients. Live entertainment is available 6 nights a week.

6307 Casino Dr. (P.O. Box SS-6307), Paradise Island, The Bahamas. © **888/666-8816** or 242/363-3500. Fax 242/363-3900. www.riu.com. 379 units. Winter $424–$454 double, $514–$576 jr. suite; off season $394–$424 double, $484–$546 jr. suite. Rates are all-inclusive. AE, DISC, MC, V. **Amenities:** 3 restaurants; 2 bars; pool; 4 tennis courts; gym; spa; Jacuzzi; sauna; kids' club; watersports equipment; salon; limited room service; massage; babysitting; laundry service; dry cleaning; nonsmoking rooms; rooms for those w/limited mobility. *In room:* A/C, ceiling fan, TV, dataport, minibar, hair dryer, safe.

Paradise Island Beach Club ⊛   Set near the eastern tip of Paradise Island, adjacent to a relatively isolated strip of spectacular beachfront, this two- and three-story timeshare complex was built in 1985. Managed by Marriott, it's more of a self-catering condo complex than a full-fledged resort. Many guests cook at least some meals in their own kitchens and head elsewhere, often to bigger hotels, for restaurants, watersports, gambling, and entertainment. Views from the bedrooms are usually ocean panoramas; overall, the setting is comfortable and, at its best, even cozy. You'll feel like you have your own Florida apartment, with easy access to the beach. Apartments have either one or two bedrooms, with wicker and rattan furnishings, and luxuries that include double basins in each bathroom, plus a tub and shower.

On the premises are both a round and a triangular-shaped swimming pool, one with a simple snack bar that's open only at lunchtime, except on Monday and Wednesday when there's a Bahamian buffet. The entertainment and casino facilities of the more densely developed sections of Paradise Island are just a short walk away. The major drawback here is the service, which is very laissez-faire.

Ocean Ridge Dr. (P.O. Box N-10600), Paradise Island, The Bahamas. © **242/363-2814** or 242/363-2992. Fax 242/363-2130. www.pibc-bahamas.com. 44 units. Winter $275 1-bedroom apt, $479 2-bedroom apt; off season $250 1-bedroom apt, $350 2-bedroom apt. AE, MC, V. **Amenities:** Pool bar; 2 pools; exercise room; salon; massage; coin-operated laundry service; rooms for those w/limited mobility. *In room:* A/C, TV, kitchen, hair dryer, iron, safe.

Sunrise Beach Club and Villas 🍴 🅺ids

This cluster of Spanish-inspired low-rise town houses occupies one of the most desirable stretches of beachfront on Paradise Island. Midway between the Hotel Riu and the One&Only Ocean Club, it's a short walk from the casino and a variety of sports and dining options. Accommodations are clustered within five separate groupings of red-roofed town houses, each with access to the resort's two swimming pools (one of which has a waterfall) and a simple snack bar. The hotel is usually full of lots of Germans, Swiss, and Austrians, many of whom stay for several weeks, preparing most of their own meals, since units have kitchens. Expect pastel colors, summery-looking furniture, and a private patio or veranda, plus king-size beds and floor-to-ceiling mirrored headboards, as well as average-size bathrooms with tub and shower. The best units are the three-bedroom apartments, situated directly on the beach. This is a good bet for "quieter" families who want a more subdued and relaxed vacation, and who want to avoid the "circus" going on 24 hours at the Atlantis.

P.O. Box SS-6519, Paradise Island, The Bahamas. © **800/451-6078** or 242/363-2250. Fax 242/363-2308. www.sunrisebeachclub.com. 100 units. Winter $315 1-bedroom apt, $551 2-bedroom apt, $695–$987 3-bedroom apt; off season $243 1-bedroom apt, $441 2-bedroom apt, $719–$987 3-bedroom apt. AE, MC, V. **Amenities:** Restaurant; bar; 2 pools; babysitting; coin-operated laundry; non-smoking rooms; rooms for those w/limited mobility. *In room:* A/C, TV, kitchen, beverage maker, hair dryer, iron, safe.

MODERATE

Bay View Village ⚘ More than 20 kinds of hibiscus and many varieties of bougainvillea beautify this 1.6-hectare (4-acre) condo complex. The condos here are near the geographic center of Paradise Island, and also only a 10-minute walk to either the harbor or the white sands of Cabbage Beach (the complex has no beach of its own). The restaurants, nightlife, and casino of Atlantis are only a few minutes away, although the modest Terrace restaurant here is nothing to be ashamed of.

We particularly recommend rooms near the center of the resort, because they are closest to the three swimming pools and laundry facilities. Each accommodation has its own kitchen with dishwasher, plus a patio or balcony and daily maid service. A shopping center is only 3 minutes away. Some units open onto views of the harbor. A full-time personal cook can be arranged on request. The units come in a wide variety of sizes; the largest can hold up to six. Rates are slightly less for weekly rentals. Penthouse suites contain roof gardens that open onto views of the harbor. Bedrooms come with king-, queen-, or twin-size beds. Bathrooms are medium in size, well maintained, and equipped with tub/shower combos.

Bayview Dr. (P.O. Box SS-6308), Paradise Island, The Bahamas. ☎ 242/363-2555. Fax 242/363-2370. 75 units. www.bayviewvillage.com. Winter $215 1-bedroom suite; $365 town house, $385 villa; off season $170 1-bedroom suite, $290 town house, $320 villa. AE, DC, DISC, MC, V. **Amenities:** Restaurant; bar; 3 pools; tennis court; babysitting; coin-operated laundry; nonsmoking rooms; rooms for those w/limited mobility. *In room:* A/C, TV, kitchen, coffeemaker, hair dryer, iron, safe.

Comfort Suites *Value* A favorite with honeymooners and a good value, this three-story, all-suite hotel is across the street from the Atlantis. If the mammoth Atlantis seems too overpowering, Comfort Suites is a nice alternative. You get the splash and wonder of the Atlantis, but you don't have to stay there all night or when the cruise-ship crowds descend. Although there are both a pool bar and a restaurant on the premises, guests are granted signing privileges at each of the drinking-and-dining spots, as well as the pool, beach, and sports facilities of the nearby Atlantis. Accommodations are priced by their views, over the island, the pool, or the garden. The medium-size bathrooms have beach towels, and ample vanities. Bedrooms are standard motel size with two double beds or one king.

Paradise Island Dr. (P.O. Box SS-6202), Paradise Island, The Bahamas. ☎ 877/424-6423 or 242/363-3680. Fax 242/363-2588. www.comfortsuites.com. 227 units. Winter $205–$255 double; off season $190–$230 double. Rates include continental breakfast. AE, DISC, MC, V. **Amenities:** Restaurant; bar; pool; tennis court; health club; babysitting; laundry service and coin-operated laundry; nonsmoking rooms; rooms for those w/limited mobility. *In room:* A/C, TV, dataport, fridge, beverage maker, hair dryer, iron, safe (in some).

INEXPENSIVE

Paradise Harbour Club & Marina   The noteworthy thing about this place is its sense of isolation, despite heavily developed Paradise Island. Built in 1991 near the island's extreme eastern tip, it's just a few steps from the also-recommended Columbus Tavern (see review later). It's pale pink, with rambling upper hallways, terra-cotta tile floors, and clean, well-organized bedrooms with tub/shower combos in the bathrooms. If available, opt for one of the top-floor accommodations so you can enjoy the view. Some of its quaint amenities, all free, include a water taxi to downtown Nassau, a beach shuttle (albeit in a golf cart), snorkeling gear, and bikes.

Paradise Island Dr. (P.O. Box SS-5804), Paradise Island, The Bahamas. ℂ 242/363-2992. Fax 242/363-2840. www.phc-bahamas.com. 23 units. Winter $150 double, $210 jr. suite, $275 1-bedroom apt, $410 2-bedroom apt; off season $120 double, $180 jr. suite, $250 1-bedroom apt, $350 2-bedroom apt. MC, V. **Amenities:** Restaurant; bar; pool; exercise room; Jacuzzi; watersports equipment/rental; golf cart shuttle to the beach; limited room service; babysitting; coin-operated laundry; rooms for those w/limited mobility. *In room:* A/C, TV, kitchen (in some), minibar, coffeemaker, hair dryer, iron, safe (in some).

4 Where to Dine

Paradise Island offers an array of the most dazzling, and the most expensive, restaurants in The Bahamas. If you're on a strict budget, cross over the bridge into downtown Nassau, which has far more reasonably priced places to eat. Meals on Paradise Island are often expensive but unimaginative. (Surf and turf appears on many a menu.) Unfortunately, you may not get what you pay for.

The greatest concentration of restaurants, all near the casino, is owned by Sun International. There are other good places outside this complex, however, including Dune at the Ocean Club, which is that hotel's showcase restaurant.

EXPENSIVE

Bahamian Club 𝕉𝕉 FRENCH/INTERNATIONAL   Overall, this is our favorite restaurant at the Atlantis. With an upscale British colonial–era feel, it's a big but civilized and clubby spot, with spacious vistas, mirrors, gleaming mahogany, and forest-green walls. The excellent food is served in two-fisted portions. Meat is king here, all those old favorites from roasted prime rib to Cornish hen, plus the island's best T-bone, along with a selection of veal and lamb chops. The retro menu also features the inevitable Dover sole, lobster, and salmon steak. All of these dishes are prepared only with top-quality ingredients imported from the mainland. Appetizers also harken back to the good old days, with fresh jumbo shrimp cocktail, baby spinach salad with a bleu-cheese dressing, and onion soup. Try the Bahamian conch chowder for some local flavor. Side dishes are excellent here, especially the penne with fresh tomato sauce and the roasted shiitake mushrooms. Proper attire required—no jeans or sneakers.

In the Atlantis, Casino Dr. ✆ **242/363-3000.** Reservations required. Main courses $41–$45. AE, DC, DISC, MC, V. Wed–Mon 6–11pm.

Blue Lagoon ✿ SEAFOOD   Across the lagoon from Atlantis, this restaurant is located two floors above the former reception area of the now closed Club Land'or, which was purchased by the Atlantis group and closed down for a major restoration and configuration. Call ahead to check on construction status.

Views of the harbor and Paradise Lake, along with music from an island combo, complements your candlelight meal here—a nice escape from the casino's glitter and glitz. Many of the fish dishes, including stone crab claws or the Nassau conch chowder, are excellent. The chef even whips up a good Caesar salad for two. The ubiquitous broiled grouper almondine is on the menu, or try some of the other dishes such as steak au poivre with a brandy sauce, or duck a l'orange. Yes, you've probably had better versions of these dishes elsewhere, but they are competently prepared and served here, even though the meats are shipped in frozen.

In the former Club Land'or, Paradise Dr. ✆ **242/363-2400.** Reservations required. Main courses $29–$75. AE, DISC, MC, V. Daily 5–10pm.

Café at the Great Hall of Waters ✿ (Kids) INTERNATIONAL This restaurant gives you a splashy look at the megaresort and water wonderland of Atlantis, even if you're not a guest of the hotel. Paradise Island has better restaurants, but none this dramatic. You feel like a scuba diver as you peer through gigantic picture windows displaying the illuminated "ruins" of Atlantis. Everywhere you look, rainbow-hued fish swim past stone archaeological remains, and rows of lobsters parade through the sand. With a ceiling that seems miles away, the Café's multilevel dining areas are located on the lower floor of the Royal Towers. There's a kids' menu, and little ones love taking walks along the aquarium walls between courses. In such a setting, the food becomes almost secondary, although it's quite good. The chef imports top-quality ingredients for such dishes as rack of lamb with an arugula pesto. Lobster is a specialty, and you can also order well-prepared versions of smoked salmon with lemon grass and jumbo lump Andros crab cakes. Desserts are uniformly delicious.

Royal Towers, Atlantis Resort, Casino Dr. ✆ 242/363-3000. Reservations required. Main courses $35–$50. AE, DC, MC, V. Thurs–Mon 7–11am, 11:30am–2:30pm, and 6–10pm.

Courtyard Terrace ☆ CONTINENTAL/BAHAMIAN   Okay, so the food isn't the island's finest, which it ought to be for these prices. The on-site Dune is better. But when the moon is right, an evening meal here can be heavenly for people who don't have to watch their wallets. You dine amid palms, flowering shrubs, and a fountain in a flagstone courtyard surrounded by colonial verandas. Live music wafts from one of the upper verandas to the patio below. This isn't the most glittering dining room, but it's the most sophisticated. Women should bring some kind of evening wrap in case it becomes chilly.

The menu includes a strong showing of the classics: beef-steak tartare, steak Diane, prime sirloin, lobster quiche, and chateaubriand. Such a menu also calls for rack of lamb; though the shrimp Provençale or the calf's liver lyonnaise, if featured, may have more zest. With candles flickering in the breeze, music floating down, and tables set with Wedgwood china and crisp linen, you might not even mind the slow service.

In the Ocean Club, Ocean Club Dr. ✆ 242/363-2501. Reservations required. Jacket and tie recommended for men. Main courses $40–$52. AE, DC, DISC, MC, V. Daily 6:30–9pm.

Dune ☆☆☆ INTERNATIONAL   The most sophisticated and cutting-edge restaurant on Paradise Island is in the west wing of the lobby level of the Ocean Club. Created and still owned by French-born restaurant guru Jean-Georges Vongerichten—who's already a big star in New York—it has a charcoal-gray and black decor that looks like it was plucked directly from a chic enclave in Milan; a sweeping view of the ocean; a teakwood floor that evokes a yacht's; and very attentive service. If you approach the place from the grounds, rather than from the interior of the hotel, you'll pass by the herb garden from which many of the culinary flavorings are derived. The chefs here invariably select the very finest ingredients, which are then handled with a razor-sharp technique. Every dish has a special something, especially shrimp dusted with orange powder and served with artichokes and arugula. A splendid choice is tuna spring rolls with soybean salsa. Also charming to the palate is a chicken-and–coconut milk soup served with shiitake cakes. The goat cheese–and-watermelon salad is an unexpected delight. Filet of grouper—that standard throughout The Bahamas—is at its savory best here when served with a zesty tomato sauce.

In the Ocean Club, Ocean Club Dr. (C) 242/363-2501, ext. 64739. Reservations required. Main courses lunch $12–$25, dinner $22–$50. AE, DC, DISC, MC, V. Daily 7–11am, noon–3pm, and 6–10:30pm.

Fathoms (R) SEAFOOD   You'll feel as if you're dining under the sea in this very dark seafood palace, with menus printed on stainless-steel sheets and an almost-mystical decor. Illuminating its glossy, metallic interior and four enormous plate-glass windows, sunlight filters through the watery aquariums that surround The Dig, Atlantis's recreation of an archaeological excavation of the underwater ruins of the Lost Continent.

At first you'll think the best appetizer is a selection of raw seafood in season. But then you're tempted by the blackened sashimi flavored with red ginger as it passes by. The lobster gazpacho is the best on the island, and you can also dig into a bowl of steamy black mussels flavored with chardonnay, garlic, and tomato. The wood-grilled yellowtail appears perfectly cooked with a wasabi potato mash and caviar, and the grilled Atlantic salmon is made extra inviting with its side dish of Parmesan garlic fries, a first for many diners. The meat devotee will find a wide selection here. Save room for dessert, and make it a light, feathery soufflé—a different one is served every night.

In the Atlantis Aquarium, Casino Dr. (C) 242/363-3897. Reservations recommended. Main courses $27–$50. AE, DC, MC, V. Daily 5:30–10pm.

Mama Loo's (R) ASIAN   Many people come here just to hang out in the bar, but if you're in the mood for a good Chinese meal, you'll be ushered to a table in a dining room with spinning ceiling fans, flaming torches from an overhead chandelier, and lots of potted palms. It evokes Shanghai during the British colonial age. The menu includes dishes from the Szechwan, Cantonese, Polynesian, and Caribbean repertoire. The best dish on the menu is Mama Loo's stir-fried lobster, beef, and broccoli with ginger. Two specialties we also like are shrimp in spicy chile sauce with a peanut sauce on the side, and deep-fried chicken filets with honey-flavored garlic sauce.

In the Coral Tower, Atlantis, Casino Dr. (C) 242/363-3000. Reservations recommended. Main courses $26–$40. AE, DC, DISC, MC, V. Tues–Sat 6–10pm.

Marketplace ⓖ (Value) INTERNATIONAL   Decorated with old vases and terra-cotta tiles, this large buffet-style restaurant is reminiscent of a sprawling market. It serves the best buffet on Paradise Island. You come here to fill up with an amazingly varied choice of food. Before you start loading onto your plate, browse past the various cooking stations and do some strategic planning. From fresh fruit to omelets, you can make breakfast as light or as heavy as you want. At lunch and dinner, you'll find everything from fresh seafood and made-to-order pastas to freshly carved roast beef and lamb. No intimate affair, this place seats some 400 diners. Sit inside or on the patio overlooking a lagoon.

Royal Towers, Atlantis Resort, Casino Dr. ⓒ **242/363-3000.** Reservations not needed. Full buffets $34–$60. AE, DC, MC, V. Daily 7–11am, 11:30am–2:30pm, and 5:30–10pm.

Villa d'Este ⓖ ITALIAN   Paradise Island's most elegant Italian restaurant offers classic dishes prepared with skill and served with flair. It's become less oriented to Tuscan dishes and is more Americanized Italian now. Italian murals decorate the walls.

Main dishes have flair, including pan-fried chicken breast with artichokes and mushrooms in a lemon-laced white-wine sauce, or a whole roasted rack of lamb coated with red-wine sauce and rosemary potatoes. The freshly made fettuccine tomato sauce and basil is almost perfect. The sea bass is quite delectable here, served with a perfect seafood broth.

In the Atlantis, Coral Tower, Casino Dr. ⓒ **242/363-3000.** Reservations required. Main courses $30–$50. AE, DC, MC, V. Fri–Tues 6–10pm.

The Water's Edge ⓖ SEAFOOD BUFFET   Three 4.5m (15-ft.) waterfalls splash into an artificial lagoon just outside the dining room's windows. Huge chandeliers illuminate the room, which has views of an open kitchen, where a battalion of chefs work to create a nightly seafood buffet. Many guests come here just to sample the pizza and pasta specialties. The pizzas are standard, but some of the pastas have a bit of zest, including penne *a l'arrabbiata* (with a spicy tomato sauce). The chef pays special attention to the antipasti, which evokes the tangy flavors of the Mediterranean, especially the *soup au pistou* (vegetables with basil and roasted garlic). Depending on the night, some of these dishes are better than others. The main problem here is that the food has a hard time competing with the ambience.

At the Atlantis, Casino Dr. ✆ **242/363-3000.** Reservations recommended. Seafood buffet $45. AE, DC, DISC, MC, V. Daily 6–10pm.

MODERATE

Blue Marlin ✿ *Finds* BAHAMIAN/SEAFOOD   This could be both your nightclub and dining choice for the evening. With a name like Blue Marlin, you expect and get fish and seafood dishes, although there are other choices as well. The catch always tastes fresh, and it's well prepared. If you've never had that famous Bahamian dish, cracked conch, here is a good place to introduce yourself to it. (Think breaded veal cutlet.) That favorite of the 1950s, lobster thermidor, is still a popular choice here, and the chef always fashions a linguine studded with morsels of fresh seafood. For the meat or poultry fancier, there are tender spare ribs basted with guava and Eleuthera coconut chicken. Every night at 7:30, a steel-pan band and limbo show is presented along with a slightly gruesome live glass-eating act. You have a choice of dining inside or out.

Hurricane Hole Plaza. ✆ **242/363-2660.** Reservations recommended. Main courses $10–$24. DISC, MC, V. Daily 5pm to "last customer."

Columbus Tavern ✿ *Finds* CONTINENTAL/BAHAMIAN   Far removed from the glitz and glamour of the casinos, the tavern seems relatively little known, even though Freddie Lightbourne of the Poop Deck restaurant has been running it for years now. It deserves to be discovered, because it serves good food at reasonable (for Paradise Island) prices. The tavern has the typical nautical decor (don't come here for the setting), with tables placed both inside and outside overlooking the harbor. The bar is worth a visit in itself, with its long list of tropical drinks. You can go local by starting off with the conch chowder, or opt for cheese-stuffed mushrooms with foie gras. Even though it's imported frozen, the rack of lamb are flawless. You can also order a decent veal cutlet and a quite good filet of grouper with a tantalizing lobster sauce.

Paradise Island Dr. ✆ **242/363-2534.** Reservations required for dinner. Main courses lunch $11–$26, dinner $20–$48. AE, MC, V. Mon–Fri 11:30am–10:30pm; Sat–Sun 8:30–10:30pm.

INEXPENSIVE

Anthony's Caribbean Grill AMERICAN/CARIBBEAN   Its owners think of this place as an upscale version of Bennigan's or TGI Fridays. But the decor is thoroughly Caribbean, thanks to psychedelic tropical colors, underwater sea themes, and jaunty maritime decorative touches. A bar dispenses everything from conventional mai tais to embarrassingly oversized, 48-ounce "sparklers"—with a combination of rum, amaretto, vodka, and fruit punch that is about all most serious drinkers can handle. Menu items include burgers, pizzas capped with everything from lobster to jerk chicken, barbecued or fried chicken, ribs with Caribbean barbecue sauce, and several meal-size salads.

Paradise Island Shopping Center, at the junction of Paradise and Casino drives. ℂ 242/363-3152. Lunch $7–$15; dinner $11–$39. AE, DISC, MC, V. Daily 7:30am–11pm.

The Cave Grill *Kids* BURGERS/SALADS/SANDWICHES This burger-and-salad joint is near the Atlantis's beach, catering to the bathing suit–and–flip-flops crowd, most often families. To reach the restaurant, you pass beneath a simulated rock-sided tunnel illuminated with flaming torches. The selection of ice cream will cool you off in the midafternoon sun.

At the Atlantis, Casino Dr. ℂ **242/363-3000.** Lunch platters $10–$24. AE, DISC, MC, V. Daily 10am–6pm.

News Café DELI Low-key and untouristy, this is where you'll find most of the island's construction workers, groundskeepers, and hotel staff having breakfast and lunch. They maintain a stack of the day's newspapers, so you can have something to read as you sip your morning cappuccino or latte. You can also stock up here on sandwiches for your beach picnic.

In the Hurricane Hole Plaza, Paradise Island. ℂ **242/363-4684.** Reservations not accepted. Breakfast, lunch sandwiches, and platters $5–$11. Assorted coffees $2–$3.50. AE, DC, DISC, MC, V. Daily 7am–11pm.

Seagrapes Restaurant *Kids* INTERNATIONAL Buffet lunches and dinners are the specialty of this pleasantly decorated tropical restaurant. This is the most affordable and family-oriented choice in the Atlantis, offering Cuban, Caribbean, and Cajun dishes. It's pretty straightforward fare, but you get a lot of food for not a lot of money—a rarity on pricey Paradise Island. The restaurant, which can seat 200 to 300 diners at a time, overlooks the lagoon and has a marketplace look, with buffet offerings displayed in little stalls and stations.

In the Atlantis, Casino Dr. ℂ **242/363-3000.** Breakfast and lunch buffet $19; dinner buffet $40. AE, DC, DISC, MC, V. Daily 7–11am, noon–3pm, and 5:30–10pm.

5 Beaches, Watersports & Other Outdoor Pursuits

Visitors interested in something more than lazing on the beaches have only to ask hotel personnel to make the necessary arrangements. Guests at the **Atlantis** (© 242/363-3000), for example, can have access to a surprising number of diversions without so much as leaving the hotel property. They can splash in private pools; play tennis, Ping-Pong, and shuffleboard; ride the waves; snorkel; or rent Sunfish, Sailfish, jet skis, banana boats, and catamarans from contractors located in kiosks.

HITTING THE BEACH

On Paradise Island, **Cabbage Beach** 𝒜𝒜 is the real showcase. Its broad white sands stretch for at least 3km (2 miles). Casuarines, palms, and sea grapes border it. It's likely to be crowded in winter, but you can find a little more elbowroom by walking to the northwestern stretch of the beach. You can reach Paradise Island from downtown Nassau by walking over the bridge, taking a taxi, or boarding a ferryboat at Prince George Dock. Cabbage Beach does not have public facilities but you can patronize one of the handful of bars and restaurants nearby and use their facilities. Technically, to use the facilities, you should be a customer—even if that means buying only a drink.

Our other favorite beach in this area is the white-sand **Paradise Beach** 𝒜𝒜, dotted with *chikees* (thatched huts), which are perfect when you've had too much of the sun. The beach is used mainly by guests of the Atlantis (p. 107), as it lies at the far western tip of the island. If you're not a resident, access is difficult. If you're staying at a hotel in Nassau and want to come to Paradise Island for a day at the beach, it's better to go to Cabbage Beach (see above).

FISHING

Anglers can fish close to shore for grouper, dolphin fish, red snapper, crabs, even lobster. Farther out, in first-class fishing boats fitted with outriggers and fighting chairs, they troll for billfish or giant marlin.

The best way to hook up with this pastime is to go to the activities desk of your hotel. All hotels have contacts with local charter operators who take their passengers out for a half or full day of fishing. For other possibilities, refer to "Beaches, Watersports & Other Outdoor Pursuits," in chapter 3.

GOLF

Ocean Club Golf Club ☆☆ on Paradise Island Drive (☏ **242/363-6682;** www.oneandonlyresorts.com), at the east end of the island, is an 18-hole championship golf course designed by Tom Weiskopf that overlooks both the Atlantic Ocean and Nassau Harbour. Attracting every caliber of golfer, the par-72 course is known for its hole 17, which plays entirely along the scenic Snorkelers Cove. Greens fees, including cart, are $245 per player, and rental clubs and shoes are available.

Golfers who want more variety will find one other course on New Providence Island (see "Beaches, Watersports & Other Outdoor Pursuits," in chapter 3).

SNORKELING & SCUBA DIVING

For more scuba sites in the area, see "Snorkeling, Scuba Diving & Underwater Walks," in chapter 3.

Bahamas Divers, East Bay Street, Yachthaven Marina Drive (☏ **242/393-5644;** www.bahamadivers.com), is the best all-around center for watersports on the island, specializing in scuba diving and snorkeling. They're located in Nassau near the Paradise Island Bridge. A one-tank dive, all equipment included, costs $55; a two-tank dive goes for $89. Snorkeling reef trips depart daily at 8:30am and 1:30pm, costing $39 with all equipment included.

6 Seeing the Sights

Most of the big hotels here have activity-packed calendars, especially for that occasional windy, rainy day that comes in winter. Hordes of Americans can be seen taking group lessons in such activities as backgammon, whist, tennis, and cooking and dancing Bahamian style. They're even taught how to mix tropical drinks, such as a Goombay Smash (spicy rum, coconut rum, apricot brandy, and orange juice served in a high-ball glass with ice) or a Yellow Bird (dark rum, white rum, Galliano herbal liqueur, and both orange and lime juice strained into a Collins glass half filled with crushed ice). To an increasing degree, hotels such as the Atlantis have configured themselves as destinations in their own right.

Atlantis Paradise Island Resort & Casino ☆☆   Regardless of where you're staying—even if it's at the most remote hotel on New Providence—you'll want to visit this lavish theme park, hotel, restaurant complex, casino, and entertainment center. It's Paradise Island's big attraction. You could spend all day here—and all night, too—wandering through the glitzy shopping malls; sampling the international cuisine of the varied restaurants; gambling at the roulette wheels, slot machines, and blackjack tables; or seeing Vegas-style revues. And once you're here, don't even think about leaving without a tour of The Dig, a Disney-style attraction that celebrates the eerie and tragic legend of the lost continent of Atlantis. During the day you can dress casually, but at night you should dress up a bit, especially if you want to try one of the better restaurants.

The most crowded time to visit Atlantis is between 9am and 5pm on days when cruise ships are berthed in the nearby harbor. (That's usually every Tues and Sat 9am–5pm.) The most crowded time to visit the casino is between 8 and 11pm any night of the week. There is no cover to enter: You pay just for what you gamble away (and that could be considerable), eat, and drink. The big shows have hefty cover charges, although some entertainment in the bars is free, except for the price of the liquor.

Casino Dr. ✆ **242/363-3000.** Free admission. Daily 24 hr.

The Cloister ⚐ Located in the Versailles Gardens of the One&Only Ocean Club, this 12th-century cloister, originally built by Augustinian monks in southwestern France, was reassembled here stone by stone. Huntington Hartford, the A&P heir, purchased the cloister from the estate of William Randolph Hearst at San Simeon in California. Regrettably, after the newspaper czar originally bought the cloister, it was hastily dismantled in France for shipment to America, but the parts had not been numbered—they all arrived unlabeled on Paradise Island. The reassembly of the complicated monument baffled most conventional methods of construction, until artist and sculptor Jean Castre-Manne set about to reassemble it piece by piece. It took him 2 years, and what you see today, pre-sumably, bears some similarity to the original. The gardens, which extend over the rise to Nassau Harbour, are filled with tropical flow-ers and classic statues. Unfortunately, although the monument retains a timeless beauty, recent buildings have encroached on either side, marring Huntington Hartford's original vision.

One&Only Ocean Club, Ocean Club Dr. ✆ **242/363-2501.** Free admission. Daily 24 hr.

7 Shopping

For serious shopping, you'll want to cross over the Paradise Island Bridge into Nassau (see chapter 3). However, many of Nassau's major stores also have shopping outlets on Paradise Island.

The Shops at the Atlantis, in the Atlantis (© **242/363-3000**), is the largest concentration of shops and boutiques on Paradise Island, rivaling anything else in The Bahamas in terms of size, selection, and style. The boutiques are part of the recently rebuilt Crystal Court Arcade within the sprawling Atlantis. Most of them are set adjacent to the resort's casino, in a well-appointed arcade that meanders between the Royal Tower and the Coral Tower, although a handful, as noted below, are scattered strategically throughout the resort. It's all about conspicuous consumption, so if you want to do more than browse, bring your platinum card and make sure it's Amex.

There are two separate branches of **Colombian Emeralds** (one in the Crystal Court arcade, another closer to the beach within the Atlantis's Beach Tower), where the colored gemstones far outnumber the relatively limited selection of diamonds. Other choices include **Mademoiselle,** with branches in both the Beach Tower and the Coral Tower, where chic but simple clothing for women focuses on festive beach and resort wear.

The richest pickings lie within the **Crystal Court Arcade.** Here, 3,252 sq. m (35,000 sq. ft.) of merchandising space features **Lalique,** France-based purveyor of fine crystal and fashion accessories for men and women; **Cartier; Versace,** the late designer to the stars (this boutique also has a particularly charming housewares division); **Armani,** whose clothes make almost any woman look like Michelle Pfeiffer and any man at least a bit thinner; **Façonnable,** a youthful, sporty designer for young and beautiful club-hoppers; **Bulgari,** purveyor of the most enviable jewels in the world, as well as watches, giftware, and perfumes; and **Gucci** and **Ferragamo,** in case you forgot your dancing shoes. And if you want a bathing suit, **Coles of Nassau** sells swimwear by Gottex, Pucci, and Fernando Sanchez. Finally, **John Bull,** known for its Bay Street store in Nassau and as a pioneer seller of watches throughout The Bahamas, also has an interesting assortment of watches, jewelry, and designer accessories at this outlet.

8 Paradise Island After Dark

Paradise Island has the best nightlife in The Bahamas, and most of it centers on the Atlantis.

The Atlantis Resort's Casino and Discothèque   No other spot in The Bahamas, with the possible exception of the Crystal Palace complex on Cable Beach, has such a wide variety of after-dark attractions and razzle-dazzle. Even if you stay in Nassau or

Cable Beach and gambling isn't your passion, drop into this artfully decorated, self-contained temple to decadence. Love it or hate it, this place is a jaw-dropper.

The only casino in the world built above a body of water, this one was designed as an homage to the lost continent of Atlantis. The gaming area is centered on buildings representing a Temple of the Sun and a Temple of the Moon with a painted replica of the zodiac overhead. Rising from key locations in and around the casino are five of the most elaborate sculptures in the world. Massive and complex, they were crafted by teams of artisans spearheaded by Dale Chihuly, the American-born resident of Venice whose glass-blowing skills are the most celebrated in the world. Other than the decor, the casino's gaming tables, open daily from 10am to 4am, are the main attraction in this enormous place, and about a thousand whirring and clanging slot machines operate 24 hours a day.

One side of the casino contains **Dragons,** a disco that manages to attract a few local hipsters as well as guests of the Atlantis. Come here anytime during casino hours for a drink. A sweaty, flirty crowd parties all night on the dance floor. Often, you can catch some of the best live music in The Bahamas, as bands take to the stage that's cantilevered above the dance floor. The disco gets going around 9pm nightly, with a cover charge of $30 required from all nonguests of the Atlantis. Ringing the casino are some 3,252 sq. m (35,000 sq. ft.) of retail shopping space (see "Shopping," above) and an impressive cluster of hideaway bars and restaurants.

Also in the same Atlantis complex, **Joker's Wild** (✆ **242/363-3000**) is the only real comedy club in The Bahamas, with a talented company of funny people who work hard to make their guests laugh. Show times are Tuesday through Sunday at 9:30pm. At least two comedians will appear on any given night, most of them hailing from The Bahamas, with occasional appearances of performers from London and New York. Midway between the Royal Tower and the Coral Tower, Casino Dr. ✆ 242/363-3000. No cover charge for casino, but a cover charge applies to clubs and shows.

THE BAR SCENE

Dune Bar Recommended as the top restaurant on Paradise Island, this deluxe dining room is also the setting for the island's most elegant and sophisticated lounge; it's becoming increasingly popular as a plush, appealing (and permissive) meeting spot for singles. The bar is centered around a translucent white marble bar skillfully illuminated from behind. At the Ocean Club, Ocean Club Dr. ℂ **242/363-2501**, ext. 64739. Call for open hours.

Plato's Lounge   This is the Atlantis resort's most romantic bar, a sensual spot where you can escape the din of the slot machines. There's a glow from dozens of flickering candles set within lavish candelabras, and ocean views through the oversize windows. A pianist sets the mood during cocktail hour and early evening. In the morning, the site doubles as a cafe, serving pastries and snacks from 6am until 4pm. It's open around the clock daily. On the lobby level of the Royal Towers, Atlantis Resort, Casino Dr. ℂ **242/363-3000**.

5

Grand Bahama (Freeport/Lucaya)

Big, bold, and *brassy* describe Grand Bahama Island, home to the resort area of Freeport/Lucaya. Though there's a ton of tourist development, it doesn't have the upscale chic of Paradise Island, but it does have fabulous white-sand beaches and a more reasonable price tag.

It may never return to its high-roller days with the gloss and glitz of the '60s, when everybody from Howard Hughes to Frank Sinatra and Rat Packers showed up, but recent improvements and massive redevelopment have brought a smile back to its face, which had grown wrinkled and tired over the latter part of the 20th century.

The second-most-popular tourist destination in The Bahamas (Nassau/Cable Beach/Paradise Island is first), Grand Bahama lies just 81km (50 miles) and less than 30 minutes by air off the Florida coast. That puts it just 122km (76 miles) east of Palm Beach, Florida. The island is the northernmost and fourth-largest landmass in The Bahamas (118km/73 miles long and 6.5–13km/4–8 miles wide).

Freeport/Lucaya was once just a dream. Wallace Groves, a Virginia-born financier, saw the prospect of developing the island into a miniature Miami Beach, and in the 1950s, almost overnight, the low-lying pine forest turned into one of the world's major resorts. Today, with the casino, the International Bazaar, high-rise hotels, golf courses, marinas, and a bevy of continental restaurants, Groves's dream is fully realized.

The Lucaya district was developed 8 years after Freeport, as a resort center along the coast. It has evolved into a blend of residential and tourist facilities. As the two communities grew, their identities became almost indistinguishable. But elements of their original purposes still exist today. Freeport is the downtown area and attracts visitors with its commerce, industry, and own resorts, whereas Lucaya is called the "Garden City" and pleases residents and vacationers alike with its fine sandy beaches.

Grand Bahama is more than an Atlantic City clone, however. If you don't care for gambling at one of the island's two casinos, or if

Grand Bahama Island

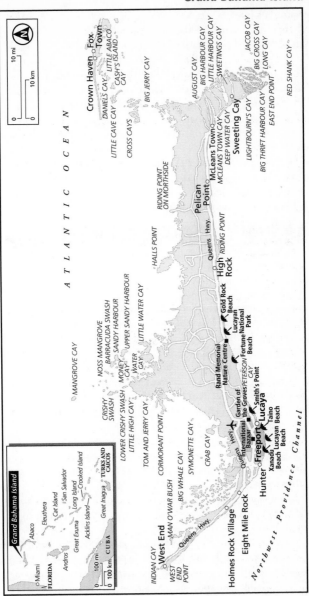

you're not interested in Vegas-style cabaret revues, try one of the alternatives. Because the island is so big, most of it remains relatively unspoiled. You can get close to nature at plenty of quiet places, including the Rand Nature Centre and the Garden of the Groves. Lucayan National Park—with its underwater caves, forest trails, and secluded beach—is another major attraction. Just kilometers from Freeport/Lucaya are serene places where you can wander in a world of casuarina, palmetto, and pine trees. During the day, you can enjoy long stretches of open beach, broken by inlets and little fishing villages.

The reviews of Grand Bahama Island are definitely mixed. Some discerning travelers who could live anywhere have built homes here; others vow never to set foot on the island again, finding it "tacky" or "uninspired." Judge for yourself.

1 Orientation

For a general discussion on traveling to The Bahamas, refer to chapter 2.

ARRIVING

A number of airlines fly to Grand Bahama International Airport from the continental United States, including **American Airlines** (© 800/433-7300; www.aa.com) and **Bahamasair** (© 800/222-4262; www.bahamasair.com), both with daily flights from Miami. **GulfStream Continental Connection** (© 800/231-0856; www.gulfstreamair.com) flies to Freeport from Miami and West Palm Beach once daily, and from Fort Lauderdale five times daily. **US Airways** (© 800/428-4322; www.usairways.com) flies once daily from Charlotte, North Carolina.

Other competing airlines include **AirTran** (© 800/247-8726), flying daily nonstop from Atlanta as well as Baltimore Thursday to Monday. **Delta Connection** (© 800/221-1212) flies daily from Atlanta.

Many visitors arrive in Nassau, then hop on one of the five daily Bahamasair flights to Freeport. These 35-minute hops run $162 round-trip.

No buses run from the airport to the major hotel zones. But many hotels will provide airport transfers, especially if you've bought a package deal. If yours does not, no problem; taxis meet arriving flights and will take you from the airport to one of the hotels in Freeport or Lucaya for about $11 to $20. The ride shouldn't take more than about 10 minutes.

A great way to get from the eastern coast of Florida to Freeport is aboard a modern ferryboat, the sleek *Cloud X,* which will transport you there in 3 hours. Launched in 2004, this 367-passenger ferry embarks from the port of Palm Beach Wednesday to Monday, offering one daily departure and one daily return. The round-trip fare is $99 for adults, $49 for children 6 to 12, and free for kids 5 and under. A $34 port charge is levied on passengers of all ages. On board are a trio of comfortable lounges, two bars, and a casino. For more information, call © **866/Go-Ferry** (fax 561/841-0472; www. cloudx.com). MasterCard and Visa are accepted. The main office for booking is at 301 Broadway, Suite 142, Riviera Beach, FL, 33404, open Monday to Friday 9am to 5pm.

Discovery Cruise Lines (© **888/213-8253;** www.discovery cruiseline.com) offers daily passage between the Fort Lauderdale Seaport and Grand Bahama Island. Frankly, the Discovery vessels making this 89km (55-mile) jaunt haven't been the newest or glitziest cruise ships sailing in the past three or four decades, but they are shipshape and fit the bill. The trip over from Florida takes about 5 hours, and they have the required pool deck and bar, along with a casino, bar show lounge, and dining facilities. They do feed passengers very well. A round-trip fare runs $157 per person, and you can make reservations online.

VISITOR INFORMATION

Assistance and information are available at the **Grand Bahama Tourism Board,** International Bazaar in Freeport (© **242/352-6909;** www.grand-bahama.com). Two other information booths are located at the **Freeport International Airport** (© **242/352-2052**) and at the Port Lucaya Marketplace (© 242/373-8988). There's also a branch at the cruise-ship docks. Hours are 9am to 5pm Monday to Saturday.

ISLAND LAYOUT

Getting around Freeport/Lucaya is fairly easy because of its flat terrain. Although Freeport and Lucaya are frequently mentioned in the same breath, newcomers should note that Freeport is a landlocked collection of hotels and shops rising from the island's center, while Lucaya, about 4km (2½ miles) away, is a waterfront section of hotels, shops, and restaurants clustered next to a saltwater pond on the island's southern shoreline.

Freeport lies midway between the northern and southern shores of Grand Bahama Island. Bisected by some of the island's largest roads, it contains the biggest hotels, as well as two of the most-visited attractions in the country: the Crowne Plaza Golf Resort & Casino at the Royal Oasis and the International Bazaar shopping complex. The local straw market, where you can buy inexpensive souvenirs, lies just to the right of the entrance to the International Bazaar.

To reach **Port Lucaya** from Freeport, head east from the International Bazaar along East Sunrise Highway, then turn south at the intersection with Seahorse Road. Within about 4km (2½ miles), it will lead to the heart of the Lucaya complex, Port Lucaya.

Set between the beach and a saltwater pond, Port Lucaya's architectural centerpiece is **Count Basie Square,** named for the great entertainer who used to have a home on the island. Within a short walk east or west, along the narrow strip of sand between the sea and the saltwater pond, rise most of the hotels of Lucaya Beach.

Heading west of Freeport and Lucaya, the West Sunrise Highway passes industrial complexes such as The Bahamas Oil Refining Company. At the junction with Queen's Highway, you can take the road northwest all the way to **West End,** a distance of some 45km (28 miles) from the center of Freeport. Along the way you pass Freeport Harbour, where cruise ships dock. Just to the east lies Hawksbill Creek, a village known for its fish market.

Much less explored is the **East End** of Grand Bahama. It's located some 72km (45 miles) from the center of Freeport and is reached via the Grand Bahama Highway, which, despite its name, is rather rough in parts. Allow about 2 hours of driving time. First you pass the **Rand Nature Centre,** about 5km (3 miles) east of Freeport. About 11km (7 miles) on is **Lucaya National Park,** and 8km (5 miles) farther lies the hamlet of **Free Town;** east of Free Town is **High Rock,** known for its Emmanuel Baptist Church. From here, the road becomes considerably rougher until it ends in **MacLean's Town,** which celebrates Columbus Day with an annual conch-cracking contest. From here, it's possible to take a water taxi across Runners Creek to the exclusive Deep Water Cay club, catering to serious anglers.

In Freeport/Lucaya, but especially on the rest of Grand Bahama Island, you will almost never find a street number on a hotel or a store. Sometimes in the more remote places, you won't even find a street name. In lieu of numbers, locate places by prominent landmarks or hotels.

2 Getting Around

BY TAXI

The government sets the taxi rates, and the cabs are metered (or should be). Metered rates are $3 for the first quarter mile (⅓ km) and 40 cents each additional mile (1.6km). Additional passengers over the age of 2 are $3 each. If there's no meter, agree on the price with the driver in advance. You can call for a taxi, although most taxis wait at the major hotels or the cruise-ship dock to pick up passengers. One major taxi company is **Freeport Taxi Company,** Logwood Road (ℂ 242/352-6666), open 24 hours. Another is **Grand Bahama Taxi Union** at the Freeport International Airport, Old Airport Road (ℂ 242/352-7101), also open 24 hours. *Note:* Typical taxi rates are as follows: From the Harbour to: Royal Oasis Golf Resort & Casino, $16; Xanadu Beach Hotel, $17; Port Lucaya Marketplace, $24; Taíno Beach Resort/The Ritz, $24; Viva Fortuna Beach, $29. From the airport to: Lucaya, $19; Viva Fortuna, $15; Royal Oasis, $11; Xanadu/Woodbourne/Running Mon Marina, $14.

BY BUS

Public bus service runs from the International Bazaar to downtown Freeport and from the Pub on the Mall to the Lucaya area. The typical fare is $1 for adults, 50¢ for children. Check with the tourist office (see "Visitor Information," above) for bus schedules. There is no number to call for information.

BY CAR

If you plan to confine your exploration to the center of Freeport with its International Bazaar and Lucaya with its beaches, you can rely on public transportation. However, if you'd like to branch out and explore the rest of the island (perhaps finding a more secluded beach), a rental car is the way to go. Try **Avis** (ℂ **800/331-2112** or 242/352-7666; www.avis.com) or **Hertz** (ℂ **800/654-3001** or 242/352-9250; www.hertz.com). Both of these companies maintain offices in small bungalows outside the exit of the Freeport International Airport.

One of the best local companies is **Dollar Rent-a-Car,** Old Airport Road (ℂ **242/352-9325;** www.dollar.com), which rents everything from a new-style Kia Sportage to a Toyota Corolla. Rates range from $49 per day manual or $55 automatic, with unlimited mileage, plus another $15 per day for a CDW (Collision Damage Waiver; $500 deductible). Gas is usually $3 per gallon, and remember to drive on the left as British rules apply.

BY SCOOTER

A scooter is a fun way to get around as most of Grand Bahamas is flat with well-paved roads. Scooters can be rented at most hotels, or, for cruise-ship passengers, in the Freeport Harbour area. Helmets are required and provided by the outfitter. You can find dozens of stands along the road in Freeport and Lucaya and also in the major parking lots, charging rates ranging from $40 to $55 a day.

ON FOOT

You can explore the center of Freeport or Lucaya on foot, but if you want to venture into the East End or West End, you'll need to rent a car, hire a taxi, or try Grand Bahama's erratic public transportation.

FAST FACTS: Grand Bahama

Banks In Freeport/Lucaya, banks are open from 9:30am to 3pm, Monday to Thursday, and 9:30am to 5pm on Friday. Most banks here have ATMs that accept VISA, MasterCard, American Express, and any other bank or credit card on the Cirrus, Honor, Novus, and PLUS networks.

Climate See "When to Go," in chapter 2.

Currency Exchange Americans need not bother to exchange their dollars into Bahamian dollars, because the currencies are on par. However, Canadians and Brits will need to convert their money, which can be done at local banks or sometimes at a hotel, though hotels tend to offer less favorable rates.

Doctors For the fastest and best service, just head to Rand Memorial Hospital (see "Hospitals," below).

Drugstores For prescriptions and other pharmaceutical needs, go to Mini Mall, 1 West Mall, Explorer's Way, where you'll find **L.M.R. Drugs** (℅ 242/352-7327), next door to Burger King. Hours are Monday to Saturday 8am to 8pm and Sunday 8am to 3pm.

Embassies & Consulates See "Fast Facts: The Bahamas," in chapter 2.

Emergencies For all emergencies, call ℅ **911,** or dial 0 for the operator.

Eyeglass Repair The biggest specialist in eyeglasses and contact lenses is the **Optique Shoppe,** 7 Regent Centre, downtown Freeport (℅ **242/352-9073**).

Hospitals If you have a medical emergency, contact the government-operated, 90-bed **Rand Memorial Hospital,** East Atlantic Drive (℅ **242/352-6735** or 242/352-2689 for ambulance emergency).

Internet Access Visit the **Cyberclub** at Seventeen Center (© 242/351-4560; cyberclub@grandbahama.net), open Monday to Saturday 9am to 8pm.

Information See "Visitor Information," earlier in this chapter.

Laundry & Dry Cleaning Try **Jiffy Cleaners and Laundry,** West Mall at Pioneer's Way (© 242/352-7079), open Monday to Saturday 8am to 6pm.

Newspapers & Magazines The Freeport News is a morning newspaper published Monday through Saturday except holidays. The two dailies published in Nassau, the *Tribune* and the *Nassau Guardian,* are also available here, as are some New York and Miami papers, especially the *Miami Herald,* usually on the date of publication. American news magazines, such as *Time* and *Newsweek,* are flown in on the day of publication.

Police In an emergency, dial © 911.

Post Office The main post office is on Explorer's Way in Freeport (© 242/352-9371).

Safety Avoid walking or jogging along lonely roads. There are no particular danger zones, but stay alert: Grand Bahama is no stranger to drugs and crime.

Taxes All visitors leaving Grand Bahama Island must pay an $18 departure tax—in cash. (Both U.S. and Bahamian dollars are accepted.) No sales tax is charged, but you will have to pay a 6% hotel tax.

Taxis See "Getting Around," earlier in this chapter.

Weather Grand Bahama, in the north of The Bahamas, has temperatures in winter that vary from about 60°F to 75°F (16°C–24°C) daily. Summer variations range from 78°F to the high 80s (26°C to the low 30s Celsius). In Freeport/Lucaya, phone © 915 for weather information.

3 Where to Stay

Your choices are in the Freeport area, near the Bahamia Casino and the International Bazaar, or in Lucaya, closer to the beach.

Remember: In most cases, a resort levy of 6% and a 15% service charge will be added to your final bill. Be prepared, and ask if it's already included in the initial price you're quoted.

Where to Stay in Freeport/Lucaya

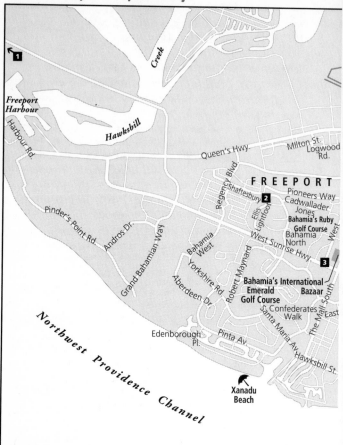

Best Western Castaways **4**

Coral Beach **7**

Crowne Plaza Golf Resort &
  Casino at the Royal Oasis **3**

Flamingo Bay Yacht Club &
  Marina Hotel **13**

Island Palm Resort **5**

Island Seas Resort **6**

Lakeview Manor Club **2**

Old Bahama Bay **1**

Paradise Cove **1**

Pelican Bay at Lucaya **9**

Port Lucaya Resort & Yacht Club **8**

Ritz Beach Resort **11**

Royal Islander **4**

Taino Beach Vacation Club **12**

The Westin & Sheraton at Our Lucaya **10**

Wyndham Viva Fortuna **14**

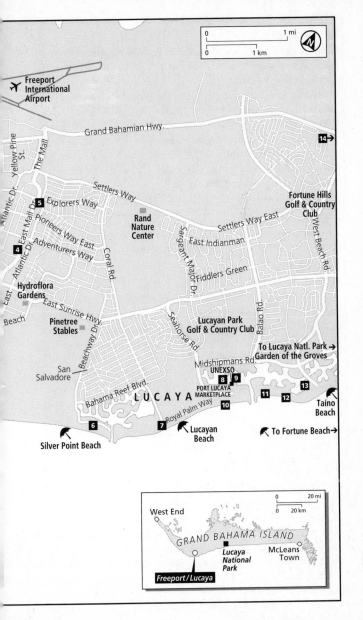

0   1 mi
0   1 km

Freeport
International
Airport

Grand Bahamian Hwy.

14 →

Yellow Pine St.

The Mall

Settlers Way

Atlantic Dr.

East Mall Dr.

5 Explorers Way

Pioneers Way East

Rand
Nature
Center

Fortune Hills
Golf & Country
Club

Settlers Way East

West Beach Rd.

Sargeant Major Dr.

East Indianman

4 Adventurers Way

East Atlantic Dr.

Coral Rd.

Fiddlers Green

Hydroflora
Gardens

East

East Sunrise Hwy.

Beach

Pinetree
Stables

Beachway Dr.

Lucayan Park
Golf & Country Club

Balao Rd.

To Lucaya Natl. Park →
Garden of the Groves

San
Salvadore

Seahorse Rd.

Midshipmans Rd.
UNEXSO

Bahama Reef Blvd.

L U C A Y A

8 **9**

PORT LUCAYA
MARKETPLACE

13

11

12

Taíno
Beach

6

7

Royal Palm Way

10

↰ Lucayan
Beach

↰ To Fortune Beach →

Silver Point Beach

0   20 mi
0   20 km

West End

GRAND BAHAMA ISLAND

Lucaya
National
Park

McLeans
Town

Freeport/Lucaya

FREEPORT
EXPENSIVE

Island Seas Resort A timeshare property open to nonmembers, this resort opens onto a secluded beach, although it also offers its own water fun in the form of a pool, hot tub, and waterfall. Also on-site is a Tiki-hut restaurant and bar. The location is convenient for the Port Lucaya Market and the Lucaya Golf and Country Club. Depending on their individual owners, each condo is different, ranging from one-bedroom units to large two-bedroom suites. Each contains a full bathroom with tub/shower, plus a full kitchen and balcony. Although not part of the hotel facilities, many watersports outfitters are right on the beach.

William's Town (P.O. Box F-44735), Freeport, Grand Bahamas, The Bahamas. © **242/ 373-1271.** Fax 242/373-1275. www.islandseas.com. 149 units. Winter $399 double, $499 2-bedroom suite; off season $219 double, $319 2-bedroom suite. AE, DISC, MC, V. **Amenities:** Restaurant; bar; pool; tennis court; bike rentals; limited room service (9am–4pm). *In room:* A/C, TV, fridge, coffeemaker, iron/ironing board, safe.

MODERATE

Crowne Plaza Golf Resort & Casino at the Royal Oasis ✿ *(Kids*

Badly hit during the 2004 hurricane, this hotel—the most famous one on the island—spent most of 2005 under restoration. It should be up and running for your visit, but ask about rates: There's a chance the prices will increase. This mammoth complex actually consists of two differently styled resorts combined under one umbrella: the 10-story Crowne Plaza tower and the less glamorous, three-story Crowne Plaza Country Club. Reinventing itself to stay competitive, the resort spent some $42 million on its once-tired, built-in-the-1960s proper-ties, hoping to revive some of their old glitz and glamour.

Flanked by a pair of fine golf courses, the Ruby and the Emerald, and thus catering to the convention crowd, the resorts are set on 1,000 hectares (2,470 acres) of tropical grounds. As it lies inland from the sea, the complex doesn't have its own natural beach. One of the grandest additions is a marine park and a man-made, landlocked beach; otherwise, you can take frequent shuttle buses to good natu-ral beaches nearby, where watersports are available. The two sections, also jointly share one of the largest casinos in the entire country, a serviceable site that's functional—though nowhere near as flashy or cutting edge as, say, the Atlantis Casino on Paradise Island.

The Crowne Plaza Country Club attracts families, honeymooners, frugal couples, golfers, and others who don't need or want luxury. The hotel's design is rather like an enormous low-rise wagon wheel, with a Disney-inspired minimountain surrounded by a swimming pool at its core. The hotel is so spread out, guests often complain that they need ground transport just to reach their bedrooms. (Nine wings radiate from the pool.) Some of the rooms have kitchenettes and are sold as timeshare units. Regular accommodations come in several classifications; even standard rooms are well equipped, with two comfortable double beds, dressing areas, and full-size bathrooms. Rooms in the 900 wing are the largest and best furnished—and are usually the ones that sell out first. Both resorts also rent out a number of suites, each furnished in summery fabrics plus beachy but durable furniture.

Crowne Plaza Tower, lying across the mall from its larger sibling, is smaller and more tranquil, and a bit more posh, containing 32 suites and 362 luxuriously furnished large units. The tower structure adjoins the Casino and the International Bazaar. A light, California-style decor prevails, with a skylit lobby and rooms that most often contain cherry hardwood furnishings. Lots of conventioneers and folks on quick getaways from Florida tend to stay here, as do high rollers.

The Mall at W. Sunrise Hwy. (P.O. Box F-207), Freeport, Grand Bahama, The Bahamas. © **800/545-1300** in the U.S. and Canada, or 242/350-7000. Fax 242/350-7002. www.theroyaloasis.com. 876 units. Crowne Plaza Country Club: Winter $145–$155 double, $240 suite; off season $115–$125 double, $180 suite. Crowne Plaza Tower: Winter $175–$205 double, $350 suite; off season $145–$155 double, $250 suite. Up to 2 children under 12 stay free in parent's room. AE, MC, V. **Amenities:** 6 restaurants; 6 bars; nightclub; casino; 3 pools; golf; 11 tennis courts; fitness center; spa; kids' activity center; limited room service (6:30am–11pm); massage; babysitting. *In room:* A/C, TV, dataport (in some), minifridge, beverage maker, hair dryer, iron/ironing board, safe.

INEXPENSIVE

Best Western Castaways *(Kids)* Castaways is a modest and unassuming hotel despite its platinum location adjacent to the International Bazaar and the casino. You stay here because of its location and the low price. It's not on the beach, but a free shuttle will take you to nearby Williams Town Beach or Xanadu Beach. Surrounded by gardens, the four-story hotel has a pagoda roof and an indoor/outdoor garden lobby with a gift shop, a clothing shop, a game room, and tour desks. Rooms are your basic motel style, and the best units are on the ground. The Flamingo Restaurant features remarkable Bahamian and American dishes daily from 7:30am to 10pm; it also serves one of the island's best breakfasts. There's also a swimming pool area with a wide terrace and a pool bar serving sandwiches and cool drinks. A children's playground adjoins the pool.

42629 E. Mall Dr., Freeport, Grand Bahama, The Bahamas. © **800/780-7234** or 242/352-6682. Fax 242/352-5087. www.bestwestern.com. 118 units. Winter

$125–$155 double, $205 suite; off season $95–$125 double, $145 suite. Children under 12 stay free in parent's room. AE, DISC, MC, V. **Amenities:** Restaurant; 2 bars; pool; bike rentals; babysitting; self-service laundry; nonsmoking rooms; rooms for those w/limited mobility. *In room:* A/C, TV, dataport, hair dryer, iron/ironing board, safe.

Island Palm Resort *(Value*

Set within the commercial heart of Freeport, this simple three-story motel consists of four buildings separated by parking lots and greenery. Within an easy walk from virtually everything in town, and 2km (1¼ miles) from the International Bazaar, it offers good value in no-frills, eminently serviceable rooms with well-kept bathrooms equipped with shower/tub combinations. Complimentary shuttle-bus service ferries anybody who's interested to nearby Williamstown Beach (also called Island Seas Beach), where you can use the beachfront facilities (including jet skis and snorkeling equipment) of its sibling resort, a timeshare unit known as Island Sea.

E. Mall Dr. (P.O. Box F-44881), Freeport, Grand Bahama, The Bahamas. ℂ 242/352-6648. Fax 242/352-6640. http://islandpalm.tripod.com. 143 units. Winter $85 double; off season $75 double. Extra person $5. AE, DISC, MC, V. **Amenities:** Restaurant; bar; nightclub; pool; nonsmoking rooms; rooms for those w/limited mobility. *In room:* A/C, TV, iron/ironing board, safe.

Lakeview Manor Club

Today this 1970s-era resort is a timeshare, but it was originally built as private apartments. It's a good bargain for those who want peace and privacy, but the staff seems a bit lax. Catering to self-sufficient types, it offers midsize one-bedroom and studio apartments, each with tropical furniture, a private balcony, plus small bathrooms with shower/tub combinations. The club overlooks the 5th hole of the PGA-approved Princess Ruby Golf Course. It's 8km (5 miles) from the beach, but it's ideal for golfers or for anyone to whom a sea view isn't important. A complimentary shuttle bus travels to the International Bazaar, the supermarket, Port Lucaya, and beach areas.

Cadwallader Jones Dr. (P.O. Box F-42699), Freeport, Grand Bahama, The Bahamas. ℂ 242/352-9789. Fax 242/352-2283. www.bahamasvg.com/lakeview. 52 units. Year-round $75 double; $100 1-bedroom apt; weekly $450 double; $600 1-bedroom apt. DC, DISC, MC, V. Closed last week of Oct. **Amenities:** Pool; 2 tennis courts; activities' desk; babysitting; self-service laundry. *In room:* A/C, ceiling fan, TV, full kitchen, beverage maker.

Royal Islander

Don't be fooled by the corny-looking, storm-battered exterior of this place. It was built during an unfortunate Disney-style period in Freeport's expansion, during the early 1980s, with an improbable-looking pyramidal roof inspired by a cluster of Mayan pyramids. Inside, it's a lot more appealing than you might think, with rooms arranged around a verdant courtyard that seems far, far removed from the busy traffic and sterile-looking landscape outside. Rooms have white-tile floors and bathrooms that are on the small side, with tiny sinks and shower stalls. Otherwise, the motif is Florida/tropical, with some pizzazz.

There's a coffee-shop-style snack bar and a small restaurant on the premises, but other than that, you'll have to wander a short distance, perhaps to the International Bazaar just across the street, to find diversions and dining. Free transport to the beach is available, but you'll have to take a bus or taxi anywhere else.

E. Mall Dr. (P.O. Box F-42549), Freeport, Grand Bahama, The Bahamas. ℭ 242/351-6000. Fax 242/351-3546. www.bahamasvacationguide.com/royalislander.html. 100 units. Winter $97 double; off season $87 double. Children under 14 stay free in parent's room. AE, MC, V. **Amenities:** Restaurant; snack bar; bar; pool; Jacuzzi; self-service laundry; nonsmoking rooms. *In room:* A/C, TV, safe.

LUCAYA
EXPENSIVE

The Westin & Sheraton at Our Lucaya ★★ *Kids* This massive $400-million resort, one of the largest in The Bahamas, is firmly anchored at the center of two of the best white sandy beaches in The Bahamas—Lucayan Beach and Taíno Beach. Expect nearly 3.2 hectares (8 acres) of soft white sand. Freeport/Lucaya, which had been losing tourist business to Paradise Island, got a big boost in 1999 when this sprawling metropolis opened its doors.

The first of the three sections was completed late in 1998 under the name **Sheraton at Our Lucaya.** It's the only one of the three branches of Our Lucaya to focus exclusively on all-inclusive holidays, whereby all meals, drinks, and most activities are included in one set price. With a vague South Beach Art Deco design, it's a massive, open-sided hexagon, with rooms facing the beach and the swimming pool. The 528-room resort is contemporary but relaxed; the developers have created a young vibe that draws a high number of families. Bedrooms are whimsical and fun, thanks to fabrics you'd expect on a loud Hawaiian shirt from the Elvis era and maple-veneered furniture, all put together with the kind of artful simplicity you'd expect in a California beach house.

In 2000, two newer subdivisions of Our Lucaya were opened, neither of which is marketed as an all-inclusive property. The smaller and somewhat more private of the two is **Westin Lighthouse Pointe,** a 322-unit, low-rise complex that focuses specifically on an adult clientele. Its larger counterpart is the 528-unit **Westin-Breakers Cay,** a grand, 10-story, white-sided tower. The three sections stretch in a glittering profile along a narrow strip of beachfront, allowing residents to drop into any of the bars, restaurants, and gardens. A complex this big contains a staggering diversity of restaurants, each designed with a different theme and ambience. The best of the resort's cuisine selections will be reviewed under "Where to Dine," later in this chapter. And consistent with the broad themes, each of the subdivisions has a dramatic and/or unconventional swimming pool. For example, the Sheraton at Our Lucaya's pool is designed around a replica of a 19th-century sugar mill, complete with an aqueduct that might be worthy of the ancient Romans.

A spa and fitness center, a quintet of tennis courts, a convention center, a state-of-the-art casino, and a shopping mall have all also been added in recent years, and there's an increasing emphasis on golf, thanks to the opening of the spectacular Reef Course (p. 165). An innovative feature for tennis players is the Fast Grand Slam of Tennis, which features replicas of the world's best known court surfaces—red clay at the French Open, manicured grass at Wimbledon, Rebound Ace at the Australian Open, and DecoTurf at the U.S. Open.

Children aged 2 to 12 can be amused and entertained throughout daylight hours every day at Camp Lucaya.

Royal Palm Way (P.O. Box F-42500), Lucaya, Grand Bahama, The Bahamas. © 877-OUR-LUCAYA in the U.S., or 242/373-1333. Sheraton fax 242/373-8804; Westin fax 242/350-5060. www.ourlucaya.com. 1,260 units. Sheraton (all-inclusive) year-round $169–$249 double; from $469 suite; $30 extra per day for 3rd and 4th occupant. Westin Lighthouse Pointe or Breakers Cay year-round $199–$259 double; from $749 suite; $30 extra per day for 3rd and 4th occupant. AE, DISC, MC, V. **Amenities:** 10 restaurants; 10 bars; 44 pools; 2 golf courses; 5 tennis courts; health club; watersports equipment/rentals; kids' camp and children's programs; business center; salon; 24-hr. room service; babysitting; laundry service; dry cleaning; nonsmoking rooms; rooms for those w/limited mobility. *In room:* A/C, TV, dataport (Westin only), kitchenette (in some units), minibar, iron/ironing board, safe.

MODERATE

Pelican Bay at Lucaya ✦✦ Here's a good choice for travelers with champagne tastes and beer budgets, a hotel with more architectural charm than any other small property on Grand Bahama. It's built on a peninsula jutting into a labyrinth of inland waterways, with moored yachts on virtually every side. Pelican Bay evokes a Danish seaside village, with rows of "town houses," each painted a different color and sporting whimsical trim, and each overlooking the harbor. The hotel opened in the fall of 1996 and later expanded with another wing in 1999. Its location couldn't be better, right next to Port Lucaya Marketplace, where restaurants and entertainment spots abound. Lucayan Beach, one of the best stretches of white sand on the island, is just across the street, and Taíno Beach, with equally good sands, lies immediately to the east of the hotel. UNEXSO, providing some of the best dive facilities in The Bahamas, is next door. If that's not enough, the extensive amenities of Our Lucaya (see previous listing) are available for use.

The spacious accommodations have Italian tile floors and white-washed furniture, with either a king-size bed or twin beds. The end rooms have cross ventilation and are the ideal choices for those who don't want to rely entirely on air-conditioning. Each unit comes with satellite TV, as well as a balcony with a view of the nearby waterway and marina. Bathrooms, although of standard size, contain oversize cotton robes and tub/shower combos.

The hotel has one main restaurant, the Ferry House, which specializes in American and Bahamian food and serves breakfast, lunch, and dinner daily. The Yellow Tail Pool Bar offers drinks and snacks all day.

Seahorse Rd. (P.O. Box F-42654), Lucaya, Grand Bahama, The Bahamas. © 800/600-9192 in the U.S., or 242/373-9550. Fax 242/373-9551. www.pelicanbayhotel.com. 186 units. Winter $165–$215 double, $275 suite; off season $135–$190 double, $250 suite. Rates include breakfast. AE, MC, V. **Amenities:** Restaurant; bar; 3 pools; Jacuzzi; business center; babysitting; nonsmoking rooms. *In room:* A/C, TV, dataport (in suites); minibar (in suites), minifridge, coffeemaker, hair dryer, iron/ironing board, safe.

Port Lucaya Resort & Yacht Club ✿
With its own 100-slip marina lying next to the Port Lucaya Marketplace, this club opened in 1993 in the heart of the Port Lucaya restaurant, hotel, and nightlife complex. The resort consists of a series of pastel-colored two-story structures that guests reach via golf cart after checking in. The wings of guest rooms separate the piers—site of some very expensive marine hardware—from a verdant central green space with a gazebo-style bar and a swimming pool. Although set back inland on a waterway, Lucayan Harbour, this resort lies within a few minutes' walk of Lucayan Beach, one of the island's finest, and is also close to Taíno Beach. Even though it's not right on the beach, it's such an easy walk that no one seems to complain. Many guests are drawn to the nautical atmosphere of the resort and its nearness to Port Lucaya Marketplace.

The medium-size rooms have tile floors and are attractively and comfortably furnished with rattan pieces and big wall mirrors. The rooms are divided into various categories, ranging from standard to deluxe, and open onto the marina (preferred by yachting guests), the Olympic-size swimming pool, or the well-landscaped garden. (If you don't want to hear the sounds coming from the lively market-place, request units 1–6, which are more tranquil and away from the noise.) Bathrooms with newer shower/tub combinations are tidy and well maintained, with adequate shelf space.

The hotel's restaurant, Tradewinds Cafe, offers standard Bahamian, American, and international dishes but only to groups of 50 or more. Finding a restaurant, however, shouldn't be difficult in the Port Lucaya Marketplace.

Bell Channel Rd. (P.O. Box F-42452), Lucaya, Grand Bahama, The Bahamas. © 800/LUCAYA-1 or 242/373-6618. Fax 242/373-6652. www.portlucayaresort.com. 160 units. Winter $100–$145 double, $175–$250 suite; off season $80–$120 double, $125–$200 suite. Extra person $25 per day. Children 12 and under stay free in parent's room. AE, DISC, MC, V. **Amenities:** Restaurant; 2 bars; pool; Jacuzzi; babysitting; nonsmoking rooms. *In room:* A/C, TV, hair dryer, iron/ironing board.

INEXPENSIVE

Coral Beach Built in 1965 as privately owned condominiums, this peacefully isolated property near a sandy beach sits amid gardens and groves of casuarinas in a residential neighborhood. Some of the apartments and rooms have verandas, and four contain kitchenettes. More suitable for older travelers, the complex rents large but rather sparsely furnished units, with shower/tub combinations in the bathroom. A poolside bar provides finger food at reasonable prices and is open daily from 10am to 4pm. A beauty salon is on the premises. You're also within walking distance of the Port Lucaya Marketplace.

Coral Rd. at Royal Palm Way (P.O. Box F-42468), Lucaya, Grand Bahama, The Bahamas. © 242/373-2468. Fax 242/373-5140. www.bahamasvg.com/coralbeach. 10 units. Winter $95–$115 double, $550–$650 weekly double; off season $80–$95 double, $490–$550 weekly double. MC, V. **Amenities:** Pool bar; pool; salon. *In room:* A/C, TV, kitchenette (in some), minifridge, coffeemaker.

TAINO BEACH
MODERATE

Ritz Beach Resort ✿ *(Kids)* Rated five stars by the government, this hotel lies adjacent to the Taíno Beach Vacation Club, sharing all the fun and amenities of its elaborate water park. Enveloped by semitropical gardens, the Ritz (not related to other fabled world hotels of the same name) also is adjacent to the Pirates of The Bahamas Beach Theme Park.

Actually, the origins of this resort date back to 1995. Over the years it was constructed in three different phases. Made up of two buildings, it also comprises a 50-room complex called Coral Suites. All the bedrooms are in concrete coral buildings, and units range from both efficiency and studio units to one-bedroom suites to elaborate villa and penthouse accommodations. The bedrooms are spacious and well furnished and handsomely maintained, with a tub-and-shower combo in the efficiency rooms and a walk-in shower in the studios.

Everything depends on how much you want to pay. Penthouses are on the fourth levels, and include such accommodations as a studio penthouse, which is multilevel with its own sun deck and private pool. The hotel's eating facilities are actually at the Taíno Beach Vacation Club where guests can patronize two international restaurants and five bars. The Ritz also has its own pool bar.

Jolly Roger Dr., Taíno Beach, Lucaya (P.O. Box F-43819), Grand Bahama Island, The Bahamas. © 888/311-7945 or 242/373-9354. Fax 242/373-4421. www.timetravel corp.com. 110 units. Year-round $199 efficiency, $299 studio, $499 penthouse. Children 12 and under stay free in parent's room. **Amenities:** Restaurant; pool bar; pool; tennis court; babysitting; laundry service; nonsmoking rooms (all); rooms for those w/limited mobility. *In room:* A/C, TV, beverage maker, hair dryer, iron/ironing board.

Taíno Beach Vacation Club   This fun resort on the southern shore offers attractively furnished and breezy one-, two-, and three-bedroom condos furnished in a semitropical motif. The setting of the beach club is near an excellent 457m (1,500-ft.) strip of white sands. Although no beach here is actually private, this one comes the closest; you won't be subject to harassment from beach vendors pestering you to sell unwanted souvenirs. Yet, when you want to remove yourself from this relatively tranquil beach, you can walk over to the adjacent water park and the Pirates of the Caribbean Theme Park, where you'll find plenty of visitors and touristy attractions. These oceanfront accommodations are highly desirable, each well equipped with several extras. The location here is only a 6-minute ride from Port Lucaya and a 15-minute drive from the International Bazaar. Accommodations are divided into a series of two buildings rising three floors in this concrete structure with ocean views. Set among tropical gardens, the emphasis here is on sports, such as volleyball and basketball.

Jolly Roger Dr., Taíno Beach, Lucaya (P.O. Box F-43819), Grand Bahama Island, The Bahamas. © 242/373-4682. Fax 242/373-4421. www.tainobeach.com. 37 units. Year-round $150 efficiency; $375 1-bedroom unit; $475 2-bedroom unit; $650 3-bedroom unit. AE, DISC, MC, V. **Amenities:** Restaurant; pool bar; pool; laundry service; nonsmoking rooms (all); rooms for those w/limited mobility. *In room:* A/C, TV, kitchenette, beverage maker, iron/ironing board.

INEXPENSIVE

Flamingo Bay Yacht Club & Marina Hotel   Unlike the Ritz Beach Resort and the Taíno Vacation Club (its sibling properties), this hotel is set back but lies only about a 5-minute walk from a strip of 457m (1,500 ft.) of white sand. A three-story concrete building, offers midsize bedrooms that are comfortable and attractively furnished in a Caribbean motif, with a sleek new bathroom with tub/shower combination. You have a choice of renting a room with a king-size bed or two double beds, and each unit comes with such extras as a microwave and toaster. Across the street is the Pirates of The Bahamas (p. 168). At a 20-slip marina, a water taxi runs every hour to the center of the Lucaya area. Although amenities are sparse, customers are permitted to use of the Ritz Beach Resort's, which are plentiful.

Jolly Roger Dr., Taíno Beach, Lucaya, Grand Bahama Island, The Bahamas. © 800/824-6623 or 242/373-4677. Fax 954/484-4757. www.timetravelcorp.com. 58 units. Year-round $70 double. Children 12 and under stay free in parent's room. AE, DISC, MC, V. **Amenities:** Coin-operated laundry; nonsmoking rooms. *In room:* A/C, TV, kitchenette, beverage maker.

OUTSIDE FREEPORT/LUCAYA
EXPENSIVE

Old Bahama Bay 🏖️🏖️   A cottage-style resort, this complex is the centerpiece of an 11-hectare (28-acre) site with home sites and a marina. In an oceanfront setting, the boutique hotel has cottages adjacent to the 72-slip marina complex; a private beach is steps away. The colonial-style architecture graces a setting 40km (25 miles) west of Freeport, consisting of suites set in six two-story beach houses and three spacious buildings overlooking the marina. The living space is the most generous on the island, with custom-designed furnishings along with private beachfront terraces. The elegant marble bathrooms are luxurious with deluxe toiletries, and a whirlpool tub. The most recent addition added 12 "beachcomber" junior suites and four two-bedroom Grand Bay suites, each designed in a British colonial style. Dockside Grille serves quite good Bahamian and international dishes for three meals a day. The gourmet restaurant on-site is Aqua, featuring Caribbean, Asian, and Bahamian-inspired dishes.

West End (P.O. Box F-42546), Grand Bahama Island, The Bahamas. © 800/572-5711 in the U.S. or 800/444-9469. Fax 242/346-6546. www.oldbahamabay.com. 49 units. Winter $259–$509 suite, from $649 2-bedroom suite; off season $199–$399 suite, from $569 2-bedroom suite. $50 per extra person. Breakfast and dinner $80 per person extra per day. AE, MC, V. **Amenities:** 3 restaurants; 2 bars; pool; 2 tennis courts; fitness center; watersports equipment/rentals; car rental; limited room service (7am–10pm); massage; babysitting; laundry service; nonsmoking rooms (all). *In room:* A/C, TV, dataport, kitchenette, minifridge, beverage maker, hair dryer, iron/ironing board, safe.

MODERATE

Paradise Cove 🐾 *(Finds)* Paradise Cove teems with rainbow-hued tropical marine life and a vast array of coral to delight the snorkeler in you. If you want to escape the glitz and glam of Freeport or Lucaya, this secluded hideaway on a beach is the perfect place. You'll find an informal series of one-bedroom apartments and two-bedroom cottages for rent here. Away from the crowds, Paradise Cove is like Grand Bahama used to be before the tourist hordes invaded. Yet you are only a 20-minute drive east of West End. Snorkeling, swimming, kayaking, and sunbathing fill the day here. At twilight, attend the breathtaking sunset bonfire. All units are good size and have full kitchens for those who want to cook their own grub.

Paradise Cove (P.O. Box F-42771), Freeport, Grand Bahama Island. ℂ **242/349-2677.** Fax 242/352-5471. www.deadmansreef.com. 12 units. Year-round $100 1-bedroom apt, $575 weekly; $195 2-bedroom villa, $1,225 weekly. Extra person $15 per day. **Amenities:** Bar; watersports equipment/rentals. *In room:* A/C, TV, kitchen.

Wyndham Viva Fortuna 🐾 *(Kids)* Think of this as an Italian Club Med. It caters to a mostly European, relatively young crowd, who appreciate the 14 secluded hectares (35 acres) of beachfront and the nonstop sports activities that are included in the price. Established in 1993, Viva Fortuna lies 9.5km (6 miles) east of the International Bazaar in the southeastern part of the island, amid an isolated landscape of casuarinas and scrubland. Midsize bedrooms lie in a colorful group of two-story outbuildings. About three-quarters have ocean views; the others overlook the garden. Each has a private balcony, and two queen-size beds, with a small bathroom with shower stalls. Singles can book one of these rooms, but they are charged 40% more than the per-person double-occupancy rate.

All meals, which are included in the rates, are served buffet-style in a pavilion near the beach, and the Italian cuisine is actually some of the best on Grand Bahama Island. In addition to the buffet, you'll find a casual Italian restaurant, La Trattoria, where you can order sit-down dinners within a candlelit setting.

1 Dubloon Rd. (P.O. Box F-42398), Freeport, Grand Bahama, The Bahamas. ℂ **800/898-9968** or 242/373-4000. Fax 242/373-5594. www.wyndham.com. 276 units. Winter $124 double, $74 per extra person; off season $98 double, $59 per extra person. Rates are all-inclusive. AE, DC, MC, V. **Amenities:** 2 restaurants; 3 bars; disco; pool; 2 tennis courts; gym; sauna; watersports equipment/rentals; kids' club; babysitting; nonsmoking rooms; rooms for those w/limited mobility. *In room:* A/C, TV, hair dryer, iron/ironing board, safe.

4 Where to Dine

Foodies will find that the cuisine on Grand Bahama Island doesn't match the more refined fare served at dozens of places on New Providence (Nassau/Paradise Island). However, a few places in Grand Bahama specialize in fine dining; others get by with rather standard fare. The good news is that the dining scene is much more affordable here.

FREEPORT
EXPENSIVE

Rib Room ℛ SEAFOOD/STEAKS The Rib Room serves the island's best steaks, in huge portions. Everything is served in the atmosphere of a British hunting lodge. If you don't want one of the steaks, opt instead for the blue-ribbon prime rib of beef with a passable Yorkshire pudding. Special praise goes to the broiled Bahamian lobster, but steer clear of the grouper. Shrimp can be succulent when it's not overcooked, and steak Diane, although rather fully flavored, is meltingly textured. The wine list is reasonably priced.

Crowne Plaza Golf Resort & Casino at the Royal Oasis, the Mall at W. Sunrise Hwy. ℭ 242/352-6721. Reservations recommended. Jackets required for men. Main courses $22–$36. AE, DC, MC, V. Fri–Wed 5:30–10:30pm.

MODERATE

Silvano's ℛ ITALIAN The only authentic Italian dining spot in Freeport, this 80-seat restaurant with its Mediterranean decor serves a worthy but not exceptional cuisine. The standard repertoire from Mama Mia's kitchen is presented here with quality ingredients, most often shipped in from the United States. Service is polite and helpful. The grilled veal steak is our favorite, although the homemade pastas are equally alluring. They're served with a wide variety of freshly made sauces. The chef also works his magic with fresh shrimp. Other traditional Italian dishes round out the menu.

Ranfurley Circle. ℭ 242/352-5111. Reservations recommended. Lunch specials $5.50–$11; main courses $13–$36. AE, DISC, MC, V. Daily noon–3pm and 5–11pm.

INEXPENSIVE

Becky's Restaurant BAHAMIAN/AMERICAN Go here to rev up before a day of serious shopping at the International Bazaar, which is right at hand. Owned by Becky and Berkeley Smith, this pink-and-white restaurant offers authentic Bahamian cuisine and a welcome dose of down-to-earth, non-casino reality. Breakfasts are either all-American or Bahamian and are available all day. Also popular are minced lobster, curried mutton, fish platters, baked or curried chicken, and conch salads. Stick to the local specialties instead of the lackluster American dishes.

E. Sunrise Hwy. and E. Beach Dr. ℰ **242/352-5247.** Breakfast $5–$11; main courses $7–$22. AE, MC, V. Daily 7am–10pm.

Geneva's BAHAMIAN/SEAFOOD If you want to eat where the locals eat, head for Geneva's, where the food is made the old-fashioned way. This restaurant is one of the best places to sample conch, which has fed and nourished Bahamians for centuries. The Monroe family will prepare it for you stewed, cracked, or fried, or in a savory conch chowder that makes an excellent starter. Grouper also appears, prepared in every imaginable way. The bartender will get you into the mood with a rum-laced Bahama Mama.

Kipling Lane and E. Mall, at W. Sunrise Hwy. ℰ **242/352-5085.** Lunch sandwiches and platters $6–$12; dinner main courses $9–$25. DISC, MC, V. Daily 7am–11pm.

The Pepper Pot BAHAMIAN This might be the only place on Grand Bahama that specializes in Bahamian takeout food. You'll find it after about a 5-minute drive east of the International Bazaar, in a tiny shopping mall. You can order takeout portions of the island's best guava duff (a dessert specialty of The Bahamas that resembles a jelly roll), as well as a savory conch chowder, the standard fish and pork chops, chicken souse (an acquired taste), cracked conch, sandwiches and hamburgers, and an array of daily specials. The owner is Ethiopian-born Wolansa Fountain.

E. Sunrise Hwy. (at Coral Rd.). ℰ **242/373-7655.** Breakfast $3–$5; main courses $7–$9; vegetarian plates $3–$5. No credit cards. Daily 24 hr.

The Pub on the Mall INTERNATIONAL Located on the same floor of the same building and under the same management, three distinctive eating areas lie across the boulevard from the International Bazaar and attract many locals. The **Prince of Wales** serves such Olde English staples as shepherd's pie, fish and chips, platters of roast beef or fish, and real English ale. One end of the room is devoted to the **Red Dog Sports Bar,** with a boisterous atmosphere and at least four TV screens blasting away for dedicated sports fans. **Silvano's** (see above) is an Italian restaurant serving lots of pasta, usually with verve, as well as veal, chicken, beefsteaks, seafood, and such desserts as tiramisu. The Bahamian-themed **Islander's Roost** has a tropical decor of bright island color and a balcony overlooking the Bazaar. The food is good if not great; the main platters are a good value, usually very filling and satisfying. Menu items include sandwiches, salads, grilled fish, beefsteaks, and prime rib.

Where to Dine in Freeport/Lucaya

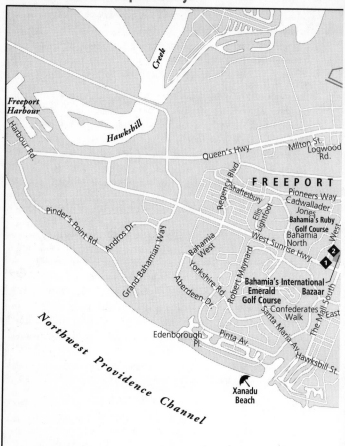

Barracuda's **6**	Georgie's **6**
Becky's Restaurant **2**	Giovanni's Café **6**
Bishop's Restaurant **10**	La Dolce Vita **6**
Café Michel **2**	Luciano's **6**
China Beach **10**	Margarita Villa Sand Bar **10**
China Temple **2**	Oasis Café **1**
Churchill's **6**	Outrigger's Native Restaurant /
Club Caribe **12**	White Wave Club **11**
Fatman's Nephew **5**	Palm Grill & Coconut Bar **1**
Ferry House **8**	Paradiso **1**
Geneva's **3**	The Pepper Pot **5**

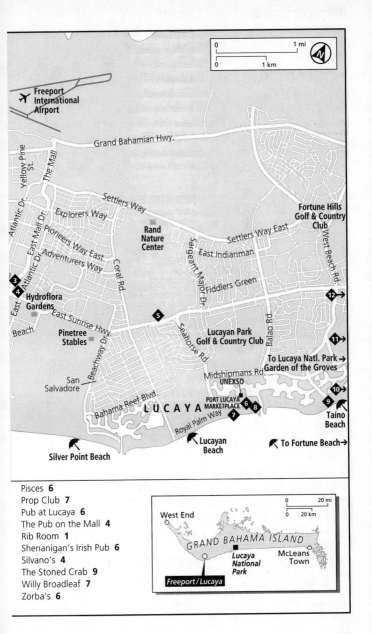

Pisces **6**
Prop Club **7**
Pub at Lucaya **6**
The Pub on the Mall **4**
Rib Room **1**
Shenanigan's Irish Pub **6**
Silvano's **4**
The Stoned Crab **9**
Willy Broadleaf **7**
Zorba's **6**

Ranfurley Circle, Sunrise Hwy. ℂ 242/352-5110. Reservations recommended. Main courses $6–$36. AE, MC, V, DISC. Prince of Wales and Red Dog daily noon–midnight; Silvano's daily noon–3pm and 5–11pm; Islander's Roost Mon–Sat 5–11pm.

IN THE INTERNATIONAL BAZAAR
INEXPENSIVE

Café Michel BAHAMIAN/AMERICAN   The name implies that you've found a real French bistro set amid the bustle of the International Bazaar, but alas, it turns out to be a mere coffee shop. Nevertheless, it's a good place for refueling when you're shopping the bazaar. About 20 tables are outside under red and white umbrellas and bistro-style tablecloths. Inside are about a dozen more. Local shoppers know to come here not only for coffee, but also for platters, salads, and sandwiches throughout the day. Both American and Bahamian dishes are served, including seafood platters, steaks, and, of course, grouper. The house specialty is a Bahamian lobster platter with all the fixings.

International Bazaar. ℂ 242/352-2191. Reservations recommended for dinner. Main courses $5–$36. AE, MC, V. Mon–Sat noon–11pm. Closes at 6pm in off season.

China Temple CHINESE   This is a Chinese joint—and don't expect more than just that—that also does takeout. Over the years it's proved to be the dining bargain of the bazaar. The menu is familiar and standard: chop suey, chow mein, and sweet-and-sour chicken. It's certainly not gourmet Asian fare, but it's cheap, and it might hit the spot when you're craving something different.

International Bazaar. ℂ 242/352-5610. Lunch $7–$9; main courses $10–$14. AE, MC, V. Mon–Sat 11am–10pm.

LUCAYA
EXPENSIVE

Churchill's ℛ AMERICAN   One of the island's most elegant restaurants, Churchill's lures discerning palates to the Westin & Sheraton at Our Lucaya—even guests staying in Freeport. We like to arrive early for drinks in the colonial-style bar with its dark-wood floors, potted plants, and ceiling fans, even a grand piano. (All the setting needs to feel complete is a new Bogie-and-Ingrid-Bergman combo willing to remake *Casablanca* on-site.) This is the island's best chophouse, featuring both succulent steaks flown over from the mainland and locally caught seafood. The manor house setting is a perfect foil for the finely honed service and top-quality ingredients, deftly prepared.

At the Westin & Sheraton at Our Lucaya, Royal Palm Way. ℂ 242/373-1333. Reservations required. Main courses $25–$65. AE, DC, DISC, MC, V. Mon–Sat 6–11pm.

The Stoned Crab ℱ SEAFOOD   Tired of frozen seafood shipped in from the mainland? Come here for the sweet stone crab claws and the lobster, both caught in Bahamian waters. There's none better on the island. You can't miss this place—a triple pyramid (ca. 1968) whose four-story wood-and-steel framework is strong enough to withstand any hurricane. Swiss-born Livio Peronino is the manager and chef, preparing a seafood platter with everything on it, including grouper, conch fritters, and all kinds of shellfish. The best pasta on the menu is linguine al pesto with lobster and shrimp. For starters, try the zesty conch chowder. Have a lobster salad with your meal and finish with Irish coffee.

At Taíno Beach, Lucaya. ℭ 242/373-1442. Reservations recommended. Main courses $22–$45. AE, MC, V. Daily 5–10pm.

Willy Broadleaf ℱ INTERNATIONAL   At the first-class Westin & Sheraton at Our Lucaya, you're treated to one of the most lavish buffet dinners in the entire Bahamian chain. The chefs conceive of their offering as a giant spread of exotic dishes based on recipes from around the globe. The decor fits the cuisine, evoking a courtyard patio in Mexico, a marketplace in old Cairo, the dining hall of an Indian maharajah, even an African village; from India comes tandoori chicken, from Greece moussaka. Another tasty treat is a sausage made from wild boar. Expect freshly made salads, both hot and cold dishes, and luscious, often fruit-based desserts.

The Westin & Sheraton at Our Lucaya, Royal Palm Way. ℭ 242/373-1333. Breakfast buffet $20, Tues–Fri $34 buffet, Sat–Sun $50 seafood buffet. AE, DC, DISC, MC, V. Daily 6:30–11am and 6–10pm.

MODERATE

Barracuda's ℱ AMERICAN   With high ceilings and big windows, this space is the size of an airplane hanger, and it's done up with playful art and a whimsical, hip decor that would be at home in Miami's South Beach. The kitchen turns out hearty breakfast dishes that are loaded with flavor. The best examples are omelets and French toast. The weekend buffet is a table-groaning event of freshly made American and Bahamian dishes—it's one of the best food values on island.

At the Westin & Sheraton at Our Lucaya, Royal Palm Way, Lucaya. ℭ 242/373-1333. Breakfast $14 or under; buffet $16. DC, MC, V. Daily 7–10:30am; Sat–Sun 6:30pm–midnight.

China Beach ℱ ASIAN FUSION   At the Westin & Sheraton at Our Lucaya, you can cruise the Pacific Rim, feasting on exotic delights, including the spicy hot cuisines of Vietnam and Thailand, with calls at Korea, Indonesia, and Malaysia. The menu changes every month but some dishes appear with regularity. Our favorites among these are a savory Hong Kong roast duckling and a zesty Thai chicken. The beef marinated in soy sauce is served with fresh spring onion, and the grouper filet appears with fresh ginger and scallions. Other Far East specialties include a seafood teppanyaki and stir-fry conch.

At the Westin & Sheraton at Our Lucaya, Royal Palm Way. $\textcircled{C}$ **242/373-1333.** Reservations recommended. Main courses $19–$33. AE, DC, DISC MC, V. Tues–Sat 6–11pm.

Oasis Café BAHAMIAN/AMERICAN
This restaurant on the lobby of the Royal Oasis resort adjoins the casino. As you eat, you can view the gamblers winning and losing (mostly the latter). If you order a la carte, the menu consists mainly of snacks and sandwiches. But many diners come here for the hot and cold dishes on the buffet. The chefs do a good job with their roasting at night, especially with the prime rib, which can be carved for you. Homemade soups are featured daily, along with fresh salads and tasty desserts. The best time to come for island flair and fun is on Bahamian night each Friday. During most of 2005, the Royal Oasis resort—including this restaurant—underwent renovations. It expects to reopen in 2006, but call ahead before visiting.

Crowne Plaza Golf Resort & Casino at the Royal Oasis, the Mall at W. Sunrise Hwy. $\textcircled{C}$ **242/350-7000.** Buffet lunch $18–$19 daily; buffet dinner $23 daily. AE, DC, MC, V. Call for hours.

Palm Grill & Coconut Bar BAHAMIAN/INTERNATIONAL/SEAFOOD
Off the lobby at the Royal Oasis resort, this eatery offers two distinct dining experiences. The Palm Grill is a fashionable bistro with tables inside or out; the kitchen serves a beautifully roasted prime rib at whatever doneness you prefer, fettuccine Alfredo with the tantalizing addition of fresh shrimp, and Bahamian snapper cooked just right—still moist—and served with grilled vegetables. At the more convivial Coconut Bar, you can order your fill of well-stuffed sandwiches, juicy burgers and fries, freshly made salads, and, of course, conch and other main courses from the same kitchen.

Crowne Plaza Golf Resort & Casino at the Royal Oasis, the Mall at W. Sunrise Hwy. $\textcircled{C}$ **242/350-7000.** Palm Grill main courses lunch $6.25–$12, dinner $12–$22. Coconut Bar main courses $7.50–$18. AE, DC, DISC, MC, V. Palm Grill daily 6:30–11:30am, noon–3pm, and 5:30–11pm. Coconut Bar daily 10am–1am.

Paradiso 🕭 ITALIAN
Set among dark woods and high booths both elegant and tasteful, you'll find yourself in an oasis of fine Italian

dining here. As you enjoy an aperitif, peruse the menu of selections representing some of the best recipes from the Italian kitchen. Veal saltimbocca (the word literally means "jump in your mouth") is a concoction with cheese and ham, and is most rewarding, as is the marinated filet mignon wrapped in pancetta. Nothing is finer nor more expensive than the lobster al Sardinia (with fresh tomatoes and vegetables). Dishes for the most part, are spiced, flavored, and sauced, especially the tender cutlets of oregano-flavored scaloppine and the fettuccine with "fruits of the sea," including Bahamian conch, scallops, lobster, and shrimp (among other seafood). Waiters are prompt and attentive, and there's a good wine list.

Crowne Plaza Golf Resort & Casino at the Royal Oasis, the Mall at W. Sunrise Hwy. *(C)* 242/352-7000. Reservations required. Main courses $18–$22. AE, DC, DISC, MC, V. Tues, Thurs–Sun 5:30–11pm.

Prop Club AMERICAN/INTERNATIONAL   With a name like Prop Club, you expect a kind of laid-back airplane hangar decor. Instead, you get parts of aircraft that crashed off the coast of Grand Bahama Island. When the weather's right, which it is most of the time, large doors open to bring the outdoors inside, and the party overflows onto the beach. You won't find the most enticing menu on the island here, but the place is a lot of fun—and the offerings far exceed most pub grub. Dig into a "mountain of ribs," or else savor the crab cakes (which actually contain a lot of crab, not just stuffing). Ever had a grilled margarita chicken sandwich? You can order one here, along with juicy burgers, fajitas, and the like.

At the Westin & Sheraton at Our Lucaya, Royal Palm Way. *(C)* 242/373-1333. Main courses $12–$23. AE, DC, MC, V. Lunch noon–5pm. Dinner 5–10pm. Bar noon–1am on weeknights; noon–2am on weekends.

AT PORT LUCAYA MARKETPLACE
EXPENSIVE

Ferry House *(R)* CAJUN/SEAFOOD   This restaurant's bar floats on pontoons, beneath a canvas canopy, above the waters of Bell Channel, the waterway that funnels boats from the open sea into the sheltered confines of Port Lucaya Marina. Lunches are relatively simple affairs, consisting of pastas, catch of the day, and meal-size salads. Dinner might feature a seafood platter laden with calamari, fish, and shrimp; a delectable duck breast with potatoes and vegetables; fresh salmon with hollandaise sauce; and savory grilled rack of lamb. But our favorite meal here is the ginger-and-honey-glazed tiger shrimp, served with a lobster bisque.

Beside Bell Channel, Port Lucaya. ℂ 242/373-1595. Reservations recommended for dinner. Lunch platters $15–$19; dinner main courses $27–$39. AE, MC, V. Mon–Fri noon–2pm; Tues–Sun 6–9pm.

Luciano's ✿ FRENCH/CONTINENTAL

With its tables usually occupied by local government officials and deal makers, Luciano's is the grande dame of Freeport restaurants, with a very European atmosphere. It's the only restaurant in Port Lucaya offering caviar, foie gras, and oysters Rockefeller, all served with a flourish by a formally dressed waitstaff wearing black and white. You can go early and enjoy a cocktail in the little bar inside or on the wooden deck overlooking the marina. Lightly smoked and thinly sliced salmon makes a good opener, as do snails in garlic butter. Fresh fish and shellfish are regularly featured and delicately prepared, allowing their natural flavors to shine through, with no heavy, overwhelming sauces. Steak Diane is one of Luciano's classics, along with an especially delectable veal medallion sautéed with shrimp and lobster.

Port Lucaya Marketplace. ℂ 242/373-9100. www.portlucaya.com/lucianos. Reservations required in winter. Main courses $27–$44. AE, MC, V. Daily 5:30–9:45pm (last order).

MODERATE

Fatman's Nephew ✿ BAHAMIAN

In another location, "Fatman" became a legend on Grand Bahama Island. Although he's no longer with us, the Fatman must have left his recipes and cooking skills to another generation of cooks. Today the place, which used to cater mainly to locals, has gone touristy, but much of the same traditional fare is still served with the same unflagging allegiance to Bahamian ways. The restaurant overlooks the marina at Port Lucaya from an eagle's-nest position on the second floor. You can enjoy drinks or meals inside, but we like to head out to an outdoor covered deck to watch the action below. At least eight kinds of game fish—including both wahoo and Cajun blackened kingfish—plus curried chicken, mutton, or beef are usually offered. Bahamian-style shark soup, made from the flesh of hammerheads ("little tender ones," according to the chef), is sometimes featured on the menu. Most dishes, except for expensive shellfish, fall at the lower end of the price scale. Beware, as the local staff can be flighty.

Port Lucaya Marketplace. ℂ 242/373-8520. Main courses $10–$40. AE, DISC, MC, V. Wed–Mon 5–11pm.

Giovanni's Cafe ✿ ITALIAN/SEAFOOD

Tucked away into one of the pedestrian thoroughfares of Port Lucaya Marketplace, you'll find a yellow-sided clapboard house that opens into a charming

38-seat Italian trattoria. The chefs (including head chef Giovanni Colo) serve Italian-influenced preparations of local seafood, specializing in seafood pasta (usually prepared only for two diners) and a lobster special. Giovanni stamps each dish with his Italian verve and flavor, whether it be Bahamian conch, local seafood, or scampi. Dishes show off his precision and rock-solid technique, exemplified by sirloin steak with fresh mushrooms, delectable shrimp scampi, and fattening, but extremely good, spaghetti carbonara.

Port Lucaya Marketplace. © 242/373-9107. Reservations recommended. Main courses lunch $8–$12, dinner $13–$33. AE, MC, V. Mon–Sat 8:30am–10pm; Sun 5–10pm.

La Dolce Vita ⚘ ITALIAN   Next to the Pub at Lucaya (see listing below), this small upscale Italian restaurant has a modern decor and traditional food. Enjoy freshly made pastas and Italian-style pizzas on a patio overlooking the marina or in the 44-seat dining room. Start with portobello mushrooms, fresh mozzarella with tomatoes, and a vinaigrette, or else carpaccio with arugula and spices. Homemade ravioli appears with different fillings such as cheese, lobster, or spinach. An excellent risotto flavored with black ink is served, or else you can order roast pork tenderloin or a crisp and perfectly flavored rack of lamb.

Port Lucaya Marketplace. © 242/373-8652. Reservations recommended. Main courses $11–$31. AE, MC, V. Daily 5:30–11pm. Closed Sept.

Pisces ⚘ INTERNATIONAL   This is our favorite among the many restaurants in the Port Lucaya Marketplace, and we're seconded by a healthy mix of locals and yacht owners who pack the place every weekend. Decorated with Tiffany-style lamps and captain's chairs, it boasts the most charming waitstaff on Grand Bahama Island. Pizzas are available and come in 27 different varieties, including a version with conch, lobster, shrimp, and chicken as well as one with Alfredo sauce. Dinners are more elaborate, with a choice of curries (including a version with conch); lobster in cream, wine, and herb sauce; all kinds of fish and shellfish; and several kinds of pasta.

Port Lucaya Marketplace. © 242/373-5192. Reservations recommended. Pizzas $12–$28; dinner main courses $9–$30. AE, DISC, MC, V. Mon–Sat 5pm–1:30am.

Pub at Lucaya ENGLISH/BAHAMIAN   Opening onto Count Basie Square, this restaurant and bar lies at the center of the Port Lucaya Marketplace. Returning visitors might remember the joint when it was called Pusser's Pub, named after that popular brand of rum.

You can come here to eat, but many patrons visit just for the drinks, especially rum-laced Pusser's Painkillers. You can order predictable pub grub such as shepherd's pie or steak-and-ale pie. Juicy American-style burgers are another lure. But you can also dine on substantial Bahamian fare at night, especially Bahamian lobster tail, cracked conch, chicken breast with herbs, or the fresh grilled catch of the day. The tables outside overlooking the water are preferred, or else you can retreat inside under a wooden beamed ceiling, where the rustic tables are lit by *faux* Tiffany-style lamps.

Port Lucaya Marketplace. © 242/373-8450. Sandwiches and burgers $8–$9; main courses $13–$40. AE, MC, V. Daily 11am–11pm (bar until 1am).

Shenanigan's Irish Pub CONTINENTAL Dark and beer-stained from the thousands of pints of Guinness, Harp, and Killian's that have been served and spilled here, this is the premier Irish or Boston-Irish hangout on Grand Bahama Island. Many visitors come just to drink, sometimes for hours at a time, soaking up the suds, and perhaps remembering to eventually order some food. If you get hungry, there's surf and turf, French-style rack of lamb for two, seafood Newburg, and several preparations of chicken. Most dishes, except for lobster, are at the low end of the price scale.

Port Lucaya Marketplace. © 242/373-4734. Main courses $9–$43. AE, DISC, MC, V. Mon–Thurs 5pm–midnight; Fri–Sat 5pm–2am (last order at 9:45pm).

INEXPENSIVE

Georgie's BAHAMIAN/AMERICAN This laid-back, informal restaurant allows you to dine harborside at Port Lucaya for breakfast, lunch, or dinner. It gets particularly busy at happy hour in the late afternoon when prices on drinks are reduced. Service shows more effort than polish, but dishes do arrive and they are quite flavorful time-tested recipes, a repertoire of old favorites like cracked conch (similar to breaded veal cutlet) served with tasty coleslaw. The catch of the day is usually pan-fried grouper or snapper served with peas 'n' rice. The chef almost daily prepares hot roast beef, serving it with mashed potatoes and mixed vegetables; for lunch, try one of the island's better chef's salads, loaded with turkey, ham, fresh tomatoes, cheese, and other good things. Other favorites here include fresh lobster, conch fritters, and barbecue chicken.

Port Lucaya Marketplace. © 242/373-8513. Breakfast $5; main courses lunch $6–$19, dinner $8–$19. DC, MC, V. Thurs–Tues 7am–11pm.

Outrigger's Native Restaurant/White Wave Club BAHAMIAN Cement-sided and simple, with a large deck extending out toward the sea, this restaurant was here long before the construction of the nearby Port Lucayan Marketplace, which lies only 4 blocks away. The restaurant area is the domain of Gretchen Wilson, whose kitchens produce a rotating series of dishes that include such lip-smacking dishes as lobster tails, minced lobster, steamed or cracked conch, pork chops, chicken, fish, and shrimp, usually served with peas 'n' rice and macaroni. Every Wednesday night, from 5pm to 2am, the restaurant is the venue for Outrigger's Famous Wednesday Night Fish Fry, when as many as a thousand diners will line up for platters of fried or steamed fish, priced at $10 each, which are accompanied by a DJ and dancers. Drinks are served within the restaurant, but at any time of the week, you might consider stepping into the nearby ramshackle bar, the White Wave Club, which serves only drinks.

Smith's Point. ℂ 242/373-4811. Main courses $10–$16. No credit cards. Sun–Fri 4pm–midnight; Sat 11am–midnight.

Zorba's BAHAMIAN/GREEK   First thing in the morning, you'll see locals standing in line for the Bahamian breakfasts served at Zorba's. From chicken souse to corned beef and grits, all the island eye-openers are on the menu. Eggs snag less daring early risers. Lunch could be a fat gyro or a souvlakia kabob. Dinner can begin with a Greek salad and then move on to moussaka, with baklava for a sweet finish. We won't pretend the food here is like a trip to the Greek isles, but it's satisfying and filling. At this casual dining spot, you can eat either inside or enjoy your meal alfresco.

Port Lucaya Marketplace. ℂ 242/373-6137. Main courses lunch $4–$13, dinner $11–$24. AE, DISC, MC, V. Daily 7am–10:30pm.

OUTSIDE FREEPORT/LUCAYA

Bishop's Restaurant 🅐 *Finds* BAHAMIAN   This eatery, known mainly to East End locals, is patronized for its real down-home cooking. Just over 50km (32 miles) east of Lucaya, the restaurant opens onto views of the sea. Far from the high-rise hotels, this little restaurant and lounge looks the way they did in The Bahamas of the 1920s and 1930s. Some of the best cracked conch we've sampled on Grand Bahama Island is served here, rolled in a light batter and fried in piping hot oil so that its crust is slightly crunchy. Another favorite, always on the menu, is fried grouper with classic peas 'n' rice. Or, for a savory dish, order the chicken barbecued in zesty sauce.

High Rock. ℂ 242/353-4515. Main courses $10–$15. MC, V. Daily 9am–5pm.

Club Caribe AMERICAN/BAHAMIAN   Set about 11km (7 miles) east of the International Bazaar, beside a beach and an offshore reef, this restaurant is a funky and offbeat charmer. You can spend a day on the beach here, renting the club's snorkeling equipment, sunbathing or swimming, and perhaps enjoying one of the house-special cocktails (try a Caribe Delight, made with bananas, banana-flavored liqueur, and rum). When it's lunchtime, you might order up a heaping platter of cracked conch; barbecued ribs; snapper or wahoo that's fried, steamed, or grilled; or a sandwich or salad. This place is simple, out-doorsy, and a refreshing change from the more congested parts of Grand Bahama. On Friday, they're usually open until 9pm or later, with live music. Oysters on the half shell, mussels, and clams are all bought fresh on Friday for a tasty weekend treat.

Churchill Beach, Mather Town, off Midshipman Rd. ✆ 242/373-6866. Main courses $5–$25. AE, MC, V. Tues–Sun 11am–6pm (or later, depending on business).

Margarita Villa Sand Bar BAHAMIAN/AMERICAN   Known for making the island's best Bahama Mama drink, this funky little local hangout with a rustic deck sits under coconut palms overlook-ing the ocean. It's an extremely casual place, with handmade barrel tables, and sand on the floor, a small menu, and an offbeat location in the little island settlement of Mather Town. When not downing some of the best margaritas and burgers in the area, patrons can be seen on the beach sunning, snorkeling, or swimming. Dig into a basket of conch fritters, a "cheeseburger in paradise," fish and chips, or steak and fries. The big event of the week is the bonfire on the beach, Tuesday from 6:30 to 10pm. A full dinner and all the activ-ities, including music, dancing, and games, goes for $41 per person.

Mather Town. ✆ 242/373-4525. Reservations required for bonfire night. Main courses $5–$14. DISC, MC, V. Daily 11am–10:30pm (or later, depending on business).

5 Beaches, Watersports & Other Outdoor Pursuits

HITTING THE BEACH

Grand Bahama Island has enough beaches for everyone, the best ones opening onto Northwest Providence Channel at Freeport and sweeping east for some 97km (60 miles) to encompass Xanadu Beach, Lucayan Beach, Taíno Beach, and others, eventually ending at such remote eastern outposts as Rocky Creek and McLean's Town. Once you leave the Freeport/Lucaya area, you can virtually have your pick of white sandy beaches all the way east. Once you're past the resort hotels, you'll see a series of secluded beaches used mainly by locals. If you like people, a lot of organized watersports, and easy access to hotel bars and rest rooms, stick to Xanadu, Taíno, and Lucayan beaches.

Though there's fine snorkeling offshore, you should book a snorkeling cruise aboard one of the catamarans offered by Paradise Watersports (see below) to see the most stunning reefs.

Xanadu Beach 𝒜𝒜 is one of our favorite beaches, immediately east of Freeport and the site of the famed Xanadu Beach Resort. The 1.6km-long (1-mile) beach may be crowded at times in winter, but that's because of those gorgeous, soft, powdery white sands, which open onto tranquil waters. The beach is set against a backdrop of coconut palms and Australian pines. You can hook up here with some of the best watersports on the island, including snorkeling, boating, jet-skiing, and parasailing.

Immediately east of Xanadu is **Silver Point Beach,** a little white-sandy beach, site of a timeshare complex where guests are out riding the waves on water bikes or playing volleyball on the beach. You'll see horseback riders from Pinetree Stables (see below) taking beach rides along the sands.

Most visitors will be found at **Lucayan Beach,** right off Royal Palm Way and immediately east of Silver Point Beach. This is one of the best beaches in The Bahamas, with kilometers of white sand. It might be crowded for a few weeks in winter, but most of the time you can find beach-blanket space. At any of the hotel resorts along this beach, you can hook up with an array of watersports or get a frosty drink from a hotel bar. It's not for those seeking seclusion, but it's a fun beach-party scene.

Immediately to the east of Lucayan Beach is **Taíno Beach,** a family favorite and a good place for watersports. This, too, is a fine, wide beach of white sands, opening onto generally tranquil waters.

Another choice not too far east is **Gold Rock Beach,** a favorite picnic spot with locals on weekends, although you'll usually have this beach to yourself on weekdays. Gold Rock Beach is a 19km (12-mile) drive from Lucaya. At Gold Rock you are at the doorstep to the **Lucayan National Park** (see below), a 16-hectare (40-acre) park filled with some of the longest, widest, and most fabulous secluded beaches on the island.

BIKING

A guided bike trip is an ideal way to see parts of Grand Bahama that most visitors miss. Starting at **Barbary Beach,** you can pedal a mountain bike along the southern coast parallel to the beach. Stop for a snack, lunch, and a dip. Finally, you reach **Lucayan National Park,** some 19km (12 miles) away. Explore the cave were the Indians buried their dead in the days when Grand Bahama was theirs, centuries before the coming of Columbus. Crabs here have been known to come up through holes in the ground carrying bits of bowls once used by the Lucayans. **Kayak Nature Tours** (℃ 242/ 373-2485), the company that sponsors these trips, transports you home to your hotel by van, so you don't have to exhaust yourself in the heat cycling back. The cost is $79 for adults, half price for children ages 10 to 16. All equipment, sustenance, and round-trip transportation from your hotel is included.

BOAT CRUISES

Ocean Wonder, Port Lucaya Dock (℃ **242/373-5880**), run by Reef Tours, is a gargantuan 18m (60-ft.) Defender glass-bottom boat. Any tour agent can arrange for you to go out on this vessel. You'll get a panoramic view of the beautiful underwater life that lives off the coast of Grand Bahama. Cruises depart from Port Lucaya behind the Straw Market on the bay side at 9:30am, 11:15am, 1:15pm, and 3:15pm, except Friday, when only two tours leave at 9:30 and 11:15am. The tour lasts 1½ hours, costs $25 for adults and $15 for children 6 to 12, and is free for children 5 and under. Make reservations a day or two ahead, as the boat does fill up quickly.

Superior Watersports (P.O. Box F-40837, Freeport; ℃ **242/ 373-7863;** www.superiorwatersports.com), offers trips on its *Bahama Mama,* a two-deck 22m (72-ft.) catamaran. Its Robinson Crusoe Beach Party, offered daily from 11am to 4pm from October through March, but from noon to 5pm from April through September, costs $59 per person and $39 for children under 12. There's also a shorter sunset booze cruise that goes for $29. (From Apr–Sept, these cruises are on Tues, Thurs, and Sat night from 6:30–8:30pm, and from Oct–Mar the same nights, but from 6–8pm.) Call for information about how to hook up with this outfitter.

For an underwater cruise, try the company's quasi-submarine, the *Seaworld Explorer.* The sub itself does not descend; instead, you walk down into the hull of the boat and watch the sea life glide by. The "semisub" departs daily at 9:30 am, 11:30am, and 1:30pm, and the two-hour ride costs $39 for adults and $25 for children age 2 to 12.

THE DOLPHIN EXPERIENCE

A pod of bottle-nosed dolphins is involved in a unique dolphin/human familiarization program at Dolphin Experience, located at **Underwater Explorers Society (UNEXSO),** next to Port Lucaya, opposite Lucayan Beach Casino (℃ **800/992-DIVE** or 242/373-1244; www.unexso.com). This "close encounter" program allows participants to observe these intelligent and friendly animals close up and to hear an interesting talk by a member of the animal-care staff. The world's largest dolphin facility, the conditions aren't cramped here, and dolphins can swim out to sea. You can step onto a shallow wading platform and interact with the dolphins; the experience costs $75 and is an educational, fun adventure for all ages. Children under 3 participate free, while it costs $38 for those aged 4 to 12. You'll want to bring your camera. Dolphins also swim out from Sanctuary Bay daily to interact with certified scuba divers in a "dolphin dive" program, costing $159.

Swimming with dolphins has its critics and supporters. You may want to visit the Whale and Dolphins Conservation Society's website at www.wdcs.org. For more information about responsible travel in general, check out these websites: Tread Lightly (www.treadlightly.org) and the International Ecotourism Society (www.ecotourism.org).

FISHING

In the waters off Grand Bahama, you can fish for barracuda, snapper, grouper, yellowtail, wahoo, and kingfish, along with other denizens of the deep.

Reef Tours, Ltd., Port Lucaya Dock (© **242/373-5880** or 242/373-5891; www.bahamasvg.com/reeftours), offers one of the least expensive ways to go deep-sea fishing around Grand Bahama Island. Adults pay $90 if they fish, $45 if they only go along to watch. Four to six people can charter the entire 13m (42-ft.) craft for $540 per half-day or $1,050 per whole day. The 9.6m (32-ft.) boat can be chartered for $375 half-day and $720 for a whole day. Departures for the 4-hour half-day excursions are daily at 8:30am

---

⸌Moments Land & Sea Eco-Tours

If you're a nature lover, escape from the casinos and take one of the **East End Adventures** (© **242/373-6662**; www.bahamas ecotours.com) bush and sea safaris. You're taken through dense pine forests and along deserted beaches, going inland on hikes to such sites as blue holes, mangrove swamps, and underground caverns. You may even learn how to crack conch. A native lunch is served on a serene beach in Lightbourne's Cay, a remote islet in the East End. Most of the tour is laid-back, as you can snorkel in blue holes or shell hunt. Safaris are conducted daily between 8am and 5:30pm; the cost is $110 for adults and $55 for kids ages 2 to 12.

and 1pm, while the 8-hour full-day excursions leave daily at 8:30am. Bait, tackle, and ice are included in the cost.

GOLF

This island boasts more golf links than any other in The Bahamas. The courses are within 11km (7 miles) of one another, and you usually won't have to wait to play. All courses are open to the public year-round, and clubs can be rented from all pro shops on the island.

Emerald Golf Course, the Mall South, at Crowne Plaza Golf Resort & Casino at the Royal Oasis (✆ **242/350-7000**), was the site of The Bahamas National. Open some years back, and more recently, in conjunction with the Ruby course (see below), it's the site of the annual January Grand Bahama Pro-Am Tournament. The course has plenty of trees along the fairways, as well as an abundance of water hazards and bunkers. The toughest hole is the 9th, a par 5 with 545 yards from the blue tees to the hole. In winter, greens fees to either of these courses are $95 per day, reduced to $85 in summer.

The championship **Ruby Golf Course,** Sunrise Highway, also at Crowne Plaza Golf Resort & Casino at the Royal Oasis (✆ **242/350-7000**), received a major upgrade in 2001 by Jim Fazio Golf Design, Inc. The Ruby course was lengthened to increase the rating and to enhance play. A fully automated irrigation system was also installed. For greens fees, see the Emerald Golf Course, above. It's a total of 6,750 yards if played from the championship blue tees.

Fortune Hills Golf & Country Club, Richmond Park, Lucaya (✆ **242/373-2222**), was originally intended to be an 18-hole course, but the back 9 were never completed. You can replay the front 9 for 18 holes and a total of 6,916 yards from the blue tees. Par is 72. Greens fees are $26 for 9 holes, $35 for 18. Electric 2-seater carts cost $38 for 9 and $48 for 18 holes. Club rental costs $18 for 18 holes and $14 for 9 holes.

The best-kept and most-manicured course on Grand Bahama is the **Lucayan Park Golf & Country Club,** Lucaya Beach at Our Lucaya (✆ **242/373-1333**). Made over after hurricane Jeanne of 2004, this beautiful course is known for the hanging boulder sculpture at its entrance. Greens are fast, with a couple of par 5s more than 500 yards long, totaling 6,824 yards from the blue tees and 6,488 from the whites. Par is 72. Greens fees are $120 for 18 holes, including a mandatory shared golf cart. We'll let you in on a secret: Even if you're not a golfer, sample the food at the club restaurant—everything from lavish champagne brunches to first-rate seafood dishes is delicious.

The first golf course to open in The Bahamas since 1969 made its premiere late in 2000. **The Reef Course** ★★ Royal Palm Way, at Our Lucaya (© **242/373-1333**; www.ourlucaya.com/reef_course.asp), was designed by Robert Trent Jones, Jr., who called it "a bit like a Scottish course but a lot warmer." This course requires precise shot-making to avoid its numerous lakes. You'll find water on 13 of the 18 holes and various types of long grass swaying in the trade winds. The course boasts 6,920 yards of links-style playing grounds. Residents of Our Lucaya, with which the course is associated, pay $110 for 18 holes or $50 for 9 holes. Nonresidents are charged $120 for 18 holes, $65 for 9 holes.

HORSEBACK RIDING

Pinetree Stables, Beachway Drive, North, Freeport (© **242/373-3600** or 305/433-4809; www.pinetree-stables.com), are the best riding stables in The Bahamas, superior to rivals on New Providence Island (Nassau). Pinetree offers trail rides to the beach in winter Tuesday through Sunday at 9 and 11:30am, 9 and 11am off season. The cost is $75 per person for a ride lasting 2 hours. No children under 8 are allowed. The weight limit per person is 200 pounds.

SEA KAYAKING

If you'd like to explore the waters off the island's north shore, call **Kayak Nature Tours** (© **242/373-2485**), who'll take you on trips through the mangroves, where you can see wildlife as you paddle along. The cost is $79 per person (children half-price), with lunch included. Double kayaks are used on these jaunts, and children must be at least 3 years of age. For the same price, you can take a 30-minute trip by kayak to an offshore island, with 1½ hours of snorkeling included along with lunch. Call ahead for reservations for either of these tours. A van will pick you up at your hotel at 9am and deliver you back at the end of the tours at 3pm.

SNORKELING & SCUBA DIVING

Serious divers are attracted to such Grand Bahama sites as the Wall, the Caves, Theo's Wreck, and Treasure Reef. **Theo's Wreck** ★★ is the most evocative site; it was a freighter that was deliberately sunk off Freeport to attract marine life. Today it does just that, as it teems with everything from horse-eyed jacks to moray eels. Other sites frequented by UNEXSO include Spit City, Ben Blue Hole, Pygmy Caves, Gold Rock, Silver Point Reef, and the Rose Garden. Keep in mind that UNEXSO's specialty is diving, while Paradise Watersports primarily entertains snorkelers.

Underwater Explorers Society (UNEXSO) 𝔸𝔸𝔸 (© **800/992-DIVE** or 242/373-1250; www.unexso.com), one of the premier dive outfitters in The Bahamas and the Caribbean, offers seven dive trips daily, including reef trips, shark dives, wreck dives, and night dives. Divers can even dive with dolphins in the open ocean here—a rare experience offered by very few facilities in the world (see "The Dolphin Experience," above).

A popular 3-hour learn-to-dive course is offered daily. Over UNEXSO's 30-year history, more than 50,000 people have successfully completed this course. For $85, students learn the basics in UNEXSO's training pools and dive the beautiful shallow reef with their instructor.

6 Seeing the Sights

Several informative tours of Grand Bahama Island are offered. One reliable company is **H. Forbes Charter Services Ltd.,** the Mall at West Sunrise Highway, Freeport (© **242/352-9311;** www.forbes charter.com). From headquarters in the International Bazaar, this company offers half- and full-day bus tours. The most popular option is the half-day Super Combination Tour, priced at $25 per adult and $20 per child age 5 to 12. It includes drive-through tours of residential areas and the island's commercial center, stops at the island's deepwater harbor, shopping, and a visit to a wholesale liquor store. Departures are Monday through Saturday at 9am and 1pm; the tour lasts 3½ hours.

See also "Beaches, Watersports & Other Outdoor Pursuits," earlier, for details on UNEXSO's Dolphin Experience, and "Shopping," below, for coverage of the International Bazaar and the Port Lucaya Marketplace.

Lucayan National Park This 16-hectare (40-acre) park, filled with mangrove, pine, and palm trees, contains one of the loveliest, most secluded beaches on Grand Bahama, a long, wide, dune-covered

---

Finds A Sudsy Look at Grand Bahama

The **Grand Bahama Brewing Co.**, Logwood Road, Freeport (© 242/351-5191), offers tours Monday to Friday of its brewery at 10am, 12:30pm, and 4:40pm. In addition to Hammerhead Ales, Lucayan Lager is also made here. Tours cost $5, but the fee is credited to any lager or ale purchases you might make.

stretch of sandy beach that you'll reach by following a wooden path winding through the trees. Bring your snorkeling gear so you can glimpse the colorful creatures living beneath the turquoise waters of a coral reef offshore. As you wander through the park, you'll cross Gold Rock Creek, fed by a spring from what is said to be the world's largest underground freshwater cavern system. There are 36,000 entrances to the caves—some only a few feet deep. Two of the caves can be seen, because they were exposed when a portion of ground collapsed. The pools in the caves are composed of 2m (6½ ft.) of freshwater atop a heavier layer of saltwater. Spiral wooden steps have been built down to the pools.

The freshwater springs once lured native Lucayans, those Arawak-connected tribes who lived on the island and depended on fishing for their livelihood. They would come inland to get fresh water for their habitats on the beach. Lucayan bones and artifacts, such as pottery, have been found in the caves, as well as on the beaches.

Settlers Way, eastern end of East Sunrise Hwy. © 242/352-5438. Admission $3; tickets available only at the Rand Nature Centre (see below). Daily 9am–4pm. Drive east along Midshipman Rd., passing Sharp Rock Point and Gold Rock.

Parrot Jungle's Garden of the Groves *Kids*

One of the island's major attractions is this 12-acre (4.8 hectares) garden, which honors its founder, Wallace Groves, and his wife, Georgette. Eleven kilometers (7 miles) east of the International Bazaar, this scenic preserve of waterfalls and flowering shrubs has some 10,000 trees, free-form lakes, footbridges, ornamental borders, lawns, and flowers. Tropical birds flock here, making this a lure for bird-watchers and ornithologists. The new managers—Parrot Jungle of Miami—have introduced a number of animals to the site, including macaws, cockatoos, pygmy goats, potbelly pigs, and American alligators. Other species introduced include the park's first Bahamian raccoons and the white-crowned pigeon, the latter on the endangered species list. The park also has a children's playground. A lovely little nondenominational chapel, open to visitors, looks down on the garden from a hill. **The Palmetto Café** serves snacks and drinks, and a Bahamian straw market is located at the entrance gate. At press time, the garden was closed due to renovations. Please call ahead or check the website for updates.

Midshipman Rd. and Magellan Dr. © 242/373-5668. www.gardenofthegroves.com. Admission $10 adults, $7 children 3–10, free for children under 3. Garden and cafe daily 9am–4pm.

Pirates of The Bahamas Beach Theme Park *(Kids)*   Islanders think of this amusement park as their Disney World. One of the largest watersports centers in The Bahamas, it features pools for diving and swimming, along with an array of activities such as parasailing, banana boating, snorkeling, kayaking, paddle-boating, and jet-skiing. Children have their own Captain Kidd's Camp with a supervised playground. Something's always happening here, including beach or bonfire parties along with such attractions as an 18-hole minigolf course. Although you don't pay a general admission fee, you are charged for some of the attractions, such as $6 for the minigolf and varying fees for the watersports. The Bonfire Party Night on Thursday and Sunday, lasting from 5 to 9pm, costs adults $50, children $40, including free transportation from your hotel, live entertainment, and an all-you-can-eat buffet dinner. A restaurant and bar are housed on-site here in a wooden structure that evokes a Spanish galleon.

Jolly Roger Dr., Taíno Beach. ℂ **242/373-8456.** Daily 9am–9pm.

Rand Nature Centre   This 100-acre (40-hectare) pineland sanctuary, located 3km (2 miles) east of the center of Freeport, is the regional headquarters of The Bahamas National Trust, a nonprofit conservation organization. Nature trails highlight native flora and "bush medicine" and provide opportunities for bird-watching; as you stroll, keep your eyes peeled for the lush blooms of tropical orchids or the brilliant flash of green and red feathers in the trees. Wild birds abound at the park. You can join a bird-watching tour on the first Saturday of every month at 8am. Other features of the nature center include native animal displays, an education center, and a gift shop selling nature books and souvenirs.

E. Settlers Way. ℂ **242/352-5438.** Admission $5 adults, $3 children 5–12, free for children under 5. Mon–Fri 9am–4pm.

7 Shopping

Shopping hours in Freeport/Lucaya are generally Monday to Saturday 9am to 6pm. However, in the International Bazaar, hours vary widely. Most places are open Monday through Saturday. Some begin business daily at 9:30am; others don't open until 10am, and closing time ranges from 5:30 to 6pm.

THE INTERNATIONAL BAZAAR

One of the world's most unusual shopping complexes, the International Bazaar, at East Mall Drive and East Sunrise Highway, covers

4 hectares (10 acres) in the heart of Freeport. Although it remains one of the most visited sites in The Bahamas, it frankly is a bit tarnished today and is due for a makeover. Its rising competitor, the Port Lucaya Marketplace (see below), is looking better every day. Buses at the entrance of the complex aren't numbered, but those marked INTERNATIONAL BAZAAR will take you right to the gateway at the Torii Gate on West Sunrise Highway. The fare is $1. Visitors walk through this much-photographed gate, a Japanese symbol of welcome, into a miniature World's Fair setting (think of it as a kitschy Bahamian version of Epcot). Continental cafes and dozens of shops loaded with merchandise await visitors. The bazaar blends architecture and cultures from some 25 countries, each recreated with cobblestones, narrow alleys, and authentically reproduced architecture. True, it's more theme-park-style shopping than authentic Bahamian experience, but it's fun nevertheless. In the nearly 100 shops, you're bound to find something that is both unique and a bargain. You'll see African handcrafts, Chinese jade, British china, Swiss watches, Irish linens, and Colombian emeralds—and that's just for starters.

On a street patterned after the Ginza in Tokyo, just inside the entrance to the bazaar, is the Asian section. A rich collection of merchandise from the Far East can be found here, including cameras, handmade teak furniture, fine silken goods, and even places where you can have clothing custom-made.

To the left, you'll find the Left Bank of Paris, or at least a reasonable facsimile, with sidewalk cafes where you can enjoy a café au lait and perhaps a pastry under shade trees. In the Continental Pavilion, you can find leather goods, jewelry, lingerie, and gifts at shops with names such as Love Boutique.

A narrow alley leads you from the French section to East India, where shops sell such exotic goods as taxi horns and silk saris. Moving on from the India House, past Kon Tiki, you arrive in Africa, where you can purchase carvings or a colorful dashiki.

10 A narrow alley leads you from the French section to East India, where shops sell such exotic goods as taxi horns and silk saris. Moving on from the India House, past Kon Tiki, you arrive in Africa, where you can purchase carvings or a colorful dashiki.

For a taste of Latin America and Iberia, make your way to the Spanish section, where serapes and piñatas hang from the railings, and imports are displayed along the cobblestone walks.

Many items sold in the shops here are said to cost 40% less than if you bought them in the United States, but don't count on that. If you were contemplating a big purchase, it's best to compare prices before you leave home. You can have purchases sent anywhere you wish.

The **Straw Market,** next door to the International Bazaar, contains items with a special Bahamian touch—colorful baskets, hats, handbags, and place mats—all of which make good gifts or souvenirs from your trip. (Be aware that some items sold here are actually made in Asia.)

Here's a description of the various shops in the bazaar.

ART

Flovin Gallery   This gallery sells original Bahamian and international art, frames, lithographs, posters, and Bahamian-made Christmas ornaments and decorated coral. It also offers handmade Bahamian dolls, coral jewelry, and other gift items. Another branch is at the Port Lucaya Marketplace (see below). In the Arcade section of the International Bazaar. ② 242/352-7564.

CRYSTAL & CHINA

Island Galleria   There's an awesome collection of crystal here. Fragile, breakable, and beautiful, it includes works of utilitarian art in china and crystal by Waterford, Aynsley, Lenox, Dansk, and Swarovski. Anything you buy can be carefully packed and shipped. Another branch is located in the Port Lucaya Marketplace (② **242/ 373-4512**). International Bazaar. ② **242/352-8194.**

FASHION

Cleo's Boutique   This shop offers everything from eveningwear to lingerie. A warm and inviting destination, Cleo's prides itself on capturing the Caribbean woman in all of her moods. You can also find a wide array of costume jewelry beginning at $25 per piece. International Bazaar. ② **242/352-3340.**

HANDCRAFTS & GIFTS

Caribbean Cargo   One of the island's best, this gift shop specializes in such items as picture frames, T-shirts that change color in sunlight, and a variety of other clothes. Another branch of this store is at the Port Lucaya Marketplace (② **242/373-7950**). In the Arcade section of the International Bazaar. ② **242/352-2929.**

Far East Traders   Look for Asian linens, hand-embroidered dresses and blouses, silk robes, lace parasols, smoking jackets, and kimonos here. A branch is located inside the Island Galleria at the Port Lucaya Marketplace (② **242/373-8697**). International Bazaar. ② **242/352-9280.**

Paris in The Bahamas This shop contains the biggest selection of luxury goods under one roof in the International Bazaar. The staff wears couture black dresses like you might have expected in Paris, and everywhere there's a sense of French glamour and conspicuous consumption. You can find both Gucci and Versace leather goods for men and women; crystal from Lalique, Baccarat, Daum, and Kosta Boda, and a huge collection of cosmetics and perfumes. International Bazaar. © 242/352-5380.

Unusual Centre Where else can you get a wide array of items made of walrus skin or goods made from exotic feathers such as peacock? There's another branch at the Port Lucaya Marketplace (© 242/373-7333). International Bazaar. © 242/352-3994.

JEWELRY
Colombian Emeralds International This branch of the world's foremost emerald jeweler offers a wide array of precious gemstone jewelry and one of the island's best watch collections. Careful shoppers will find significant savings over U.S. prices. The outlet offers certified appraisals and free 90-day insurance. Two more branches are at the Port Lucaya Marketplace (© 242/373-8400). South American section of the International Bazaar. © 242/352-1138. www.dutyfree.com.

PERFUMES & FRAGRANCES
The Perfume Factory Fragrance of The Bahamas This is the top fragrance producer in The Bahamas. The shop is housed in a model of an 1800s mansion, in which visitors are invited to hear a 5-minute commentary and to see the mixing of fragrant oils. There's even a "mixology" department where you can create your own fragrance from a selection of oils. The shop's well-known products include Island Promises, Goombay, Paradise, and Pink Pearl (with conch pearls in the bottle). The shop also sells Guanahani, created to commemorate the 500th anniversary of Columbus's first landfall, and Sand, the leading Bahamian-made men's fragrance. At the rear of the International Bazaar. © 242/352-9391. www.perfumefactory.com.

PORT LUCAYA MARKETPLACE
Port Lucaya Marketplace on Seahorse Road is a shopping and dining complex set on 2.4 hectares (6 acres). Free entertainment, such as steel-drum bands and strolling musicians, adds to a festival atmosphere. A boardwalk along the water makes it easy to watch the frolicking dolphins.

The complex rose on the site of a former Bahamian straw market, but the craftspeople and their straw products are back in full force after having been temporarily dislodged.

The waterfront location is a distinct advantage. Many of the restaurants and shops overlook a 106-slip marina, home of a "fantasy" pirate ship featuring lunch and dinner/dancing cruises. A variety of charter vessels are also based at the Port Lucaya Marina, and dockage at the marina is available to visitors coming by boat to shop or dine.

Androsia   This is the Port Lucaya outlet of the famous batik house of Andros Island. Its designs and colors capture the spirit of The Bahamas. Fabrics are handmade on the island of Andros. The store sells quality, 100%-cotton resort wear, including simple skirts, tops, jackets, and shorts for women, and it also offers a colorful line of children's wear. Port Lucaya Marketplace. ☏ 242/373-8387.

Bandolera   The staff can be rather haughty here, but despite its drawbacks, the store carries a collection of chic women's clothing that's many cuts above the usual run of T-shirts and tank tops that are the norm within many of its competitors. Port Lucaya Marketplace. ☏ 242/373-7691.

Flovin Gallery II   This branch of the art gallery located in the Port Lucaya Marketplace sells a collection of oil paintings (both Bahamian and international), along with lithographs and posters. In its limited field, it's the best in the business. It also features a number of gift items, such as handmade Bahamian dolls, decorated corals, and Christmas ornaments. Port Lucaya Marketplace. ☏ 242/373-8388.

Harley-Davidson of Freeport   This is one of only two registered and licensed Harley outlets in The Bahamas. You can special order a motorcycle if you feel flush with funds from a casino, but it's more likely that you'll content yourself with T-shirts, leather vests, belts, caps, sunglasses, and gift items. Port Lucaya Marketplace. ☏ 242/373-8269.

Jeweler's Warehouse   Bargain hunters looking for good buys on discounted, closeout 14-karat gold and gemstone jewelry should come here. Discounts range up to 50%, but the quality of many of these items remains high. Guarantees and certified appraisals are possible. Port Lucaya Marketplace. ☏ 242/373-8401.

Les Parisiens   This outlet offers a wide range of fine jewelry and watches. It also sells crystal, Versace wear, and perfumes, including the latest from Paris. Port Lucaya Marketplace. ☏ 242/373-2974.

UNEXSO Dive Shop   This premier dive shop of The Bahamas sells everything related to the water—swimsuits, wet suits, underwater cameras, video equipment, shades, hats, souvenirs, and state-of-the-art diver's equipment. Port Lucaya Marketplace. ℂ **800/992-3483** or 242/373-1244.

8 Grand Bahama After Dark

Many resort hotels stage their own entertainment at night, and these shows are open to the general public.

ROLLING THE DICE

Casino at Westin & Sheraton at Our Lucaya   We call this casino the best on the island. It far exceeds the glamour of its rival casino in Freeport. The casino's 30 tables offer guests their choice of games, ranging from baccarat to Caribbean stud poker. Blackjack and roulette are also popular games of chance here; for the frugal gambler, some 400 slot machines await. The casino is open daily from 10am to 2am or later. Entrance is free. The Westin & Sheraton at Our Lucaya, Royal Palm Way. ℂ **242/373-1333.**

Royal Oasis Casino   Most of the nightlife in Freeport/Lucaya centers around this glittering, giant, Moroccan-style palace, one of the largest casinos in The Bahamas and the Caribbean. Under this Moorish-domed structure, visitors play games of chance and attend Las Vegas–inspired floor shows. Open daily 10am to 2am. Entrance is free. In the Crowne Plaza Golf Resort & Casino at the Royal Oasis, the Mall at W. Sunrise Hwy. ℂ **242/350-7000.**

THE CLUB & BAR SCENE

Located in the center of the **Port Lucaya Marketplace** waterfront restaurant and shopping complex, **Count Basie Square** contains a vine-covered bandstand where the best live music on the island is performed on Tuesday, Friday, and Saturday evenings from about 7:30 to 8pm. And it's free! The square honors the "Count," who used to have a grand home on Grand Bahama. Steel bands, small Junkanoo groups, and even gospel singers from a local church are likely to be heard performing here, their voices or music wafting across the 50-slip marina. You can sip a beer or a tropical rum concoction at one of the bars in the complex. (See "Where to Dine," earlier in this chapter, for details on a few of these, including **Fatman's Nephew** and **Shenanigan's Irish Pub.**)

John B. Lounge   Inside a formidable pile, this club offers some of the best live entertainment on the island. At the outdoorsy John B.

Lounge, live music is presented Friday to Sunday. The bar lounge and adjoining dance club are open nightly from 9pm to 2am. Most visitors attend, however, for the Goombay production on Tuesday and Saturday. If you want dinner and a show, arrive at 6:30pm; otherwise, showtime is at 7:30pm. The cost of both is $45. Or you can attend just to see the show, paying from $5 per drink. In the Crowne Plaza Golf Resort & Casino in the Royal Oasis, the Mall at W. Sunrise Hwy. © 242/350-7000.

Prop Club   At this action-oriented sports bar and dance club, each night something different is happening: karaoke on Tuesday and Thursday, sumo wrestling on Wednesday, cultural show nights on Thursday, island "jam nights" on Friday, and '70s revival nights on Saturday. But also expect a "get down with the DJ" snooze-a-thon on Sundays, and game nights on slow Mondays. The highlight is the cultural show with a live Junkanoo finale. You can also dine here, enjoying the likes of coconut shrimp, blackened grouper, and sirloin steak, paying from $10 for a full meal. For decor, as the name suggests, remnants of an old airplane and antique propellers adorn the walls. The kitchen is open daily from noon to 10pm, but the bar is open noon to 1am. The DJ arrives at 10pm every night. The Sheraton at Our Lucaya, Royal Palm Way. © 242/373-1333.

Index

See also Accommodations and Restaurant indexes below.

The only guide independent travelers need to make smart choices, avoid rip-offs, get the most for their money, and travel like a pro.

Frommer's
Italy 2006

Frommer's®

WILEY

Available at

THE NEW TRAVELOCITY GUARANTEE

EVERYTHING YOU BOOK WILL BE RIGHT, OR WE'LL WORK WITH OUR TRAVEL PARTNERS TO MAKE IT RIGHT, RIGHT AWAY.

*To drive home the point,
we're going to use the word "right" in every single sentence.*

Let's get right to it. Right to the meat! Only Travelocity guarantees everything about your booking will be right, or we'll work with our travel partners to make it right, right away. Right on!

Here's a picture taken smack dab right in the middle of Antigua, where the guarantee also covers you.

The guarantee covers all but one of the items pictured to the right.

Now, you may be thinking, "Yeah, right, I'm so sure." That's OK; you have the right to remain skeptical. That is until we mention help is always right around the corner. Call us right off the bat, knowing that our customer service reps are there for you 24/7. Righting wrongs. Left and right.

For example, what if the ocean view you booked actually looks out at a downright ugly parking lot? You'd be right to call – we're there for you. And no one in their right mind would be pleased to learn the rental car place has closed and left them stranded. Call Travelocity and we'll help get you back on the right track.

Now if you're guessing there are some things we can't control, like the weather, well you're right. But we can help you with most things – to get all the details in righting,* visit **travelocity.com/guarantee**.

*Sorry, spelling things right is one of the few things not covered under the guarantee.

I'd give my right arm for a guarantee like this, although I'm glad I don't have to.

You'll never roam alone.

©2005 Travelocity.com LP. CST # 2056372-50.

IF YOU BOOK IT, IT SHOULD BE THERE.

Only Travelocity guarantees it will be, or we'll work with our travel partners to make it right, right away. So if you're missing a balcony or anything else you booked, just call us 24/7. **1-888-TRAVELOCITY.**

travelocity
You'll never roam alone.